Media Representations of Macau's Gaming Industry in Greater China

Yuxi Wu

Media Representations of Macau's Gaming Industry in Greater China

A Corpus-based Critical Discourse Analysis

Springer

Yuxi Wu
City University of Macau
Macau, China

ISBN 978-981-19-7726-8 ISBN 978-981-19-7724-4 (eBook)
https://doi.org/10.1007/978-981-19-7724-4

This Springer imprint is published by the registered company Springer Nature Singapore Pte Ltd.
The registered company address is: 152 Beach Road, #21-01/04 Gateway East, Singapore 189721, Singapore

Acknowledgments

First of all, I would like to express my heartfelt gratitude to my thesis supervisor Prof. Winnie Cheng, who has dedicated so much of her time to reading through every version of my thesis and giving me insightful comments and invaluable guidance on my research and my thesis. Her MA course *Corpus Linguistics for Professional Communication* inspired me a lot, as it has guided me through the world of corpus linguistics. Her books and publications have also offered me many invaluable ideas and references for my academic studies. Without her constant encouragement and supervision, this work could not have been accomplished. It was my great honour to study under her guidance. I am also very thankful to Prof. Martin Warren as his DALS course *Discourse Analysis and Corpus Linguistics*, which has offered me a comprehensive perspective on critical discourse analysis and corpus linguistics, is very enlightening.

I would like to extend my sincere gratitude to Prof. Franca POPPI and Dr. Wang Lixun for their constructive advice and insightful comments on my thesis. My heartfelt appreciation also goes to Prof. Tao Wenhao and Prof. Hung Tong Ning, Tony for their firm and kind support for my study. Special gratitude is also extended to my dear friend Ms. Linda Visner for her always generous help and encouragement.

Last but not least, I want to thank my dear family for giving me unconditional support and understanding!

Contents

List of Tables

Chapter 1
Why Study Media Representations of Macau's Gaming Industry in Greater China?

This introductory chapter starts by describing the background information of this book: Macau and the brief history of its pillar industry gaming. This is followed by the rationale for the volume which explains the reasons why Macau's gaming industry in 2014 was chosen as the research topic, why the media discourse of three regions was chosen and analysed, why corpus-based critical discourse analysis was conducted to address how Macau's gaming industry is represented in the news discourse, and why Sinclair's (2004) notion of extended units of meaning of the lexical item is used to examine the semantic and pragmatic meanings associated with frequently occurring lexical items in the news article corpora. Then, the research objective and questions and the structure of this book are described.

1.1 General

The present study adopts a corpus-based critical discourse analysis approach to examining and comparing news articles in order to find out media representations of Macau's Gaming Industry in 2014 in three territories of Greater China Region, namely Mainland China, Hong Kong and Macau. The comparison of media representations is achieved by combining two approaches, namely critical discourse analysis (CDA) and corpus linguistics (CL). CDA is based on Fairclough's (1989, 2001, 2015) notion of "language as a form of social practice" (p. 55). Three research methods of CL, namely frequency, trigrams, and key semantic fields, are employed to obtain quantitative results from the news article corpora. Sinclair's (2004) model of five categories of co-selection of a lexical item is applied to analyse the co-selection patterns of the most frequent lexical words in the three news article corpora.

Y. Wu, *Media Representations of Macau's Gaming Industry in Greater China*,
https://doi.org/10.1007/978-981-19-7724-4_1

1.2 Background: Macau's Political, Cultural, and Economic Situation and the Brief History of Gaming in Macau

Macau, a former Portuguese colony west of Hong Kong, is a very special place located in the Pearl River Delta region of Southern China. From the 16th to nineteenth centuries, Eastern and Western cultures mingled in Macau, guiding Macau's evolution into a place with its own unique political, economic and social features (Hao, 2011). Macau was administered by Portugal and it therefore followed the Portuguese economic structure of capitalism. In accordance with the Sino-Portuguese Joint Declaration on the Question of Macau in 1987, the Government of the People's Republic of China (PRC) resumed the exercise of sovereignty over Macau effective 20 December 1999. From that day on, Macau was handed over from Portugal to the People's Republic of China, like the return of Hong Kong's sovereignty on 1 July 1997. It became the second Special Administrative Region (SAR) of China, marking a new period in the history of Macau. Due to discussions of reunification with China in the 1980s, Hong Kong and Macau were allowed to retain their economic and administrative systems by practising the constitutional principle of "One Country, Two Systems" as proposed by the former Chinese leader, Deng Xiaoping. The principle hence allows the co-existence of two different socio-political systems, namely "socialism with Chinese characteristics" in Mainland China and capitalism in the Hong Kong Special Administrative Region (SAR) and Macau SAR (Leng, 2009).

Macau's economic influence was relatively small and had always been neglected by the public and the mass media (Tang & Sheng, 2009), as well as by the "scholarly community due to its territorial size, geographical marginality and historical isolation" (Hao et al., 2017, p. 2) before its handover to China. Macau has been overshadowed by its neighbouring British-ruled city, Hong Kong in the twentieth century and "lacks the political and commercial significance" of the other former colony (Hao et al., 2017, p. 2). From the mid-1970s until 1993, the economic development of Macao mainly relied on the manufacturing sector. In the 1990s, this sector was in decline, and by contrast, both the gaming and tourism industries gradually became crucial to Macau. After 20 December 1999, "Macau experienced a tremendous success in economic development" (Tang & Sheng, 2009, p. 220), especially its spectacular economic growth with double-digit rates between 2002 and 2013 (Hao et al., 2017). Sheng and Tsui (2009) observed that the major cause contributing to the economic boom in the post-colonial period was the rapid growth of casinos.

In the twenty-first century, gaming has become a pillar industry in Macau, playing a leading role in its economy; in addition, the gaming industry provides the most significant source of revenue for Macau's government (Gaming Inspection and Coordination Bureau [DICJ], n.d.). In terms of per capital gross domestic product (GDP), Macau is one of the richest economies. Macau's GDP soared from USD 5.84 billion in 1999 to USD 19.02 billion in 2007, with the city's GDP reaching USD 179.35 billion by 2014 (Macao Statistics and Census Services, 1999, 2002, 2007). In 2007, Macau became the largest gaming market in the world, exceeding the Las Vegas Strip in scale, with its gross gaming revenue reaching USD 7.08 billion. The casino boom in Macau not only benefits the region's GDP, but also government revenues. The gross gaming revenue in Macau has reached USD 44.97 billion, and tax revenues from gaming are USD 0.17 trillion, accounting for 74.41 percent of the Macao SAR's total financial revenue (USD 0.22 trillion), suggesting that the gaming industry is extremely significant for Macau's society (Statistics and Census Service, 2016). In other words, gaming revenue is the most sizable contributor to Macau's economic development. Specifically, the public and social services provided by Macau's government are primarily funded from tax revenue generated from gaming revenue.

Macau has been characterised by its gaming activities for many centuries (Wan & Pinheiro, 2011). The history of gaming in Macau can be traced back to the late sixteenth century (Gaming Inspection and Coordination Bureau, [DICJ], n.d.) when the form of gambling was very simple, "mainly on tables laid out across the streets" (Sheng, 2017, p. 97). In its initial period, gambling was illegal in Macau; however, at that time, gambling was considered to be a favourite leisure activity. According to Kwan and Mccartney (2005), after the 150-year deregulation of the gaming business, in 1847 Macau became the only place where gaming was permitted when the Portuguese authority legalised casino gambling in Macau in order to compensate for the economic recession. In the early 1960s, the Portuguese central government declared Macau to be a casino city (Sheng, 2017).

Macau has been well-known for its gaming industry from then on. This post-colonial economic boom of Macau is primarily driven by two stimuli (Lai, 2014). Firstly, the liberation of the gaming industry proposed by the government of Macau in 2002 was considered the primary force to accelerate the expansion of Macau's gaming scale. Specifically, prior to 2002, Macau's gaming sector was monopolised by Stanley Ho, who gained the concession in 1962, and was operated by Sociedade de Turismo Diversões de Macau (STDM). The Macau government decided to liberalise its gambling operations and broke this monopoly into three concessions, granting access through a bidding process to operators including Sociedade de Jogos de Macau (SJM), Wynn Resorts and Galaxy to "introduce the competitive mechanism into the gaming sector of gaming" (Sheng, 2017). The end of a 70-year monopoly and the opening of the market environment marked a historic step for Macau's gaming industry and allowed foreign investment and capital in Macau's gaming sector, leading to the rapid development of gaming in the Macau SAR.

Secondly, the "Facilitated Individual Travel" (FTS) policy (Statistics and Census Service, 2004) implemented in 2003 by the Chinese central government also boosted Macau's economic development as it offered a more convenient way for visitors from Mainland China to enter Macau. Before the implementation of the FTS scheme, group travel tours to Hong Kong and Macau were the preferred way for Mainlanders to visit these two regions, as the application for individual travel permits was more complicated.

1.3 Rationale for the Book

1.3.1 Why Study Macau's Gaming Industry in 2014?

As described in Sect.1.2, Macau's unique political, social and economic system and the remarkable development of Macau's economy, particularly in its gaming industry, indicate the value of research on this topic. In terms of Macau's news value, the rise of a robust gaming industry and its transformation from a sleepy fishing village to a city of wealth, without doubt, have attracted extensive and international attention in recent years (Hao et al., 2017; Lai, 2014). A number of mass media outlets, such as The Economist, CNN, BBC, and The Guardian, etc., have reported on Macau's gaming industry. In addition, issues and topics related to the gaming industry can also be found in official government reports, such as the Gaming Sector Survey published by the Statistics and Census Service (DSEC), and the research report entitled Interim Review of Gaming *Liberalization for Games of Fortune in Macao: Economic, Social, Livelihood Impacts and Operating Conditions of the Concessionaires*, published by the Gaming Inspection and Coordination Bureau (DICJ).

An increasing number of research studies has focused on different aspects of the gaming industry in Macau. For example, Fong et al. (2011) investigated the social cost of gambling in Macau before and after the liberalisation of gambling from a welfare economic aspect. Wang (2012) explored the impacts of casino gaming in Macau since 2002 from social, economic and environmental perspectives through interviewing 17 key community leaders. Wu and Chen (2015) investigated and compared the view-points of Singaporean and Macau residents on gaming and its social, economic and environmental impacts. Liu et al. (2015) reviewed the development of casino gaming in the last decades and described potential challenges and difficulties. Wan and Pinheiro (2011) examined the economic growth of casino gaming, and its subsequent problems of urban land use. Some studies are interested in the relationship between tourism and casino gaming in Macau. The relationship between tourism and the gaming industry is very close due to the Macau government's unique strategy for developing its casino-oriented tourism market. Wong and Rosenbaum (2012) explored tourists' motivation for visiting casinos in Macau by conducting a questionnaire survey. Zeng et al. (2014) surveyed the perceptions of Macau's gaming held by Mainland Chinese and Hong Kong visitors using the adaptation theory.[1] Tang et al. (2009) examined the internal image projection of Macau for different target tourists. Their study examined how Macau's image was represented by five English and Chinese language websites, namely a travel agency, the Macau Governmental Tourism Office (MGTO), a tourism magazine, guidebook and tourist blog, and made a comparison between the Chinese and English versions through adopting frequency analysis to check the top 35 words, content analysis and correspondence analysis (CA). Their findings reveal that "Macau's images projected on English and

---

[1] Adaptation theory means "when one is exposed to gambling for the first time, out of novelty, he or she is highly likely to participate" (Zeng et al., 2014, p.111).

Chinese websites are quite different" (Tang et al., 2009, p. 90). Specifically, Chinese-language sources tended to highlight the gambling aspect of Macau, as Chinese tourists tended to be attracted by gambling activities in Macau, neglecting its cultural traits. In contrast, the gaming image of Macau tended to be constructed by English-language sources as an "adult playground", with comparisons to Las Vegas. Several other studies have focused on legal problems related to Macau's gaming industry (Siu Lam & Greenlees, 2017; Liu et al., 2015); for example, Siu Lam and Greenlees (2017) examined and compared the implementation of anti-money laundering rules in casinos in the USA and Macau.

The year 2014 is chosen for the study of media representations of the gaming industry of Macau as this year was notable for Macau, due to several significant events which happened. These were treated as newsworthy events of huge value. First, 2014 marked the 15th anniversary of Macau's return to China. Chinese President Xi Jinping went to Macau in person to attend a series of celebration ceremonies for the 15th anniversary of the establishment of the Macau Special Administrative Region (MSAR). Second, the election of the fourth-term Chief Executive of the Macau government was held in August 2014 and the inauguration ceremony of the fourth-term MSAR government was held on 20 December 2014. On the other hand, a series of anti-corruption campaigns in Mainland China and stricter visa requirements and border controls have led to a considerable loss for Macau's gaming revenues (Riley, 2015). Liu et al. (2015) found that the gaming revenue decline in 2014 in Macau was primarily associated with both macroeconomic and political factors in China.

2014 is the year for Macau with a great news value (Harcup & O'Neil, 2001). Harcup and O'Neil (2001) listed 10 factors of news value, namely power elites, good news, bad news, surprise, magnitude, celebrities, entertainment, follow-up, relevance, and individual newspapers' agendas. The news value of the news articles published in 2014 was found to satisfy four of the ten factors. The first factor is the pinnacle of elite power, Chinese President Xi Jinping's visit to the Macau SAR to attend the 15th anniversary of Macau's return to China; The second factor is the stricter visa policies for visitors from mainland China to enter Macau (as "most gaming revenues were contributed by mainland visitors") (Zeng et al., 2014). The third factor is the Macau's junket gaming revenue decline due to the anti-corruption campaign in China. The fourth factor is a series of celebration activities centred around the 15th year anniversary of Macau's handover. The above four factors suggest that Macau's gaming industry in 2014 is a worthy topic for investigation.

1.3.2 Why Study the Media Representations of Macau's Gaming Industry in Three Territories?

Media discourse is a very important and common type of discourse, which can be found everywhere in our daily lives, and consequently very few people are not affected by the media (Talbot, 2007). As defined by O'keeffe (2006), media discourse is "a totality of how reality is represented in the broadcast and printed media from television to newspaper" (p. 1). It is recognized that the media have a huge influence on shaping people's ideas and behaviours (Bednarek & Caple, 2012; Fairclough, 1995; Thornborrow, 1999). The power of media discourse cannot be underestimated, as it can "influence knowledge, beliefs, values, social rations and social identities" (Fairclough, 1995, p. 2) and the media discourse exerts power through representing news events in a particular way (Fairclough, 1995). This study examined newspaper articles as newspapers contain more hard news than other printed media such as television and broadcast (Baker, Gabrietos & McEnery, 2013).

The study examines media representations of Macau's gaming industry by different newspapers published in the Greater China Region, namely the Chinese Mainland, Hong Kong and Macau. Although these three regions belong to the territory of the People's Republic of China (PRC), each is characterised with different historical backgrounds, economic statuses, political systems and social norms.

Mainland China is based on the socialist economic system and the state-owned economy, namely the socialist economy under ownership by the whole people (Constitution of the People's Republic of China, 2004). Since its reforming and opening-up in 1978, China has gradually become one of the most important economic powers in the world, transforming from the previous fully planned economy before 1978 to the socialist market economy in the 21st Century (The State Council of the People's Republic of China, n.d.).

By comparison, Hong Kong and Macau have been ruled by Britain and Portugal for more than one century. Currently, they are two special administrative regions (SARs) of the PRC under the national policy of "One Country, Two Systems", which was designed by China's paramount leader Deng Xiaoping in 1981 for the purpose of the peaceful reunification of these two capitalist societies to the communist PRC (Chan & Lo, 2010). They have still retained their previous capitalist systems after the transfer to Chinese sovereignty, according to the stipulation of the Basic Laws of Hong Kong SAR and Macau SAR. According to Leng (2009), "the socialist system and policies will not be practiced in Hong Kong and Macau" (p. 51). Each of them has their own unique economies (Woronoff, 2010). Specifically, Macau's economy mainly relies on gaming and tourism revenues (Gaming Inspection and Coordination Bureau [DICJ], n.d.) whereas Hong Kong's economy depends on four key industries, namely financial services, tourism, trading and logistics, and professional and producer services (Census and Statistics Department, 2018).

Apart from the diverse economic situations between these two regions, Hong Kong SAR and Macau SAR are also different in terms of socio-cultural backgrounds: for instance, Hong Kong's sociocultural distinctiveness or Hong Kong identity has been stated as being much stronger than Macau's. Macau's local identity is relatively weaker, instead, the Chinese identity of Macau people is stronger than Macau identity (Lee et al., 2013).

1.3.3 Why Corpus-Based Critical Discourse Analysis?

Two types of linguistic studies, namely corpus linguistic (CL) and critical discourse analysis (CDA), are combined to examine and compare the news articles in the present study.

CL is a widely utilized approach to analysing news discourse, making use of the computer corpus software to deal with the large amounts of news articles, with a particular emphasis on comparing the dominant themes and topics of news discourse through calculating keywords, frequency, etc. CL can reveal the repeated and regularly framing issues or events in media discourse (O'Halloran, 2010). The present study adopts corpus methods to generate three kinds of results for analysis, namely single lexical word frequency lists, trigrams, and key semantic fields to examine and compare news articles published in Chinese Mainland, Hong Kong and Macau.

As one of the most commonly utilized linguistic approaches in the news discourse, CDA concentrates on examining the relationship between language, power and ideology. Fowler (1991) contended that "nearly all meanings are socially constructed" (p. 8), and therefore all discourse can be treated as a social product or social practice. CDA sees language as social practice, suggesting that language is seen as part of society as well as a social process (Fairclough, 1989, 2015). According to Fairclough (2015), the relationship between language and society is internal and dialectical rather than external as language is a part of society and the dialectal relationship refers to "the relations between discourse and other elements of social phenomena" (Fairclough, 2007, p. 12). The goal of CDA is to go beyond the text, taking socio-cultural contexts into consideration (Bednarek & Caple, 2012). According to Baker (2010b) and Baker et al. (2013), the CDA approach requires a detailed examination of language in the discourse. The present study is based on Fairclough's (1995) notion of a three-dimensional conception of discourse, namely text, discourse practice, and sociocultural practice (p. 97). CDA was conducted to examine the news discourse, taking account of the broader historical, social and political contexts, in order to explain the corpus findings regarding Macau's gaming industry.

The corpus-based CDA can make use of the advantages of CL and CDA to examine news discourse. As noted by Mautner (2016), the role of CL cannot only contribute to the study of CDA in order to reduce the bias of CDA analysts for the arbitrary selection of research texts, but also can enlarge the empirical data of the study. The corpus-based CDA approach has generally been employed to examine different political, ideological and social issues. This includes, for example, the media's representations of human rights in Hong Kong (Cheng & Lam, 2010), western perceptions of Hong Kong before and after 1997 (Cheng & Lam, 2013), media attitudes towards the representations of Islam in the British press (Baker et al., 2013), and Chinese environmental issues (Liu & Li, 2017).

1.3.4 Why Extended Units of Meaning of the Lexical Item?

Single lexical wordlists have indicated the starting point of the study and the examination of extended units of meaning of frequent lexical words between different items of news discourse. Sinclair's (2004) descriptive model of lexical item is utilised as a basis for analysing frequency data. The notion "lexical item", proposed by Sinclair (2004), tends to be phrasal, and it refers to "an abstract category distinct from the word requires us to take meaning in to account" (Sinclair, 2004, p. 133). As Cheng (2012) noted, the individual word does not create meaning, instead "meaning resides in extended units" (p. 154) as "the word is not the best starting point for a description of meaning, because meaning arises from words in particular combinations" (Sinclair, 2004, p. 148) and lexical items can be considered as the composition of an extended unit of meaning.

Sinclair's (2004) descriptive model of five categories of co-selection of the lexical item consists of two obligatory categories (i.e. core and semantic prosody) and three optional categories (i.e. colligation, collocation and semantic preference). The core is invariable, constituting the evidence of the occurrence of the item as a whole, and the semantic prosody determines the meaning of the whole. Collocation is defined as "the co-occurrences of particular word, colligation is the co-occurrence of a grammatical class or pattern with a word, phrase or another set of grammatical choices" (Sinclair, 2004, p. 41). Semantic preference of a lexical item refers to "the restriction of regular co-occurrences to items which share a semantic feature" (Sinclair, 2004, p. 142). In comparison to semantic preference, the semantic prosody of a lexical item is the determiner of the meaning as a whole, expressing attitudinal and pragmatic meaning (Sinclair, 2004). It is the "consistent aura of meaning with which a form is imbued by its collocates" (Louw, 1993, p. 157) and it is attitudinal.

The extended unit of meaning of a lexical item is very necessary for analysing the frequent lexical words in each news discourse. Simple comparison of single word frequency lists is not enough, instead their co-selection patterns, such as collocation, semantic preference and prosody, can uncover the topical concerns and attitudes of different news discourse and media (Cheng & Ho, 2014).

1.4 Research Objective and Research Question

Based on the rationale described above, the present study aims to examine how Macau's gaming industry was represented in different English-language newspapers from three territories of China, namely Mainland China, Hong Kong SAR, and Macau SAR, as published in 2014 in order to compare media representations of Macau's gaming industry in the three territories.

For comparative purposes, three news article corpora were built, namely *Xinhua & China Daily* corpus (*XH&CDC*) in Mainland China, *South China Morning Post* corpus (*SCMPC*) in Hong Kong and *Macau Post Daily* corpus (*MPDC*) in Macau (see details in Sect. 3.3). The study aims to address the research question as follows:

> How do English-language newspapers published in Mainland China, Hong Kong SAR, and Macau SAR compare in terms of their representations of Macau's gaming industry?

The study compared the media representations of Macau's gaming industry of Chinese Mainland, Hong Kong SAR and Macau SAR through comparing the language use among three news article corpora in terms of frequent lexical words and co-selections of these frequent lexical words based on Sinclair's (2004) model of five categories of co-selection (i.e., collocation, semantic preference, and semantic prosody), frequent trigrams, and significant key semantic fields.

Specifically, collocation, semantic preference and semantic prosody are of five categories of co-selection (Sinclair, 2004) and examination of these three categories helps in understanding what kinds of co-selection patterns are made by writers in each news article corpus. Specifically, collocation refers to the "co-selection of words" (Cheng, 2012, p. 114). Collocation, "the frequent co-occurrences of words" (Sinclair, 2004, p. 28) can be helpful for comprehending the patterns of meaning of words in each news article corpus (Cheng, 2012). The semantic preference is related to "the co-occurrences of words with semantic choices" (Sinclair, 2004, p. 142) and therefore the examination of semantic preference of the same lexical item in each news article corpus can reveal the respective semantic choice of the same words in different news corpuses. Semantic prosody is significant for the present study as it tends to be evaluative and can reveal the writer's or speaker's attitudes and stances (Baker et al., 2008). The attitudinal meaning expressed by the semantic prosody of the same lexical words in the three news corpora can be compared to unveil the attitudes of news media.

The most frequent 20 trigrams can uncover similarities and differences between phraseological patterns among the three news article corpora.

Examining the top 20 key semantic fields can uncover the salient semantic fields in each news article corpus in order to reveal the differences and similarities among three news article corpora at the semantic level.

1.5 Structure of the Book

This book comprises six chapters in total. This Chapter is the introduction. Chapter 2 is a review of the relevant literature, mainly addressing two aspects: the features and functions of news discourse and the major research approaches to the study of news discourse. This is followed by a review of the theoretical frameworks of CL and CDA and relevant corpus-based CDA studies. Chapter 3 describes the research methods, focusing on the research procedures adopted to build the three news article corpora, a description of the news article corpora, and the analytical frameworks adopted by the study. In Chaps. 4 and 5, the findings of the study are described with reference to the research questions and the previous literature. The final chapter draws conclusions from this study, discusses both the implications and contributions of this study, some of the limitations, and suggests directions for future research.

References

Baker, P. (2010). Representations of Islam in British broadsheet and tabloid newspapers 1999–2005. *Journal of Language and Politics, 9*(2), 310–338.

Baker, P., Gabrielatos, C., Khosravinik, M., Krzyżanowski, M., McEnery, T., & Wodak, R. (2008). A useful methodological synergy? combining critical discourse analysis and corpus linguistics to examine discourses of refugees and asylum seekers in the UK press. *Discourse & Society, 19*(3), 273–306.

Baker, P., Gabrielatos, C., & McEnery, T. (2013). *Discourse analysis and media attitudes: The representation of Islam in the British press*. Cambridge University Press. https://doi.org/10.1017/CBO9780511920103

Bednarek, M., & Caple, H. (2012). *News discourse*. Continuum.

Census and Statistics Department, The Government of the Hong Kong Special Administrative Region. (2018). *Monthly Digest of Statistics*, Retrieved May, from https://www.statistics.gov.hk/pub/B71805FB2018XXXXB0100.pdf.

Chan, M. K., & Lo, S. H. (2010). *The A to Z of the Hong Kong SAR and the Macao SAR*. Scarecrow Press.

Cheng, W. (2012). *Exploring corpus linguistics: Language in action*. Routledge.

Cheng, W., & Ho, J. (2014). Brainwashing or nurturing positive values: Competing voices in Hong Kong's national education debate. *Journal of Pragmatics, 74*, 1–14.

Cheng, W., & Lam, P. W. Y. (2010). Media discourses in Hong Kong: Change in representation of human rights. *Text & Talk, 30*(5), 507–527.

Cheng, W., & Lam, P. W. Y. (2013). Western perceptions of Hong Kong ten years on: A corpus-driven critical discourse study. *Applied Linguistics, 34*(2), 173–190.

Constitution of the people's republic of China. (2004). Retrieved, from http://www.npc.gov.cn/englishnpc/Constitution/node_2825.htm.

Fairclough, N. (1989). *Language and power* (1st ed.). Longman.

Fairclough, N. (1995). *Media discourse*. Oxford University Press.

Fairclough, N. (2001). *Language and power* (2nd ed.). Longman.

Fairclough, N. (2015). *Language and power* (3rd ed.). Routledge.

Fairclough, N. (2007). Introduction. In F. Norman, C. Giuseppina, & P. Ardizzone (Eds.), *Discourse and contemporary social change* (Vol. 54, pp. 9–21). Germany: Peter Lang.

Fong, D. K., Fong, H. N., & Li, S. Z. (2011). The social cost of gambling in macao: Before and after the liberalisation of the gaming industry. *International Gambling Studies, 11*(01), 43–56.

Fowler, R. (1991). *Language in the news: Discourse and ideology in the press*. Routledge.

Hao, Z. (2011). *Macau history and society*. Hong Kong University Press.

Hao, Y., Sheng, L., & Pan, G. (2017). *Political economy of Macao since 1999*. Springer Singapore.

Harcup, T., & O'Neill, D. (2001). What is news? galtung and ruge revisited. *Journalism Studies, 2*(2), 261–280.

Kwan, A. V. C., & Mccartney, G. (2005). Mapping resident perceptions of gaming impact. *Journal of Travel Research, 44*(2), 177–187.

Lai, D. W. L. (2014). Social policy in the macao special administrative region of China. In K. H. Mok & M. K. W. Lau (Eds.), *Managing social change and social policy in greater China: Welfare regimes in transition* (pp. 126–146). Routledge.

Lee, F. L., Lee, C. C., Yao, M. Z., Chang, T. K., Lin, F. J., & Shen, C. F. (2013). *Communication, public opinion, and globalization in urban China*. Routledge.

Leng, T. X. (2009). On the fundamental characteristics of the "One Country, Two Systems" policy. *Academic Journal of "One Country, Two Systems"*, *1*(1), 50–59.

Liu, M., & Li, C. (2017). Competing discursive constructions of china's smog in Chinese and anglo-american english-language newspapers: A corpus-assisted discourse study. *Discourse & Communication, 11*(4), 386–403.

Liu, M. T., Chang, T. T. G., Loi, E. H., & Chan, A. C. H. (2015). Macau gambling industry: Current challenges and opportunities next decade. *Asia Pacific Journal of Marketing and Logistics, 27*(3), 499–512.

Louw, B. (1993). Irony in the text or insincerity in the writer? The diagnostic potential of semantic prosodies. In M. Baker, G. Francis, & E. Tognini-Bonelli (Eds.), *Text and technology: In honour of John Sinclair* (pp. 157–176). John Benjamins Publishing.

Macao Statistics and Census Services. (1999). *Yearbook of statistics*. Retrieved, from https://www.dsec.gov.mo/Statistic.aspx?NodeGuid=d45bf8ce-2b35-45d9-ab3a-ed645e8af4bb.

Macao Statistics and Census Services. (2002). *Yearbook of statistics*. Retrieved, from https://www.dsec.gov.mo/Statistic.aspx?NodeGuid=d45bf8ce-2b35-45d9-ab3a-ed645e8af4bb.

Macao Statistics and Census Services. (2004). *Yearbook of statistics*. Retrieved, from https://www.dsec.gov.mo/Statistic.aspx?NodeGuid=d45bf8ce-2b35-45d9-ab3a-ed645e8af4bb

Macao Statistics and Census Services. (2007). *Yearbook of statistics*. Retrieved from https://www.dsec.gov.mo/Statistic.aspx?NodeGuid=d45bf8ce-2b35-45d9-ab3a-ed645e8af4bb

Macao Statistics and Census Services. (2016). *Yearbook of statistics*. Retrieved, from https://www.dsec.gov.mo/Statistic.aspx?NodeGuid=d45bf8ce-2b35-45d9-ab3a-ed645e8af4bb

Mautner, G. (2016). Checks and balances: How corpus linguistics can contribute to CDA. In R. Wodak & M. Meyer (Eds.), *Methods of critical discourse studies* (pp. 154–179). Sage Publications.

O'Halloran, K. (2010). How to use corpus linguistics in the study of media discourse. In A. O'Keeffe & M. McCarthy (Eds.), *The Routledge handbook of corpus linguistics* (pp. 563–577). Routledge.

O'Keeffe, A. (2006). *Investigating media discourse*. Routledge.

Riley, C. (2015). Macau's economy slumps 17% after anti-corruption drive. *CNN Business*. Retrieved from https://money.cnn.com/2015/03/16/news/economy/macau-gambling-gdp-revenue/

Sheng, L. (2017). Explaining urban economic governance: The city of Macao. *Cities, 61*, 96–108.

Sinclair, J. (2004). *Trust the text: Language, corpus and discourse*. Routledge.

Siu Lam, C., & Greenlees, M. (2017). Casino money laundering regulations–Macao and USA. *Journal of Money Laundering Control, 20*(1), 52–69. https://doi.org/10.1108/JMLC-04-2016-0015

Talbot, M. (2007). *Media discourse: Representation and interaction: Representation and interaction*. Edinburgh University Press.

Tang, U. W., & Sheng, N. (2009). Macao. *Cities, 26*(4), 220–231.

Tang, L., Choi, S., Morrison, A. M., & Lehto, X. Y. (2009). The many faces of Macau: A correspondence analysis of the images communicated by online tourism information sources in English and Chinese. *Journal of Vacation Marketing, 15*(1), 79–94. https://doi.org/10.1177/1356766708098173

The State Council of the People's Republic of China. (n.d.). Retrieved, from http://english.gov.cn

Thornborrow, J. (1999). Language and the media. In L. Thomas, W. Shân, I. Singh, J. S. Peccei, J. Thornborrow, & J. Jones (Eds.), *Language, society and Power: An Introduction* (pp. 56–73). Routledge.

Wan, Y. K. P. (2012). The social, economic and environmental impacts of casino gaming in Macao: The community leader perspective. *Journal of Sustainable Tourism, 20*(5), 737–755.

Wan, P., & Pinheiro, F. V. (2011). The development of the gaming industry and its impact on land use. In N. M. K. Lam & I. Scott (Eds.), *Gaming, governance and public policy in Macao* (pp. 19–35). Hong Kong University Press.

Wong, I. A., & Rosenbaum, M. S. (2012). Beyond hardcore gambling: Understanding why mainland Chinese visit casinos in Macau. *Journal of Hospitality & Tourism Research, 36*(1), 32–51.

Woronoff, J. (2010). Editor's foreword. In M. K. Chan. & S. H. Lo., The A to Z of the Hong Kong SAR and the Macao SAR. (pp. 25-28). Plymouth: Scarecrow Press.

Wu, S. T., & Chen, Y. S. (2015). The social, economic, and environmental impacts of casino gambling on the residents of Macau and Singapore. *Tourism Management, 48*, 285–298.

Zeng, Z., Prentice, C., & King, B. E. (2014). To gamble or not? perceptions of Macau among Mainland Chinese and Hong Kong visitors. *International Journal of Tourism Research, 16*(2), 105–112.

Chapter 2
News Discourse and Relevant Linguistic Studies

This chapter reviews the literature relevant to this book in the areas of news discourse, the major research approaches employed in the study of news discourse, and relevant studies with their findings, especially those using CL and CDA, in terms of their research objectives, questions, and approaches (2.1). Then, relevant news discourse studies in the contexts of Mainland China, Hong Kong, and Macau are reviewed (2.2). This is followed by a review of the research approaches of corpus linguistics (2.3) and critical discourse analysis (2.4). The last section reviews the application of the integration of CL and CDA to investigate the different topic areas under the different contexts (2.5) other than news discourse, as it has been reviewed in (2.1) and (2.2).

2.1 Major Research Approaches to News Discourse

This section reviews different research approaches and methods of news discourse research studies, together with their findings. To begin with, news reports in both the press and on TV constitute a particular type of discourse (van Dijk, 1988). News discourse, as defined by Bednarek & Caple (2012), is "the type of discourse that audiences encounter in news bulletins, news programmes, on news websites, or in the newspaper-discourse that reports on newsworthy events, happening and issues" (p. 2). News discourse is not only limited to print news discourse, but also covers various kinds of media, such as online news, radio news, and television news. Bednarek & Caple (2012) view news discourse as multimodal or multi-semiotic, which does not only include the semiotic system of language, but also contains the semiotic system of images. For example, still and moving images can be found in TV news, online, and print news discourse, in which meanings are created through both text and image.

With the advent of technology, the internet has become widely used in people's daily lives. By the end of the twentieth century, an emerging product of the internet was online news (Boczkowski, 2004), in which more multimodal features such as

Y. Wu, *Media Representations of Macau's Gaming Industry in Greater China*,
https://doi.org/10.1007/978-981-19-7724-4_2

digital interactivity (e.g., general email, comment sections), hyperlinks and multimedia services (e.g., animation, audio and video) are merged into the traditional unidirectional print newspaper (Greer & Mensing, 2004). As Baker et al. (2013) observed, most print newspapers have corresponding online versions to keep up with social trends. Some studies have been conducted to explore the multi-modal elements in news discourse. For example, Knox (2009) explored the multi-modal features in the homepages of three online news websites.

A wide range of approaches has been adopted in the research of news discourse. Five major linguistic approaches have been adopted to examine news discourse, namely conversation analytical approach, systemic functional linguistic approach, sociolinguistic approach, corpus linguistic approach, the critical approach, and integration of CL and CDA. These approaches are discussed in turn.

2.1.1 Conversation Analysis

Research on news discourse based on conversation analysis specially focuses on the detailed analysis of spoken news discourse. Clayman & Heritage (2002), for instance, examined 250 television political news interviews broadcast in the UK and the USA by employing the sociological technique of conversation analysis to analyse the interaction phenomenon in the news discourse. The findings reveal that both British and American news interviews mixed the adversarial and naturalistic questions by examining the linguistic features of interviews in the design of questions. Montgomery (2010) explored interviews in broadcast news based on the close discourse analysis of interviews about the news related to the 2008 Beijing Olympics and the London Bombings, with a special focus on personal experience, emotions, and findings reveal that the news interviews from Beijing Olympics and London bombings are different from each other, for instance, the interviewees in the former are successful performers to demonstrate their emotions and interviewees in the latter are victims to narrate their experiences.

2.1.2 The Systemic Functional Approach

The systemic functional approach is informed by systemic functional linguistics (Halliday & Matthiessen, 2013), taking the genre and register of the news discourse into consideration. For instance, Feez et al. (2008) distinguished various genres in news discourse, such as hard news, soft news, media anecdotes, media features, etc. In another study, Caple (2010) focused on the meaning making in news, investigating the use of *allusion* in the 40 image-nuclear news stories based on systemic functional linguistics (SFL). The finding shows that the use of *allusion* can form a bond with the readers through the shared knowledge of these allusions.

2.1.3 The Sociolinguistic Approach

The sociolinguistic approach mainly underlines the socio-cultural analysis of news discourse with a special focus on the correlations between variable linguistic features and social contextual factors in a rather narrow sense (Fairclough, 1995), such as the correlation between the style and social context. For example, Bell (1991) examined the linguistic features in various newspapers, *The Times, the Guardian, the Sun* and *Daily Mirror*. The findings demonstrate that the linguistic features are diverse in terms of their different groups of target readers, such as the middle class and the working class. For instance, the determiner is employed more frequently in the middle-class newspapers than the working-class newspapers. The advantage of the socio-linguistic approach is to highlight the detailed linguistic features, to "the form and 'texture' of texts" (Fairclough, 1995, p. 21).

2.1.4 The Critical Approach

The critical approach is a well-known and commonly adopted approach to study news discourse, and is used to uncover power relations and ideologies hidden in the language (Bednarek & Caple, 2012) with the goal of going beyond the language and taking the socio-contextual factors into consideration (Fairclough, 1995).

For critical discourse analysts, news discourse is a complex communicative event, in which the social context is embedded (Van Dijk, 1988). By the same token, Conboy (2006) notes that language is of public nature and deeply rooted in social activities, and therefore it has the tendency to signal the social positioning of the writer and the reader. Moreover, he observes that "social difference is embedded within our language and therefore inevitably within the language of our news media" (p. 10).

Various studies have found that different newspaper types can have different topical focuses and the use of language when reporting the same news events. Regarding newspaper styles, newspapers can be categorized into different types based on style and format. Tabloids are smaller than broadsheets in paper size and have short articles focusing on the national news. In contrast, broadsheets are generally larger in paper size, with more text, concentrating on international and political news (Baker et al., 2013). They found that the language style in tabloids is more informal through the use of words such as cops and pal, and abbreviations such as TV, as opposed to more formal terms such as Mr and television. In another study, Conboy (2006) found that various language features are applied in different types of newspapers; for example, the specific rhetorical features (e.g., the use of political slang and metaphors) are used in tabloids to satisfy the interest of readers from working class compared with the broadsheets. In another study, Baker (2010b) observed that more emotive forms of language, such as terrorist, evil, maniac and henchman, were employed to describe Osama Bin Laden in the UK tabloids compared to broadsheets.

Additionally, in the view of critical discourse analysts, the power of news is great, which helps them "to construct a normative view of the world and set parameters for how we interact with the world" (Conboy, 2006, p. 4), indicating the potential of news to affect people's ways of thinking and shape their opinions, attitudes and ideologies. News exerts its control through the manifestation of language, as contended by Thornborrow (1999), who points out that an important aspect of "the potential power of the media from a linguistic point of view is the way that people and events get reported" (p. 58). Her study exemplifies how the same event is represented and interpreted differently by means of diversity in the employment of linguistic choices between two newspapers, and thus indicating different perspectives and focuses on that event. As expressed by Bednarek & Caple (2012), the power of the media cannot be underestimated, and the media can also wield an influence on governments and institutions. A number of studies (Blider & Allen, 2016; Dietrich et al., 2006; Esses et al., 2013; Lido et al., 2006; Walgarve et al., 2008) have shown that newspapers can exert great influence and power on public opinions. For example, Walgarve et al. (2008) found that newspapers can exercise more power than television, especially on the political agenda of Parliament and government. They also found that Belgian's parliament could be more easily influenced by the media than the government and besides, print media could have the larger effects on some particular issues such as law and order, and environment than foreign policy and economic issues. Dietrich et al. (2006) surveyed 167 students between the ages of 13–18, with the findings showing that some of the respondents who had read news articles related to the mentally ill and violence tended to associate those special groups with "violent" and "dangerous" and a negative attitude is revealed in the self-administrated questionnaire.

In another study, Lido et al. (2006) found that the negative representation of asylum seekers in the press tends to affect the readers' opinions and attitudes directly towards these people by conducting five experiments on British participants, including 86 students and staff from the University of Sussex. Esses et al. (2013) explored the effect of media coverage in Canada related to immigrants and refugees by checking whether participants who had read editorials related to the negative portrayal of refugees had a negative mental association. Their findings demonstrated that the media might cause extreme reactions of the readers toward immigrants and refugees. Blider & Allen's (2016) study shows that the British news press influences readers' opinions on the issue of immigration by distancing migrants and minorities from mainstream society by comparing migrant policies with newspaper portrayals.

Apart from the power of news, news can be biased and positioned. There are no absolutely neutral media without any biases or political tendencies in terms of selecting stories for publishing or giving priority to certain quotes or highlights in a particular article (Baker et al., 2013). According to Fowler (1991), newspapers normally employ various ways to report on the same thing, and this representation is neither random nor accidental as it carries different types of ideological load. According to van Dijk (1988), the stance is a vital part of news discourse due to different ways of thinking, as well as historical, cultural, social, political and ideological differences in different contexts. As Baker et al. (2013) suggest, the standpoint of news cannot be presented completely and fully impartially or accurately; instead, the media provide potential readers with different representations of events through the use of language. According to Baker (2006b), journalists and news reporters can produce or tailor news articles with a particular purpose, aiming at affecting the perception and views of newsreaders or even shaping the public's ideology through citing perspectives which are powerful and privileged.

This view is shared by Conboy (2010) who states that news agencies can select and adopt different strategies to report a particular topic, which is a decision-making process. Representation in media discourse is a constructive practice; therefore, events or ideas are transmitted under the influence of social, economic, political and historical factors, and not neutrally. Conboy (2010) also contends that the content and the style of a newspaper is determined by the voice of the political economy as the press must expend concentration on making a profit through their choice of political stances; more specifically, a newspaper can select particular linguistic forms, including lexical choice and language structure, so as to satisfy particular social groups' needs. The view is summarised as "newspapers have always created reader, not news, as the primary function" (ibid., p. 7). This suggests that, apart from the basic informational function, news discourse seems to transfer potential ideological effects to particular readers. Brindle (2016b) also observed that the particular choice of language or usage in news reports could result in the divergence of interpretations towards particular social issues. Accordingly, long-term repetition of a particular ideology or stance will consequently influence the views of the audience. Thus, news may be biased or partial toward the same events, depending on different news agencies' interests and political stances.

To conclude, news reports can exert huge power and influence, having "the ability to shape people's behaviours and ideas" (Bednarek & Caple, 2012, p. 6) through language choices, the recycling of certain news events, and the strengthening or weakening of particular topics. Studying news discourse can, therefore, reveal the ideologies, media attitudes and political stances behind a newspaper.

This study aims to examine newspapers in three territories of China to find out how language is employed in each newspaper and across the three newspapers to represent the topic of gaming in Macau in 2014.

CDA is commonly used to examine how particular social and political issues are represented in the news discourse in different types of contexts. The studies of Joye (2010), Yin (2007) and Li (2011) adopt CDA to examine the diversities of news discourse between China and the USA. Joye (2010) applied the CDA approach to investigate the news discourse related to the global SARS outbreak in 2003 with the finding showing that the term SARS was positively constructed in Belgium for its effective control and anti-crisis capacity and stressed safety and sufficient medical support in their own country. In contrast, this term in China was constructed negatively and Chinese people were going through the disease. Yin (2007) utilised the CDA approach to examine discursive strategies concerning the issue of human rights in the *New York Times* and *The People's Daily*, with the finding showing that the news discourse of *The New York Times* seemed to be on the offensive, criticising the abuse of the human rights, whereas Chinese news discourse in *The People's Daily* acted in the defensive role to resist American remarks. Li (2011) investigated news reports about the terrorist attack in 2001 in two newspapers, *The China Daily* published in China and *The New York Times* in the USA. The findings show that Chinese media tried to portray the USA in the role of actor who instigated the incident, whereas American media tended to portray the USA as the agent to calm and address the conflict.

The following studies have utilised CDA approach to examine the news discourse in the global contexts, such as the UK, Australia, South Korea, Sweden, and Brazil. Fowler (1991) used the CDA approach to analyse the representation of women in British press, with the findings suggesting that women are treated as a special group of people, namely women are constructed as a vulnerable group, and by comparison men are depicted as professionally and politically successful. Adopting CDA, Teo (2000) examined the ideological construction of racism in relation to gangs made up of Vietnamese minorities in two major Australian newspapers, revealing that racial inequality and prejudice existed in the news discourse towards Vietnamese people. Kim (2012) investigated how migrants were represented in Korean news discourse from 1990 to 2009 and found that the Korean media expressed a positive attitude towards these groups of people. However, she found that these positive expressions are not real and indeed negative, and that Korean media in actuality are attempting to marginalize immigrants within mainstream society and portray them as the victims. Persson (2016) investigated how immigrant rights activists are represented in 30 Swedish news articles, including both regional and national sources, by investigating the use of modality in the journalists' discourse. The findings demonstrate that activists are positioned as dreamers who are not strongly connected with political reality. Pereira & Biachi (2016) explored how discursive strategies about the female candidates in the Brazilian presidential election were employed in two domestic weekly magazines in 2011. Findings show that both magazines were found to contain diverse cultural and historical stereotypes regarding the understanding of women, and both publications held an unfavourable attitude towards both female candidates.

2.1.5 The CL Approach

Apart from the CDA, CL is also an important linguistic approach for the news discourse research, especially when dealing with a large number of news texts. For example, Baker & McEnery (2005) carried out a corpus-based discourse analysis on refugees and asylum seekers between the British newspapers and the UN (i.e., texts from the Office of the United Nations High Commissioner for Refugees website) by calculating the relative frequency and collocates of *refugee(s)* and *asylum seeker(s)*. They found that the media texts show different attitudes compared with the UN discourse. Specifically, British news corpora indicated a more complicated and ambivalent view towards refugees and asylum seekers and centred their influence on British society, whereas the UN corpus tended to employ a global view towards this issue. Johnson et al. (2003) explored the notion of 'political correctness' (PC) in three British broadsheet newspapers, namely *The Sunday Times*, *The Independent on Sunday* and *The Observer* (1994–1999), by employing two corpus analytical methods (i.e., frequency and keywords). The finding reveals that the use of the term PC decreases during the five-year period in three newspapers and the frequencies of the terms related to PC are closely related to the debate over Prime Minister Tony Blair and the polity party in the UK Labour party.

In another study, Kim (2014) examined the collocational patterns concerning *North Korea* published in three mainstream US news sources (i.e., *CNN*, *Newsweek*, and *The New York Times*). The corpus findings show that the US media tend to divide countries into specific sets in terms of those countries' political stance towards America. Specifically, the three US media corporations tend to classify Iraq and Pakistan as the "enemy group", like North Korea, through a detailed examination of collocate lists pertaining to North Korea. In Gabrielatos & Baker's (2008) corpus-based study, they examined the discursive representation of refugees and asylum seekers in the UK press. They also noted that the manner of representation of news in broadsheets and tabloid news may be diversified, and therefore they employed keyword analysis to compare themes and topics between the two types of newspaper. Gabrielatos & Baker's (2008) research found that there is an annual diachronic change towards asylum applications in the UK press from 1982 to 2005.

2.1.6 Integration of CDA and CL in the News Discourse

In recent years, a large number of studies have integrated CL and CDA to examine how particular political or social issues are represented in the news discourse. Some scholars examined the representation of several synonyms in the media discourse. For example, Orpin (2005) investigated the ideology of eight synonymous words in a corpus of 800 texts collected from four British newspapers.

The synonymous words are found to be *corruption*, *sleaze*, *bribery*, *graft*, *malpractices*, *impropriety*, *nepotism*, and *cronoyism*. Corpus tools were used to generate the related concordance lines and collocations, and capture the semantic profile of words, connotational differences, and the geographic locations that words refer to. The media coverage concerning these words was found to be quite negative when they were related to South Korea, Italy, India and Malaysia, whilst the British media show less negative attitudes towards similar events transpiring in Britain. Similarly, Mautner (2007) examined media discourse related to the term *elderly*. Based on the findings, the word *elderly* is found to co-select with words with negative meanings, such as *infirm* and *frail*. A few positive adjectives, such as *charismatic* and *sharp-minded*, are also found to modify the term *elderly*.

In addition, some studies are interested in how the controversial groups of people are represented in the British newspapers. Baker et al. (2008) extended their research to examining refugees, asylum seekers, immigrants and migrants (RASIM) and developed a nine-step model of corpus-assisted CDA, which integrates the discourse-historical approach in CDA (DHA) with CL. It involves moving recursively between different levels of analysis, "using frequency and concordance information to derive and test new hypotheses" (Baker, 2014, p. 213). In addition, Baker et al. (2013) conducted a large-scale corpus-driven study aiming at examining how the word *Muslim* is represented and manifested in the 140 million-word media corpus collected from various types of British newspapers from 1998 to 2009. The online computer tool Sketch Engine was used to analyse collocations of the noun *Muslim*. The findings show that the term *Muslim* tends to co-select with words with negative meanings such as conflicts. In another study, Baker (2010b) investigated how subjects related to Islam and Muslims are represented in the British press by examining the top keywords. Baker (2010b) subsequently compared two types of newspapers (i.e., tabloid press and broadsheet) by making a comparison between significant keyword lists. The results show that the themes and topics of news reports in the two sets of newspaper are diverse. Tabloids tend to focus on the individual terrorist while broadsheets do not pay much attention to individuals; instead, the coverage of news reports relevant to global, Muslim-related conflicts is broader than that in the tabloids.

In a recent study, Baker (2014) investigated the representation of *trans people* in the British press by adopting CL which demonstrates how corpus techniques can assist CDA in a detailed way, finding that there is evidence to suggest that the British media show a marked treatment towards these people by portraying this group of people as weird objects, villains, etc.

In recent decades, more researchers have focused on bilingual and multilingual news discourse. CDA and CL are combined to uncover the ideological differences in the news discourse in two or three different languages. For example, Taylor (2014) conducted a cross-linguistic discourse analysis to examine how migrants are represented in two countries' news media with the research findings revealing that migrants tend to be negatively represented in regional news reports in Italian and British tabloids, and that geographical nationalities are foregrounded in both countries' corpora. Vessey (2013) conducted a cross-linguistic corpus-assisted discourse study to examine and compare ideologies in multi-lingual articles published in Anglophone and Francophone Canadian newspapers, in order to ascertain the ideological differences between newspapers in these two languages. Vessey (2013) found that the English-speaking and French-speaking newspapers served different purposes. The English version contains more positive features such as success and intelligence, and the special focus is given to the importance of bilingualism and language education; in contrast, the French version gives a less positive evaluation of bilingualism and paid little attention to language education.

Bayley et al. (2012) examined multilingual newspapers related to *citizenship* published in France, Italy and the UK. Their findings indicate that *citizenship* co-occurs with words related to the education field in the three corpora with different representations. The Italian news mentioned education and citizenship in an abstract way, whereas the British news paid more attention to specific educational institutions. The French corpus contains both of these features. The Italian corpus revealed the political uncertainty towards issues regarding the right to citizenship associated with the problem of immigrants. In the UK corpus, the term *citizenship* was closely related to education with positive value.

Morley & Taylor (2009) investigated how immigrants are represented in Italian and British newspapers, highlighting relevant discussions related to the notion "us" and "them". Immigrants were shown as tending to be constructed by the Italian press in a negative light, underlining their illegality.

2.2 News Discourse in Chinese Mainland and Hong Kong

In the context of China, many studies have examined how a particular social event or topic is represented in the news media, addressing ideologies and attitudes.

In the Hong Kong SAR, Cheng & Lam (2010) examined the media representation of the human rights issue in Hong Kong's leading English newspaper: *the South China Moring Post* (SCMP) between two particular periods, namely before (1993–1994) and after (2003–2004) Hong Kong's return to China. They studied the co-selection patterns associated with the lexical item *human rights* based on the Sinclair's (2004) descriptive model of five categories of co-selection in order to track the ideological changes between these two periods. Results show that the ideologies represented in the *SCMP* concerning human rights issues had shifted over the two periods. In another study, Cheng & Lam (2013) examined western perceptions of Hong Kong during two particular periods of time: 1996–1998 and 2006–2008 before and after Hong Kong's handover to China through examining the co-selection patterns associated with the lexical item *Hong Kong/ political*. The findings of their study revealed that western media discourse has changed across these two periods, shifting from a focus on the general business environment in British Hong Kong to a concentration on politically-related events or issues in the Hong Kong SAR. In contrast, the Chinese media tend to quote more Hong Kong political parties or individuals' unfavourable opinions on the current Hong Kong political situation in post-1997.

Cheng & Ho (2014) explored the social issues concerning the introduction of "Moral and National Education" (MNE) in Hong Kong in 2012 through comparing collocations, semantic preferences, semantic prosodies and metaphors between news reports and Hong Kong government press releases. Their results showed that various metaphors related to fighting are applied in the news discourse to describe the actions and attitudes respond to the government, whereas government press releases maintained a neutral and positive attitude towards this plan.

Flowerdew et al. (2002) examined the discriminatory discursive practices in the *South China Morning Post* regarding immigrants from Chinese Mainlanders claiming right-of-abode in 1999 to 2000 with the finding showing that the metaphorical language with negative meanings, such as *influx*, *flood* and *burden*, are used to describe immigrants from mainland China.

Zhang & Mihelj (2012) investigated the discursive constructions concerning the collective identity in Hong Kong by examining two pro-democratic news media outlets, *Apple Daily* and *The Hong Kong Economic Journal*, and the pro-government outlets *Oriental Daily News and Wen Wei Po*. Findings show that the two pro-democracy newspapers tend to label China as a unit, not including Hong Kong, underlining various issues between Hong Kong and China. By comparison, pro-government newspapers are inclined to highlight unity, representing Hong Kong as an integral part of China. Feng (2017) targeted at the recent social issue that happened in Hong Kong. A corpus-based study was adopted based on the Attitude framework to investigate how the Occupy Central Movement is represented in 120 news articles collected from four Chinese-language newspapers of Hong Kong, including *Apple Daily*, *Ming Pao*, *Oriental Daily News*, and *Ta Kung Pao*. The results demonstrate that their attitudes towards the Occupy Central Movement have changed, moving from the initially supportive to neural and finally antipathetic toward this event.

In the Chinese Mainland context, relevant research studies have combined CL and CDA to reveal respective ideological differences towards the same news events or themes represented between the newspapers published in Mainland Chinese and those published in the English-speaking countries, such as the UK and the USA. For example, Qian (2010) merged CDA and CL to examine and compare the news language related to terrorism before and after the 9/11 attack in *The People's Daily* in China and the *The Sun* in the UK. Qian (2010) determined that *terrorism* is constructed differently in the above two newspapers. More emotive expressions, such as *unspeakable* and *unbelievable*, as well as the strongly subjective adjective *evil* were employed in *The Sun* to describe terrorism and by contrast, *The People's Daily* tends to employ the implicit and careful language.

In another study, Wang (2009) conducted a corpus-based study to explore the media representations regarding Taiwan's KMT Chairman Lien Chan's visit to China, by examining the frequencies, part-of-speech of respective lexical choices, and semantic category frequencies in two English-language newspapers published in different social contexts, namely *China Daily* in Mainland China and *The China Post* in Taiwan. The findings revealed that *China Daily* primarily marked the significance of his visit to China with a very positive attitude while the reporting perspectives of *The China Post* in Taiwan were varied, including detailed descriptions of such incidents as the protests caused by the visit. Wang (2013) examined the lexical item *depression* in English and its Chinese equivalent *Yiyuzheng* between the Chinese and the British newspapers from 1984 to 2009 through corpus analysis of wordlists, keywords, semantic prosody, etc. The findings suggest that the media construction of *depression* between the British and the Chinese media is different. Specifically, improvement of the social environment is constructed by the Chinese press as being more important than medical treatment, whereas *depression* in the British news corpus was constructed variously as a psychological problem and a biochemical condition for which pharmaceutical intervention and psychotherapy are needed. Yang (2015) examined how the 2008 Summer Olympics torch relay was represented in the British (*BBC News* and *The Guardian*) and the Chinese press (*China Daily*), with the findings implying that ideological clashes are found in both countries' press towards the Beijing Olympic Games. The Chinese press emphasised the value of Chinese pride, honour, and harmony with a very positive attitude towards this significant sports event; by comparison, the British media reported more controversial issues caused by the torch relay, with a focus on human rights issues in China, including the lexical item *Tibet problem* with the largest number of occurrences due to the diverse historical and political context. Liu et al. (2015) investigated how the metaphorical language concerning currency dispute is represented in two English-language newspapers between *China Daily* and *New York Times*, based on the corpus-based critical metaphor analysis. The findings demonstrate that five dominant metaphors, namely Physical, Movement, Health, Conflict Machine, and Victim, are framed differently in each newspaper. Currency dispute is constructed as the physical conflict and Renminbi (i.e., Chinese current unit) is described as the victim of government control and manipulation in the western news. By comparison, the Chinese press tends to conceptualize the dispute and the USA made the Renminbi of scapegoat. The diversity between these two newspapers is attributed to the differences in socio-political contexts.

Wang & Chen (2015) conducted a comparative study to examine how the 2008 Sichuan Earthquake was represented between *China Daily* (*CD*) and the *New York Times* (*NYT*) by examining word frequencies, parts of speech (POS) and semantic fields. The findings demonstrate the political stances and ideologies hidden in the language in the context of two different countries are different. The Chinese press tends to construct a positive image of the Chinese government and the united Chinese nation whereas the American media show their concern about the technological backwardness and the incompetence of government with a negative attitude. Liu & Li (2017) conducted a corpus-assisted discourse study (CADS) to compare the representation of the topic of the Chinese smog between 2011 and 2014 in *China Daily*, published in China and three English language newspapers, namely *The New York Times*, *The Times* and *The Guardian*, by examining and comparing the top 100 lexical keywords and top 10 evaluative lexical collocates in each newspaper corpus. The results demonstrate that *China Daily* tends to construct China's smog as a normal weather phenomenon, highlighting the positive image of the Chinese central government as having a strong responsibility; by contrast, the western media are more likely to project China's smog as a severe pollution, affecting human health, and to hold a negative, adverse attitude towards the Chinese government.

As noted, to date scarce research has been conducted to explore the news discourse of Macau, not to mention employing a combined CL and CDA approach. The majority of the studies is interested in examining the stylistic features of news articles at a lexical and syntactic level. For example, Yao & Huang (2014) explored the lexical differences in the Chinese language news discourse between mainland China and Macau, with their finding showing that the Chinese particle *LE* (了) is employed more frequently in Macau's newspapers, which has a more subjective reporting perspective than that of mainland Chinese newspapers.

2.3 The CL Approach in Non-media Discourse

This section describes the CL approach in detail and reviews the literature about the application of the CL approach in discourse types other than news discourse. With the advancement of computer technology, many scholars have taken advantage of different corpus methods to examine a large sample of text data.

Corpus linguistics has always been seen as a quantitative method. According to Hunston (2002, p. 2), a corpus is "a large collection of naturally occurring data specialised for language study and in which data is readable and calculated by computer programs". In other words, "corpora are interrogated through the dedicated software" (Hunston, 2006, p. 234). Corpus is described as "an empirical method, which is used to analyse and describe language, and the use of corpora is seen as the primary data and starting point" (Cheng, 2013, p. 1). Mautner (2008, p. 55) argues that quantitative indicators illuminate particularly promising entry points into the discourse data. Normally, the texts are selected to compile a corpus with a specific purpose and can represent a particular type or variety of language (Hunston, 2006, p. 234).

One of the merits of the corpus is the ability to deal with large amounts of data. Hunston (2006, p. 234) states that a large corpus can be used to test hypotheses from the quantitative dimension in many linguistic studies. Stubbs (2001) summarises evaluative meaning as not only expressed by individual words but also by phrases, co-occurring nodes and collocates stating that "repeated instances of collocation across a corpus provide objective, empirical evidence for evaluative meanings" (Stubbs, 2001, p. 215). Repeated patterns reflect evaluative meanings widely shared in a discourse community rather than individual feelings. In addition, CL is a suitable approach for comparative purposes, and it provides insights into the main features of different specialised corpora to identify differences and similarities.

CL can be further divided into corpus-based, corpus-driven, and corpus-assisted approaches, based on why and how a corpus is utilised in conducting research (Cheng, 2012, p. 13). Tognini-Boneili (2001) distinguishes between the corpus-based and the corpus-driven approaches. Specifically, the use of the corpus-based approach indicates a methodology that "makes use of the corpus itself to expound, test and exemplify theories and descriptions that were generated before a large corpus become available to inform language study" (p. 65). Baker et al. (2013, p. 26) explain that the corpus-based approach is used to test hypotheses. In contrast, the corpus-driven approach refers to analysis of the integrity of the data. Therefore, the description and interpretation towards the corpus is based on the evidence which is provided by the corpus (Tognini-Boneili, 2001, p. 84). Baker (2006a) explains that the corpus-based approach utilises corpus as a source used to check researcher intuition while the corpus-driven approach is more like the inductive way which treats corpus itself the data and pattern which is noted to express regularities and exceptions. Baker & McEnery (2005) point out that the advantage of the corpus-based approach is to allow discourse analysts to gain a more complete and detailed understanding of meanings and functions of certain word choices in text (p. 223).

Flowerdew (2014) summarizes and compares eight entry points of the bottom-up approach concerning the corpus method of specialised text analysis. They are word frequency list, keyword list, n-grams, congrams, phrases frames, collocational frameworks, small words, and semantic sequences. These above corpus studies are the bottom-up approach with conclusion demonstrating that the choice of the starting points is determined by the different digital corpus tools as well as the research purpose.

Frequency data refers to "the words in a corpus can be arranged in order of their frequency in that corpus" (Hunston, 2002, p. 3). It is the most common way to approach quantified data, and is especially useful when comparing different corpora in terms of their respective frequency list. Word frequency list can be employed as the starting point to reveal the most frequently mentioned themes in the particular corpus (Brindle, 2016a; Cheng, 2012; Vessey, 2015). The frequency data is not only limited to individual words, but also appears with multi-word units, clusters or n-grams, which "tell us something about the context that a word occurs in" (Qian, 2010, p. 35).

Keywords occur statistically frequently in corpora compared to the reference corpus, and Qian (2010) points out that the analysis of keywords is very significant for CDA as it can signify the salient lexis and "reveal a preoccupation with certain ways of presenting information" (p. 35).

Collocation in this study is employed to examine concordance lines and observe the salient occurrence of node words; additionally, concordance analysis enables the analysis of semantic preference and semantic prosody. McEnery et al., (2006, p. 159) summarise that "collocation, semantic preference and prosody can only be quantified reliably on the basis of corpus data in the lexical studies". According to Sinclair (1991), the analysis of collocation is an integral approach to gain a deeper understanding of the lexical item as "collocates are extensions of meanings which can provide further semantic analysis" (p. 115). The examination of collocates in the concordance lines ascertains language patterns as well as contextual information as concordance analysis is the best way to scrutinize a text as the observation of concordances is helpful to obtain the particular word form in detail (Baker, 2006a; McEnery et al., 2006). Baker et al. (2008) explain that the semantic preference tends to be semantic rather than evaluative as semantic preference is "a class of words which share some semantic feature such as words to do with medicine" or "change" (Stubbs, 2001, p. 88).

Some studies integrating CL and CDA are based on the descriptive model of Sinclair's (2004) five categories of co-selection of a lexical item. For example, Cheng (2006) explored the top 10 most frequently occurring lexical words in the spoken data related to SARS, partly collected from the spoken corpus from the *Hong Kong Corpus of Spoken English*. The analytical framework of the study is based on lexical items (Sinclair, 2004). The findings reveal an optimistic view of "Hong Kong's post-SARS future" (p. 341). Pope (2015) examined the lexical items associated with *come* and *go* in various sub-corpora, including ICE-Canada, -GB, -India, and -Jamaica in the *International Corpora of English* (ICE) with the finding that *come* and *go* have the unique co-selections in different discourse. In another study, Ooi (2008) analysed the language of online gaming, with the results showing that the lexical item *game* preponderantly occurred in the gaming blog corpus. In addition, 5 lexemes, namely *vertically, frag, cheap, NPC* and *shmup*, are investigated using concordance analysis with a special focus on their semantic prosodies, and are then compared against online dictionaries. Ooi (2008) found that *frag* as a verb is found to have the semantic prosody of "positive violence" in the gaming corpus, whereas its dictionary definition refers to 'violent killing' (p. 319). The lexical item *vertically* co-selects with the verbs *scroll(ing)*, *flip*, *advance*, and *move*, revealing that the semantic preference is 'movement' and the semantic prosody is 'forward'. (p. 318).

Apart from the CL methods described above, semantic field analysis is also widely utilized for the comparative purpose in different kinds of genres and discourse, such as Internet forum, legal language, literature work, online Q&A forum, mission statements and political manifesto (e.g., Baker, 2017; Culpeper, 2009; L'Hôte, 2010; Potts, 2016; Potts & Baker, 2012; Potts & Semino, 2017; Prentice, 2010; Rayson, 2008; Sun & Jiang, 2014). These semantic field analyses have demonstrated that conducting semantic field analysis with the aid of the USAS program in the Wmatrix (Rayson, 2008) can draw the comparison between the target corpus and reference corpus at the semantic level through identifying overused key semantic tags. As Prentice (2010) noted, the key semantic tags (fields) can reveal the dominant themes and concepts in a particular discourse as they are statistically significant. For example, Rayson (2008) employed key semantic field analysis to compare *Labour* and *Liberal Democrats* between the Labour corpus and the LibDem corpus. The findings reveal the different focuses between party policy areas at the semantic level: the Labour corpus indicates the greater emphasis on work, employment and family issues; by comparison, the Liberal Democrats focus on transport policy, environmental issues, etc.

Potts & Baker (2012) conducted a comparative cultural study aiming at contrasting American (AmE) and British English (BrE) by comparing their significant key semantic tags. Their findings demonstrate some differences between BrE and AmE. First, in terms of topic preferences, British English focuses on topics or themes related to time, hypotheticals, modality; by contrast, American English focuses on the themes concerning military and weaponry, as well as IT and computing. Second, in terms of diachronic change, semantic field analysis reveals that BrE shows a preference for degree and suitability, whereas AmE demonstrates the tendency of comparison. Potts (2016) used a key semantic field analysis to investigate the online question-and-answer forum posts to signify the distinctive features as well as the broad theme in meaning in order to examine the differences among several sub-corpora. Specifically, Potts (2016) compared the top 2 key semantic tags, with the findings revealing a diversity of key topics and themes in three sub corpora of four countries (i.e., the UK, the Philippines, India, and the US). Key topics related to religious beliefs are found in the Indian corpus, and those related to government and education are over-represented in the Philippines corpus. In the UK corpus, "FOOD" and "GEOGRAPHY" are the top key semantic tags, and by contrast, social and military issues such as welfare and racial divisions are the focuses in the US corpus.

Baker (2017) adopted the semantic field study in one part of his study to investigate the cultural and pragmatic aspects within two varieties of English, namely British English and American English, through examining eight corpora, and calculating and comparing the semantic tags. The findings revealed that both American and British cultures are becoming more 'advanced', moving from old forms of industry to technological achievements such as computing, visual arts and flight evidenced by a growing use of semantic tags related to scientific and technological field. The references related to law and order, weapons and war are increasingly used in the American corpus. Besides, both varieties of English are found to be more concerned with themes or topics related to danger. In the American corpora, words concerning law and order are significantly more frequently mentioned compared to the British corpora.

Besides, semantic field analysis is also applied to compare the use of metaphors in different corpora. For instance, implementing a keyness comparison at the semantic level, Potts & Semino (2017) compared the "violence" metaphor between the MELC-US and MELC-UK corpora. Their study revealed differences of topics in terms of the use of the metaphor of violence between the UK and the US-based discourse. The US corpus contained more metaphors specific to the American healthcare system than the UK corpus to its own system.

Sun & Jiang (2014) examined the metaphorical use between the Chinese and the American mission statement in the business discourse with the finding revealing that the use of metaphor in the US and China is different: the Chinese companies tend to construct themselves as the strong competitor of business and by contrast, the American cooperation tends to underline themselves as the ethnically responsible community members.

L'Hôte (2010) investigated how globalisation was articulated in New Labour political discourse and made use of USAS tagging to examine and compare the general tendency of the text, with BNC as the baseline corpus. The findings showed that globalisation is predominantly framed as an economic phenomenon, characterised by issues related to tourism and security. Potts & Kjær (2016) adopted the semantic field analysis in their corpus-based CDA study on legal language. They calculated the dominant key semantic tags by Wmatrix so as to obtain the dominant concepts in the two trials and appeals.

The advantage of semantic analysis, different from the traditional corpus techniques, such as frequency and keywords, can allow the researcher to access the themes of a particular discourse in an indirect way; that is, by using the words to expand the contextual information (Prentice, 2010) In contrast, the adoption of semantic field analysis is a straightforward choice to access the broad themes within a corpus as "the semantic tags can reveal the semantic fields which group together word senses that are related by virtue of their being connected at some levels of generality with the same mental concept" (Archer et al., 2002, p. 1).

2.4 Critical Discourse Analysis

There are three major theoretical approaches to CDA with different emphases, aspects, and backgrounds. They are dialectical-relational approach (Fairclough, 1989, 1995), socio-cognitive studies (Van Dijk, 1993), and discourse-historical method (Wodak & Mayer, 2009).

The dialectical-relational approach (DRA) sees language as a social practice, with a special focus on sociocultural change and the change in discourse. As Fairclough

(2001) points out, unlike discourse analysis, the objective of CDA is not simply restricted to analysing the text itself, but to interpret the relationship between text and interaction, and explain the relationship between interaction and social context. DRA is to analyse the dialectal relationship between language and other elements of social practice (Wodak & Meyer, 2009).

According to Fairclough (1989, 2015), CDA research normally covers three dimensions or states. As Fairclough (2010) describes:

Each discursive event has three dimensions or facets: it is a spoken or written language text, it is an instance of discourse practice involving the production and interpretation of text, and it is a piece of social practice. These are three perspectives one can take upon, three complementary ways of reading, a complex social event (p. 94).

Fairclough (2015) suggests that CDA involves three stages. They are "description", "concerned with formal properties of the text" (p. 58); interpretation, "concerned with relationship between text and interaction" (p. 58), and explanation "concerned with the relationship between interaction and social context" (p. 59).

The discourse-historical approach (DHA) is connected with the socio-cognitive theory (Van Dijk, 1998), conceiving the term 'discourse' as structured forms of knowledge and the term 'text' as "concrete oral utterances and written documents" (Wodak & Meyer, 2015, p. 6). DHA (Reisigl & Wodak, 2015) focuses on the employment of augmentation strategy, highlighting historical analysis in which context is seen as primarily historical, based on empirical data and background information.

The following CDA studies are based on the DHA framework. For example, Lawton (2013) examined the discursive construction of "English only movements" for immigrants in the public texts made by the proponents of this movement in the context of the USA. The legitimation, and the use of metaphor are analysed based on the DHA notion with the findings revealing that the ideological opinions concerning "in group" and "out groups" are constructed to derogate and discriminate the discrimination immigration. Musolff (2014) examined the use of metaphor *body politic* in British English, French and German public discourse and explained the findings in the light of the historical, augmentative dimension of discourse. The findings show that the metaphorical use of *body politic* in three languages was not only used as metaphors but also was associated with political memories and mythologies in terms of discourse-historical perspective.

The approach to socio-cognitive discourse analysis (SCDS) (van Dijk, 1993) combines the social cognition theory with linguistic and social theories (Lin, 2014), in which discourse is seen as a communicative event compassing the written form, conversational interactivity and other semiotic elements. As van Dijk (2015) noted, SCDS connects the discourse structures with social structures through a complex socio-cognitive link. For example, Koller (2012) investigated the socio-cognitive representation concerning collective identity in the radio interview data based on SCDS, starting with describing the linguistic features from the individual text at the micro-level to the interpretation of contexts at the macro-level with the aim of examining how identities are represented through checking linguistic or other semiotic devices. The finding shows that the development of collective identity is not a linear fashion.

Although CDA is informed by various theoretical frameworks, the various approaches share some features. Firstly, CDA especially addresses social problems and "all approaches are problem-oriented" (Wodak & Meyer, 2015, p. 4), taking into account contexts of the language use (Wodak, 2001) as "CDA views language as discourse and a form of social practice" (Fairclough, 1989, p. 2). CDA also scrutinises how ideologies and power relations are represented in language as "discourse constitutes society and culture" (Fairclough & Wodak, 1997, p. 271).

Secondly, "discourse is historical" (Fairclough & Wodak, 1997, pp. 271–80). Specifically, the three factors of power, history and ideology are essential for CDA (Wodak, 2001, p. 3). Baker et al., (2008, p. 273) explain that CDA is the performance of discourse analysis from a critical perspective which goes beyond the text, addressing issues of power, domination and ideology, as well as taking historical, social, economic factors into consideration, and therefore the CDA theoretical framework is always applied to gain insights from language, power and ideology (Orpin, 2005, p. 37).

The third shared tenet of CDA is that power relations are discursive (Fairclough & Wodak, 1997). CDA is commonly used to investigate the relationship between language and power; for instance, the social inequality embedded in discourse. According to Wodak & Meyer (2015), the notion of power is central to CDA analysts as "power does not necessarily derive from language, but language can be used to challenge power, to subvert it, to alter distributions of power in the short and the long term" (p. 12). Moreover, in most cases, power is not visible, and therefore "language provides a finely articulated vehicle for the expression of differences in power in hierarchical social structure" (ibid., p. 12).

According to Wodak (1996), although CDA focuses on social problems rather than centring on the language per se, CDA still needs to take into account the linguistic features of the social and cultural processes and structures, and therefore "CDA is essentially interdisciplinary" (p. 17). Maunter (2016) suggests that CDA gives special attention to connecting linguistic evidence with a detailed analysis of extra-linguistic context (i.e., social and cultural structures). Flowerdew (2018) explains that CDA not only focuses on the discourse itself but is also interested in "discourses", the taking of many contextual factors (i.e., historical background, social factors, economic factors etc.) into consideration.

CDA is not only widely applied in the media discourse, but also in educational discourse, such as textbook and curriculum analysis (de los Heros, 2009; Gulliver, 2010). For example, de los Heros (2009) examined the use of regional varieties of Spanish in the official textbook for the first year high school students in Peru based on DRA framework, associating the findings with the wider local educational reform policy context of Peru. The results generated from examining lexical choices reveal that the ideology embedded in the textbook does not correspond to the educational policy of Peru *Talento*. The main goal of this policy is to promote the local diversification of language. However, the standard Spanish in the textbook is found to be regarded as the superior form of language, compared to the regional variety. The ingenuous variety of Spanish is described as the stigmatization or bad variety of Spanish. Gulliver (2010) investigated the immigrant success stories in English in a second language textbook for Canadian official language instruction programs based on the notion (Fairclough, 2003) that the maintenance of a low orientation to difference. The finding demonstrates that immigrants are constructed by Canada, which transforms the hard-working newcomers into a successful role model.

Out of the three major approaches to CDA, DRA (Fairclough, 1989, 2010, 2015) is found to be more suitable for this study as DRA looks to build connections between properties of texts, features of discourse practice (text production, consumption and distribution), and wider sociocultural practices (Fairclough, 2010, p. 89). Data analysis requires to combine the 'micro' forms of analysis (linguistic analysis) and 'macro' forms of analysis, which take the social, political, economic factors into account (Fairclough, 1989).

However, CDA has some obvious weaknesses and therefore has received a lot of criticism. According to Rogers (2004), CDA approach is "neither systematic nor rigorous" (p. 14). Stubbs (1997) doubts the representativeness of selected samples in CDA studies because of the limited and small-scale textual fragments (Fowler, 1996) Widdowson (2000) asserts that CDA is highly subjective due to its arbitrary selection of the text, and therefore it lacks academic rigor, making it difficult to draw reliable generalizations on language patterns. Thus, the approach that combines CDA and CL has been introduced.

2.5 Combination of CDA and CL and Its Advantages

The above two sections have reviewed the CDA and CL approaches separately. These two approaches have their own merits and flaws, and therefore this section turns to focus on the combination of these two research approaches. The findings of relevant studies are reviewed and compared to demonstrate how an integration of CL and CDA is applied in different kinds of discourse and corpora.

The emergence of digital media texts accelerates the popularity of the unification of CDA and CL. Specifically, CDA framework is utilized to study how language is constructed and manifested particularly in the media texts with the aid of corpus techniques. The purpose of the synergy of CL and CDA is to incorporate the recurring patterns of the discourse with various sociolinguistics elements (Flowerdew, 2018), as "language and the social are inextricably, and dialectally, linked" (Mautner, 2016, p. 156).

As mentioned before, the CDA approach is that the analyst intentionally selects particular texts which may be beneficial to study; as a result, the rest of the text may be neglected or underestimated by researchers. Widdowson (2000) terms this "cherry picking". In light of the limitations of CDA (e.g., fragmented and arbitrary), CL can play a vital role in the analysis of discourse as it is considered to be a useful and effective way to compensate for the shortcomings of CDA (Baker, 2006a; Baker et al., 2008). First, corpora can serve as repositories, a backup for critical discourse analysts to deal with the large amount of various resources. Stubbs (1997) advises that corpus techniques can be used to bolster or, in other words, compensate for the disadvantages of CDA, as they are capable of dealing with the large amount of data needed by CL calculation programs.

O'Halloran (2010) is of the view that critical discourse analysts can take the advantage of CL techniques to enlarge the size of texts from the media and shift from a qualitative to a quantitative method, and that the corpus-based CDA can allow analysts to go beyond single text in order to examine the large number of synchronic or diachronic data.

Second, despite the possibility of quantifying a large body of data, CL possesses other advantages. First, it can reduce researchers' bias. Compared with CDA, CL is of relatively high objectivity, allowing the researcher to approach the text without preconceived views towards the contents (Baker et al., 2008; Gabrielatos & Baker, 2008). Baker (2006a) argued that "there is no absolute objectivity and the bias cannot be cast off completely" (p. 10). The utilisation of CL can more or less restrict the researcher's cognitive bias as CL is based on linguistic evidence (Maunter, 2016) and the large amount of data is more acceptable than an arbitrary selection of samples (Baker et al., 2013).

Third, increasingly researchers have emphasised the benefits of the integration of CDA and CL for the purpose of examining discursive features in media texts. For example, as Van Dijk (1995) noted, the selection of lexical items in the discourse could represent the speaker or writers' opinions or stances, and therefore, CL program is considered to be a useful way to produce evidence, such as a list of collocations of particular lexical items. Baker et al. (2013) also note that CL is helpful to find out the typical and recurrent use of language in the news discourse.

Finally, corpus methods are helpful to identify the incremental effect of the discourse effectively, as it is difficult for researchers to make the generalisation of the typical features in a particular discourse through the observation of a single text or small number of texts. Instead, discourse including a large amount of data can indicate the cumulative effect of media discourse as the power of the media can be achieved by the repetition of certain topics, which can then be detected by the use of a corpus computer program.

However, Baker (2010b) argues that "repetition is not the only requisite of the powerful discourse and articulations made by a powerful person, such as a politician, well-known blogger or celebrity" (p. 124) can also exert influence on the audience. For example, Baker (2006a) suggests that the single or unrepresentative speech made by the leader of a country can carry more weight discursively than the repeated texts made by ordinary people.

CL is considered to be a useful and effective approach to compensate for the shortcomings of CDA (Baker, 2006a; Baker et al., 2008) as "CL can be harnessed to uncover the relationship between the language and society" (Mautner, 2007, p. 57). CDA is a suitable theoretical framework, which can be used to determine embedded ideologies, such as power and dominance, through the observation of the subtle and insidious details in the discourse (Baker & McEnery, 2015, p. 5). Using the CDA approach to examine the ideology in a small amount of text is feasible as it can be achieved through manual sorting and examination, whereas it is impossible for analysts to manually process and sort out a large amount of data; and therefore, a combination of the two approaches indicates that "it is a real progress for CDA" (O'Halloran, 2010, p. 563).

To conclude, combining CL and CDA is quite common to highlight specific language patterns, which can offer some indicators of ideology that can be used to determine the cumulative effect of the media, which may influence the reader gradually and unconsciously (Brindle, 2016a).

The following studies have combined CL with CDA effectively in the discourse other than news discourse, as reviewed in the above section. For example, Prentice (2010) investigated social attitudes towards Scottish independence in the internet discussion forum based on the automated semantic tagging and CDA framework. Their results reveal the differences in identity between England and Scotland as evidenced by two significant semantic fields as "COMPARATIVE" and "GEOGRAPHICAL NAMES". Brindle (2016a) combined CL and CDA to explore the online hate language in the supremacist web in terms of the frequency pattern and the close examination of the text. The findings demonstrate that the white supremacy movement can be found in the data of forum and the ideology is still tightly controlled by the elite group.

The literature review concerning different types of discourse is helpful for my study, which provides me with a series of theoretical frameworks regarding the application of CL and CDA in the news discourse.

References

Archer, D., Wilson, A., & Rayson, P. (2002). Introduction to the USAS category system. *Benedict Project Report*. Retrieved from ucrel.lancs.ac.uk/usas/usas%20guide.pdf.

Baker, P. (2006). *Public discourses of gay men*. Routledge.

Baker, P. (2010). Representations of Islam in British broadsheet and tabloid newspapers 1999–2005. *Journal of Language and Politics, 9*(2), 310–338.

Baker, P. (2014). Bad wigs and screaming mimis: Using corpus-assisted techniques to carry out critical discourse analysis of the representation of trans people in the British press. In C. Hart & P. Cap (Eds.), *Contemporary critical discourse studies* (pp. 211–236). Bloomsbury.

Baker, P. (2017). *American and British English: Divided by a common language?* Cambridge University Press.

Baker, P., Gabrielatos, C., Khosravinik, M., Krzyżanowski, M., McEnery, T., & Wodak, R. (2008). A useful methodological synergy? Combining critical discourse analysis and corpus linguistics to examine discourses of refugees and asylum seekers in the UK press. *Discourse & Society, 19*(3), 273–306.

Baker, P., Gabrielatos, C., & McEnery, T. (2013). *Discourse analysis and media attitudes: The representation of Islam in the British Press*. Cambridge University Press. https://doi.org/10.1017/CBO9780511920103

Baker, P., & McEnery, T. (2005). A corpus-based approach to discourses of refugees and asylum seekers in UN and newspaper texts. *Journal of Language and Politics, 4*(2), 197–226.

Baker, P., & McEnery, T. (2015). Introduction. In P. Baker & T. McEnery (Eds.), *Corpora and discourse studies: Integrating discourse and corpora* (pp. 1–20). Palgrave.

Bednarek, M., & Caple, H. (2012). *News discourse*. Continuum.

Bell, A. (1991). *The language of news media*. Blackwell.

Blinder, S., & Allen, W. L. (2016). Constructing immigrants: Portrayals of migrant groups in British national newspapers, 2010–2012. *International Migration Review, 50*(1), 3–40.
Boczkowski, P. J. (2004). *Digitizing the news: Innovation in online newspapers.* Cambridge: The MIT Press.
Brindle, A. (2016a). A corpus analysis of discursive constructions of the Sunflower Student Movement in the English-language Taiwanese press. *Discourse & Society, 27*(1), 3–19.
Brindle, A. (2016b). *The language of hate: A corpus linguistic analysis of white supremacist Language.* Routledge.
Caple, H. (2010). Doubling-up: Allusion and bonding in multi-semiotic news stories. In M. Bednarek & J. R. Martin (Eds.), *New discourse on language: Functional perspectives on multimodality, identity and affiliation* (pp. 111–134). London: Continuum.
Cheng, W. (2006). Describing the extended meanings of lexical cohesion in a corpus of SARS spoken discourse. *International Journal of Corpus Linguistics, 11*(3), 325–344.
Cheng, W. (2012). *Exploring corpus linguistics: Language in action.* Routledge.
Cheng, W. (2013). Corpus-based linguistic approaches to critical discourse analysis. In C. A. Chapelle (Ed.), *The encyclopedia of applied linguistics* (pp. 1–8). Wiley-Blackwell Publishing Ltd.
Cheng, W., & Ho, J. (2014). Brainwashing or nurturing positive values: Competing voices in Hong Kong's national education debate. *Journal of Pragmatics, 74*, 1–14.
Cheng, W., & Lam, P. W. Y. (2010). Media discourses in Hong Kong: Change in representation of human rights. *Text & Talk, 30*(5), 507–527.
Cheng, W., & Lam, P. W. Y. (2013). Western perceptions of Hong Kong ten years on: A corpus-driven critical discourse study. *Applied Linguistics, 34*(2), 173–190.
Clayman, S., & Heritage, J. (2002). *The news interview: Journalists and public figures on the air.* Cambridge University Press.
Conboy, M. (2010). *The language of newspapers: Socio-historical perspectives.* London: Continuum.
Conboy, M. (2006). *Tabloid Britain: Constructing a community through language.* Routledge.
Culpeper, J. (2009). Keyness: Words, parts-of-speech and semantic categories in the character-talk of Shakespeare's Romeo and Juliet. *International Journal of Corpus Linguistics, 14*(1), 29–59.
de los Heros, S. (2009). Linguistic pluralism or prescriptivism? A CDA of language ideologies in Talento, Peru's official textbook for the first-year of high school. *Linguistics and Education, 20*(2), 172–199.
Dietrich, S., Heider, D., Matschinger, H., & Angermeyer, M. C. (2006). Influence of newspaper reporting on adolescents' attitudes toward people with mental illness. *Social Psychiatry and Psychiatric Epidemiology, 41*(4), 318–322.
Esses, V. M., Medianu, S., & Lawson, A. S. (2013). Uncertainty, threat, and the role of the media in promoting the dehumanization of immigrants and refugees. *Journal of Social Issues, 69*(3), 518–536.
Fairclough, N. (1989). *Language and power* (1st ed.). Longman.
Fairclough, N. (1995). *Media discourse.* Oxford University Press.
Fairclough, N. (2001). *Language and power* (2nd ed.). Longman.
Fairclough, N. (2003). *Analysing discourse: Textual analysis for social research.* Routledge.
Fairclough, N. (2010). *Critical discourse analysis: The critical study of language* (2nd ed.). Routledge.
Fairclough, N. (2015). *Language and power* (3rd ed.). Routledge.
Feez, S., Iedema, R., & White, P. R. R. (2008). *Media Literacy.* Surry Hills, NSW: NSW Adult Migrant Education Service.
Feng, W. D. (2017). Ideological dissonances among Chinese-language newspapers in Hong Kong: A corpus-based analysis of reports on the occupy central movement. *Discourse & Communication, 11*(6), 549–566.
Flowerdew, J. (2018). Critical discourse studies and context. In J. Flowerdew & J. E. Richardson (Eds.), *The Routledge handbook of critical discourse studies* (pp. 165–178). Routledge.

Flowerdew, J., Li, D. C., & Tran, S. (2002). Discriminatory news discourse: Some Hong Kong data. *Discourse & Society, 13*(3), 319–345.

Flowerdew, L. (2014). Which unit for linguistic analysis of ESP corpora of written text? In M. Gotti & D. S. Giannoni (Eds.), *Corpus analysis descriptive and pedagogical purposes* (pp. 25–42). Peter Lang.

Fowler, R. (1991). *Language in the news: Discourse and ideology in the press*. Routledge.

Fowler, R. (1996). On critical linguistics. In C. R. Caldas-Coulthard & M. Coulthard (Eds.), *Texts and practices: Readings in critical discourse analysis* (pp. 3–14). Routledge.

Gabrielatos, C., & Baker, P. (2008). Fleeing, sneaking, flooding: A corpus analysis of discursive constructions of refugees and asylum seekers in the UK press, 1996–2005. *Journal of English Linguistics, 36*(1), 5–38.

Greer, J., & Mensing, D. (2004). US news web sites better, but small papers still lag. *Newspaper Research Journal, 25*(2), 98–112.

Gulliver, T. (2010). Immigrant success stories in ESL textbooks. *Tesol Quarterly, 44*(4), 725–745.

Halliday, M. A. K., & Matthiessen, C. M. (2013). *Halliday's introduction to functional grammar*. Routledge.

Hunston, S. (2002). *Corpora in applied linguistics*. Cambridge University Press.

Hunston, S. (2006). Corpus linguistics. *Linguistics, 7*(2), 234–248.

Johnson, S., Culpeper, J., & Suhr, S. (2003). From politically correct councillors to Blairite nonsense: Discourses of political correctness in three British newspapers. *Discourse & Society, 14*(1), 29–47.

Joye, S. (2010). News discourses on distant suffering: A critical discourse analysis of the 2003 SARS outbreak. *Discourse & Society, 21*(5), 586–601.

Kim, K. H. (2014). Examining US news media discourses about North Korea: A corpus-based critical discourse analysis. *Discourse & Society, 25*(2), 221–244.

Kim, S. (2012). Racism in the global era: Analysis of Korean media discourse around migrants, 1990–2009. *Discourse & Society, 23*(6), 657–678.

Knox, J. S. (2009). Punctuating the home page: Image as language in an online newspaper. *Discourse & Communication, 3*(2), 145–172.

Koller, V. (2012). How to analyse collective identity in discourse: Textual and contextual parameters. *Critical Approaches to Discourse Analysis Across Disciplines, 5*(2), 19-38. http://cadaad.net/2012_volume_5_issue_2/79-66.

L'Hôte, E. (2010). New Labour and globalization: Globalist discourse with a twist? *Discourse & Society, 21*(4), 355–376.

Lawton, R. (2013). Speak English or go home: The anti-immigrant discourse of the American "English Only Movement." *Critical Approaches to Discourse Analysis across Disciplines, 7*(1), 100–122.

Li, J. (2011). Collision of language in news discourse: A functional–cognitive perspective on transitivity. *Critical Discourse Studies, 8*(3), 203–219.

Lido, C., Brown, R., Samson, A., & Calitri, R. (2006). *Effects of the media priming asylum-seeker stereotypes on thoughts and behaviour*. Economic and Social Research Council.

Lin, A. (2014). Critical discourse analysis in applied linguistics: A methodological review. *Annual Review of Applied Linguistics, 34*, 213–232.

Liu, M. T., Chang, T. T. G., Loi, E. H., & Chan, A. C. H. (2015). Macau gambling industry: Current challenges and opportunities next decade. *Asia Pacific Journal of Marketing and Logistics, 27*(3), 499–512.

Liu, M., & Li, C. (2017). Competing discursive constructions of China's smog in Chinese and Anglo-American English-language newspapers: A corpus-assisted discourse study. *Discourse & Communication, 11*(4), 386–403.

Mautner, G. (2007). Mining large corpora for social information: The case of elderly. *Language in Society, 36*(01), 51–72.

Mautner, G. (2008). Analysing newspaper, magazines and other print media. In R. Wodak & M. Krzyżanowski (Eds.), *Qualitative discourse analysis in the social sciences* (pp. 30–53). Palgrave Macmillan.

Mautner, G. (2016). Checks and balances: How corpus linguistics can contribute to CDA. In R. Wodak & M. Meyer (Eds.), *Methods of critical discourse studies* (pp. 154–179). Sage Publications.

McEnery, T., Xiao, R., & Tono, Y. (2006). *Corpus-based language studies: An advanced resource book*. Routledge.

Montgomery, M. (2010). Rituals of personal experience in television news interviews. *Discourse & Communication, 4*(2), 185–211.

Morley, J., & Taylor, C. (2009). Us and them: How immigrants are constructed in British and Italian newspapers. In P. Bayley & G. Williams (Eds.), *European identity* (pp. 190–223). Oxford University Press.

Musolff, A. (2014). The metaphor of the 'body politic' across languages and cultures. In F. Polzenhagen, Z. Kövecses, S. Vogelbacher, & S. Kleinke (Eds.), *Cognitive Explorations into Metaphor and Metonymy* (pp. 85–99). Peter Lang.

O'Halloran, K. (2010). How to use corpus linguistics in the study of media discourse. In A. O'Keeffe & M. McCarthy (Eds.), *The Routledge handbook of corpus linguistics* (pp. 563–577). Routledge.

Ooi, V. B. (2008). The lexis of electronic gaming on the web: A sinclairian approach. *International Journal of Lexicography, 21*(3), 311–323.

Orpin, D. (2005). Corpus linguistics and critical discourse analysis: Examining the ideology of sleaze. *International Journal of Corpus Linguistics, 10*(1), 37–61.

Pereira, F. H., & Biachi, M. M. (2016). Women in the 2010 Brazilian presidential elections: Two weekly magazines' discourses on women candidates. *Critical Discourse Studies, 13*(4), 411–428.

Persson, G. (2016). Ideological struggle over epistemic and political positions in news discourse on migrant activism in Sweden. *Critical Discourse Studies, 13*(3), 278–293.

Pope, C. W. (2015). Placing come and go: locating the lexical item. PhD thesis, University of Nottingham.

Potts, A. (2016). Semantic annotation. In P. Baker & J. Egbert (Eds.), *Triangulating methodological approaches in corpus linguistic research* (pp. 57–72). Routledge.

Potts, A., & Baker, P. (2012). Does semantic tagging identify cultural change in British and American English? *International Journal of Corpus Linguistics, 17*(3), 295–324.

Potts, A., & Kjær, A. L. (2016). Constructing achievement in the International Criminal Tribunal for the Former Yugoslavia (ICTY): A corpus-based critical discourse analysis. *International Journal for the Semiotics of Law-Revue Internationale De Sémiotique Juridique, 29*(3), 525–555.

Potts, A., & Semino, E. (2017). Healthcare professionals' online use of violence metaphors for care at the end of life in the US: A corpus-based comparison with the UK. *Corpora, 12*(1), 55–84.

Prentice, S. (2010). Using automated semantic tagging in critical discourse analysis: A case study on Scottish independence from a Scottish nationalist perspective. *Discourse & Society, 21*(4), 405–437.

Qian, Y. (2010). *Discursive constructions around terrorism in the People's Daily (China) and The Sun (UK) before and after 9.11: A corpus-based contrastive critical discourse analysis*. Bern: Peter Lang.

Rayson, P. (2008). From key words to key semantic domains. *International Journal of Corpus Linguistics, 13*(4), 519–549.

Reisigl, M., & Wodak, R. (2015). The discourse-historical approach (DHA). In R. Wodak & M. Meyer (Eds.), *Methods of critical discourse analysis* (pp. 23–61). Sage.

Rogers, R. (2004). Critical approaches to discourse analysis in educational research. In R. Rogers (Ed.), *Critical discourse analysis in education* (pp. 1–20). Routledge.

Sinclair, J. (1991). *Corpus, concordance, collocation*. Oxford University Press.

Sinclair, J. (2004). *Trust the text: Language, corpus and discourse*. Routledge.

Stubbs, M. (1997). Whorf's children: Critical comments on critical discourse analysis (CDA). *British Studies in Applied Linguistics, 12*, 100–116.

Stubbs, M. (2001). *Words and phrases: Corpus studies of lexical semantics*. Blackwell publishers.

Sun, Y., & Jiang, J. (2014). Metaphor use in Chinese and US corporate mission statements: A cognitive sociolinguistic analysis. *English for Specific Purposes, 33*, 4–14.

Taylor, C. (2014). Investigating the representation of migrants in the UK and Italian press: A cross-linguistic corpus-assisted discourse analysis. *International Journal of Corpus Linguistics, 19*(3), 368–400.

Teo, P. (2000). Racism in the news: A critical discourse analysis of news reporting in two Australian newspapers. *Discourse & Society, 11*(1), 7–49. https://doi.org/10.1177/0957926500011001002

Thornborrow, J. (1999). Language and the media. In L. Thomas, W. Shân, I. Singh, J. S. Peccei, J. Thornborrow, & J. Jones (Eds.), *Language, society and power: An introduction* (pp. 56–73). Routledge.

Tognini-Bonelli, E. (2001). *Corpus linguistics at work*. John Benjamins Publishing.

Van Dijk, T. A. (1988). *News as discourse*. Routledge.

Van Dijk, T. A. (1993). Principles of critical discourse analysis. *Discourse & Society, 4*(2), 249–283.

Van Dijk, T. A. (1995). Discourse semantics and ideology. *Discourse & Society, 6*(2), 243–289.

Van Dijk, T. A. (1998). *Ideology: A multidisciplinary approach*. Sage.

Van Dijk, T. A. (2015). Critical discourse studies: A sociocognitive approach. In R. Wodak & M. Meyer (Eds.), *Methods of critical discourse analysis* (pp. 62–85). Sage.

Vessey, R. (2013). *Language ideologies and discourses of national identity in Canadian newspapers: A cross-linguistic corpus-assisted discourse study*. Doctoral dissertation, Queen Mary University of London.

Vessey, R. (2015). Corpus approaches to language ideology. *Applied Linguistics, 38*(3), 277–296.

Walgrave, S., Soroka, S., & Nuytemans, M. (2008). The mass media's political agenda-setting power: A longitudinal analysis of media, parliament, and government in Belgium (1993 to 2000). *Comparative Political Studies, 41*(6), 814–836. https://doi.org/10.1177/0010414006299098

Wang, F. (2013). *A social constructionist analysis of the discourse of mental depression in British and Chinese news: A corpus-based study*. Doctoral dissertation, University of Birmingham.

Wang, H. (2009). Divergent news representations of Lien Chan's visit to China: A corpus-based lexical comparison between the China Post and the China Daily. *Journal of Asian Pacific Communication, 19*(2), 179–198.

Wang, L., & Chen, S. Z. (2015). A corpus-based critical analysis of lexical choices in Sichuan earthquake by Chinese and American news media. *Canadian Social Science, 11*(7), 111–116.

Widdowson, H. G. (2000). On the limitations of linguistics applied. *Applied Linguistics, 21*(1), 3–25.

Wodak, R., & Fairclough, N. (1997). Critical discourse analysis. In T. A. van Dijk (Ed.), *Discourse as social interaction* (pp. 258–284). London: Sage

Wodak, R. (1996). *Disorders of discourse*. Longman.

Wodak, R. (2001). What CDA is about-a summary or its history, important concepts and its developments. In R. Wodak & M. Meyer (Eds.), *Methods of critical discourse analysis* (pp. 1–14). Sage.

Wodak, R., & Meyer, M. (2009). *Methods of critical discourse analysis* (2nd ed.). Sage.

Wodak, R., & Meyer, M. (2015). Critical discourse analysis: History, agenda, theory, and methodology. In R. Wodak & M. Meyer (Eds.), *Methods of critical discourse analysis* (pp. 1–22). Sage.

Yang, M. (2015). Olympism and the Beijing Olympic torch relay in the British and Chinese media discourses: A comparative study. *The International Journal of the History of Sport, 32*(3), 499–515.

Yao, S. Y., & Huang, Y. (2014). Aomen yu nei di xin weng yu pian chi hui cha yi de ji liang yan jiu [A quantitative study of the lexical differences in news discourses between Macau and Mainland]. *Yu Yan Wen Zi Yin Yong, 5*(2), 27–37.

Yin, J. (2007). The clash of rights: A critical analysis of news discourse on human rights in the United States and China. *Critical Discourse Studies, 4*(1), 75–94.

Zhang, M., & Mihelj, S. (2012). Hong Kong identity and the press–politics dynamics: A corpus-assisted discourse study. *Asian Journal of Communication, 22*(5), 506–527.

Chapter 3
Corpus-Based Critical Discourse Analysis: Data and Research Methods

In the previous chapter, the theoretical framework of this study was introduced. This chapter describes the methods adopted in the present study. It begins with the research question (3.1), and data description followed (3.2), which gives an account of the news data used in this study, including the background of the newspapers in the three territories as well as their respective ideologies and stances. This is followed by corpus compilation (3.3), which describes the news article corpora. The analytical frameworks for data analysis are described in 3.4, and the research design (3.5) represents the three-step research procedures. The two corpus tools, Wordsmith 7.0 (Scott, 2016) and Wmatrix (Rayson, 2008), are used to investigate the data in the three news article corpora.

3.1 Research Question

The research question addressed in this study is:

> How do English-language newspapers published in Mainland China, Hong Kong SAR, and Macau SAR compare in terms of their representations of Macau's gaming industry?

The comparison of media representations of Macau's gaming industry is achieved through the three corpus methods, namely frequent single lexical words and co-occurrences of these frequent words based on the Sinclair's (2004) model of five categories of co-selection of a lexical item, trigrams, and key semantic fields (Rayson, 2008) generated by comparing each news article corpus with the same reference corpus BNC written Sampler. This chapter describes the research methods in the present study.

Y. Wu, *Media Representations of Macau's Gaming Industry in Greater China*,
https://doi.org/10.1007/978-981-19-7724-4_3

3.2 Data Description: Introducing Four Newspapers in Chinese Mainland, Hong Kong, and Macau

The data analysed in the study were collected from four English-language newspapers from three territories in China, namely Mainland China, Hong Kong, and Macau. Although these three places belong to the territory of the People's Republic of China (PRC), they have different historical backgrounds, economic statuses, and political systems. (see Sect. 1.3.2).

Newspaper articles published from 1 January 2014 to 31 December 2014 were collected from four English newspapers as the year of 2014 is the very special year for Macau (see Sect. 1.3.1). They were *China Daily* (*CD*) and *Xinhua News Agency* (*XH*) from Chinese Mainland, *South China Morning Post* (*SCMP*) from Hong Kong and *Macau Post Daily* (*MPD*) from Macau. These four newspapers are part of the mainstream news media in their respective regions. Both *Xinhua News Agency* and *China Daily* are state-run news media in Mainland China. *Xinhua News Agency* is the largest local domestic information news provider and its core value is to "publicize China and Report the World" in an "Authoritative Voice" (Xinhuanet, n.d.). In addition to providing news releases in Chinese version, *Xinhua* also provides versions of six foreign languages, namely English, Portuguese, Spanish, Arabic, Russian and French. According to Scollon (2000), *Xinhua News Agency* is the principal official source provider where "many news stories are published in the newspaper of the Chinese government, such as *People's Daily* and *China daily*." (p. 765). As Xin (2012) noted, *Xinhua News Agency* is considered to be one of the most influential national news organizations of China and is regarded as the royal propaganda machine of the Chinese Communist Party (CCP) and the Chinese authorities. *Xinhua News* can represent the dominant ideology of CCP and "set an official tone for other news media" (Xin, 2012, p. 135). *China Daily*, established in 1981, is the largest national English-language newspaper in Mainland China. According to Li (2009), *China Daily* can be treated as the English version of *People's Daily*, serving as the 'official mouthpiece' of the Chinese Communist Party (CCP). *China Daily* is an English-language newspaper, primarily for non-Chinese readers and therefore it plays a role in promoting Chinese national images and expressing the Chinese government's politics and foreign policy concerns (Li, 2009), and aims to represent the Chinese authorities for external communication (Liu, 2017).

It is noted that the ideology and stance of *Xinhua News* is consistent with *China Daily* as the Mainland Chinese media industry is still strictly controlled by the Chinese authorities. Thus, a strict censorship system is applied in Mainland China (Frisch et al., 2017).

South China Morning Post (*SCMP*) has been the leading English newspaper in Hong Kong since 1903. The *SCMP* is characterized by the elite readership (Cheng & Lam, 2010; Flowerdew et al., 2002). The *SCMP* identifies itself as the most influential paper for Elite Business readers in Hong Kong (South China Morning Post, 2017) and 68% of its readers are university educated or above (Hong Kong Audience Survey, 2016). The reporting angles of the *SCMP* are believed to follow "the lead of western-based news agencies that reflects largely the views from Washington DC" (Chan, 2000, p. 324). As Flowerdew et al. (2002) suggested, the editorial stances of the *SCMP* tend to be more democratic and liberal, as reflected in their stances towards the right-of-abode issue. The *SCMP* is different from the state-owned news media in Mainland China, which is a corporate own media. Although the *SCMP* has undergone several ownership shifts, its reporting angle tends to be like western-style news. (Cheng & Lam, 2010). It is noted that ownership of the *SCMP* was bought by Alibaba group in 2015 and some concerns have been expressed towards the shifts of stances of the *SCMP* (Frisch et al., 2017). However, the news articles used in this present study were collected in 2014, which will not affect the previous stances held by the *SCMP*.

In Macau, *The Macau Post Daily* (*MPD*) was founded in 2004 and is the oldest local English newspaper with the largest circulation in Macau (The Macau Post Daily, n.d). *MPD* is owned by Macau Everbright Publishing, Editing & Consultancy Company Limited. (Government Information Bureau of the MSAR, n.d.). The major readers of *MPD* are the increasingly growing English business professionals working in Macau (Moody, 2008). Its director is Harald Christian Brüning, who has been working in some international agencies and *MPD* aims to convey Macau's perspective. As for the ideologies and stances of *MPD*, to date, no academic research study has been conducted. The websites of *MPD* demonstrate that the editorial principles are to "support the principle of One Country, Two Systems, which forms the constitutional basis for Macau's autonomous status as an integral part of China" (The Macau Post Daily, n.d).

3.3 Corpus Compilation and News Article Corpora

Newspaper articles published in the four newspapers were retrieved from two online databases, *Wisenews* and *Factiva*, by searching for the following items: 'Macau' OR 'Macao' AND 'gaming' OR 'gambling'. The types of news articles were not limited to news reports and editorials; there were also featured stories. News articles from *Xinhua News Agency (XH)* and *China Daily (CD)* were merged due to the relatively small number of news articles related to Macau's gaming industry in 2014. The corpus as a whole comprises 199,005 tokens: *XH&CDC* (31,247 tokens), *MPDC* (112,373 tokens), and *SCMPC* (55,385 tokens). As a result, three specialized news article corpora of three territories, characterised by diverse ideologies and stances, were compiled. According to McEnery et al. (2006), specialized corpora are very helpful to discourse analysts. As reviewed in Chap. 2, many researchers have analysed different types of specialised corpora for different purposes (e.g., Baker et al., 2013; Cheng & Lam, 2010, 2013).

The composition of the three news article corpora is described below (Table 3.1 and Fig. 3.1).

As shown in Table 3.1 and Fig. 3.1, the number of news articles published in 2014 on the topic of Macau's gaming industry across the three territories is not balanced.

Table 3.1 Number of news articles in three news article corpora

Corpus	Number and percentage of news articles	Tokens
XH&CDC	35 (9.1%)	31,247
SCMPC	93 (24.16%)	55,385
MPDC	257 (66.75%)	112,373
Total	385 (100%)	199,005

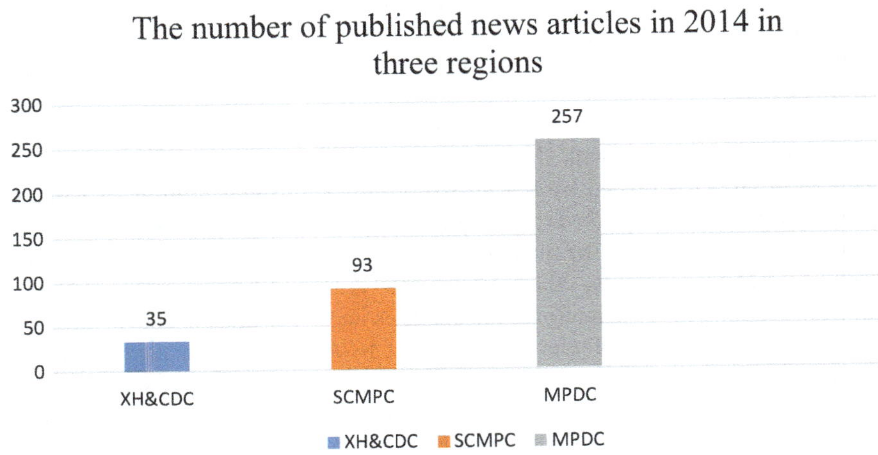

Fig. 3.1 The number of news articles collected from the three territories

The occurrence of news articles in the *MPDC* (66.75%) is the highest of the three news article corpora. It is not surprising that *The Macau Post Daily*, as Macau's regional press, puts its focus on news events closely related to Macau's gaming. As mentioned before, the gaming industry significantly influences different aspects of Macanese society, such as economy, employment rate, and so on. According to McCartney (2015), Macau has become the global leader in the gaming industry in terms of gross gaming revenue since 2006. Thus, the predominant number of news articles in the *MPDC* is expected. By comparison, the *XH&CDC* only contains of 9.1% news articles in total. In Hong Kong, the occurrence of news articles concerning Macau's gaming published in the *SCMP* is about three times (24.17%) higher than that in Mainland China.

3.4 Corpus Linguistics Methods

To address the research question, three corpus methods of CL were initially utilised to examine the language patterns in each news article corpus, as these methods can indicate to the researcher the appropriate starting point of the study, and can also be used to identify the significant distinctive linguistic features of respective news article corpora for comparative purposes.

CL has been widely and effectively used to trace differences and quantify linguistic elements among different newspapers (Gabrielatos & Baker, 2008). In this study, various methods of corpus linguistics were adopted to make sense of the linguistic patterns observed. They were the frequencies of occurrence of single lexical words, trigrams, and key semantic fields.

3.4.1 Single Word and Trigram Lists

Examining the frequency lists is considered to be a good starting point for any kinds of corpus studies and helpful in comprehending a corpus (Baker, 2006a). A frequency list can reveal the characteristics of a corpus or text through the repeated occurrences, indicating the explicit lexical preference since "choices of words and phrases are not neutral, but communicate ideology and culture" (Brindle, 2016a, p. 43). A frequency list serves as the filter to narrow the scope of the data for further analysis.

Corpus tools such as *Wordsmith* 7.0 (Scott, 2016) and *Wmatrix* (Rayson, 2008) do not only display raw frequencies but also relative frequencies. Raw frequencies in different-sized corpora cannot be compared directly as "these raw frequencies mean very little relative to each other" (Evison, 2010, p. 126), and therefore the technique of normalization is needed. In the present study, relative frequencies were examined for comparative purposes. In addition to the comparison of relative frequencies, the comparing of the rank order of linguistic items in more than two corpora helped to find out the difference of certain words and topics between corpora (Freake et al., 2011).

The study examined the most frequent single words in each news article corpus as they indicate the dominant topics and ideas of the particular corpus. Trigrams were also analysed. The importance of multi-word units, or clusters, chunks, n-grams, or lexical bundles, is well acknowledged in lexical studies. Biber (2006, p. 134) defines clusters as "lexical bundles which are the most frequently occurring sequences of words". According to Baker (2017), the frequency of clusters of more than 2 words tends to fall dramatically as length expands. Specifically, "the statistical significance of word clusters is usually measured by their recurring rate; for example, 5 or 10 occurrences in a million words." (McEnery & Xiao, 2011, p. 151).

3.4.2 Extended Units of Meaning of the Lexical Item

The notion of the lexical item (Sinclair, 2004) is central to the present study. According to Sinclair (2004), the term 'lexical item', originated from the 'idiom principle' (Sinclair, 1991), is considered to be an abstract category, different from the word, which needs to take meaning into consideration as language is all about producing meaning and the nature of language tends to be phraseological (Sinclair, 2004). The concept of 'lexical item' refers to "the apparently simultaneous choice of two words" (Sinclair, 1991, p. 110). It was then developed into, defined by Sinclair's (2004) 'phraseological tendency' referring to "tendency towards idiomaticity, where words tend to go together and make meaning by their combinations" (p. 29). The model of five categories of co-selection of the lexical item (Sinclair, 2004) has been introduced in Chap. 1.

The present study investigated and compared the extended units of meaning of the frequent single lexical words in the three news article corpora. By examining collocation, semantic preference, and semantic prosody, the study aims to identify topical concerns and attitudes in different news article corpora.

3.4.3 Key Semantic Field Analysis

In addition to manual examination of the semantic preferences (Sinclair, 2004) of specific lexical items in their concordances, the study investigated entire corpora in terms of key semantic fields. The semantic tagging adopted is based on the USAS system (http://urcel.lancs.ac.uk/usas/). As described by Rayson et al. (2004), USAS refers to the "UCREL semantic analysis system" and the tag sets were originally based on the *Longman Lexicon of Contemporary English* (McArthur, 1981).

The online interface Wmatrix (Rayson, 2008) can undertake semantic tagging automatically in the running texts. The USAS tagger function in Wmatrix can assign the semantic tagger to each word or multiword expression in the corpus to gather these words into semantic field (Rayson, 2008). The USAS tagset is:

> hierarchical, including 21 major higher-order tags (see Table 3.2), labelled with letters of the alphabet, but having finer divisions marked with subsequent letters, numbers, decimal points and arithmetic symbols (Baker, 2017, p.177).

The 21 major discourse fields are further divided into over 230 category labels (Ancher et al., 2002). Baker (2017) explained that "some words are tagged with one or more plus or minus signs depending on whether their meaning is generally positive or negative" (p. 178). It is noted that the USAS semantic tagger has an accuracy rate of 91–92%, suggesting the results need to be checked by the researcher carefully. According to Baker (2017), the tagger system tends to work better in the literal sense, requiring researchers to identify the metaphorical use or the mistagged case through reading concordance lines. Baker (2017) exemplifies that the word *honey* in the television corpus was wrongly tagged as F1 (FOOD) by the USUA. In fact, this word comes from the characters in the film who call others 'honey', instead of referring to food.

The process of semantic annotation is necessary for the present study. Firstly, semantic annotation can demonstrate the semantic relations between items within a corpus or the semantic features of words in a corpus (Cheng, 2012) and it can group words with similar meanings together and thus gaining more analysis possibilities

Table 3.2 The higher-order tags in the USAS tag set (Rayson et al., 2004, p. 2)

USUA tag set	Description
A	General & Abstract Terms
B	The Body & the Individual
C	Arts & Crafts
E	Emotional Actions, States & Processes
F	Food & Farming
G	Government & the Public Domain
H	Architecture, Building, Houses & the Home
I	Money & Commerce
K	Entertainment, Sports & Games
L	Life & Living Things
M	Movement, Location, Travel & Transport
N	Numbers & Measurement
O	Substances, Materials, Objects & Equipment
P	Education
Q	Linguistic Actions, States & Processes
S	Social Actions, States & Processes
T	Time
W	The World & Our Environment
X	Psychological Actions, States & Processes
Y	Science & Technology
Z	Names & Grammatical Words

(Potts, 2016). Baker and McEnery (2015) suggest that semantic tagging is a helpful feature of data down-sampling, which enables the researcher to narrow down the scale of texts and to focus on relatively small parts with predominant features. Secondly, semantic annotation is suitable for the comparative purpose. Rayson (2008) states that the advantages of comparison at the semantic level are in multi-word expressions and semantic field analysis, which are effective in illuminating and comparing the broad themes in the discourse. Thus, enriched perspectives concerning the themes in the news article corpora can be gained through the semantic field analysis.

Key semantic field analysis is based on the semantic annotation, adding the notion of 'keyness' to the semantic fields. Specifically, in the Wmatrix program (Rayson, 2008), a log likelihood value of ≥ 7 is statistically significant for $p < 0.01$(1 in 100 likelihood that the result could occur randomly). Specifically, a semantic field in the running text with a log likelihood value of ≥ 7 indicates it is a 'key semantic field' (O'Halloran, 2017). As explained by Rayson (2008), a key semantic field with the highest level of LL value indicates that this semantic field has the most significant difference between the study corpus and the reference corpus. Thus, LL statistical measure can illuminate the statistical significance of the study corpus when it is compared with the reference corpus.

In this study, the study corpora are three news article corpora, and each was compared with the same reference corpus BNC Sampler (Written), resulting in three lists of key semantic fields measured by LL value, which are statistically salient with regard to the reference corpus. BNC Sampler was chosen because it is regarded as the baseline corpus to identify the general tendency of each news article corpus. Since the present study focuses on written materials, namely, news articles, the BNC Sampler (Written) (1 million words), which only contains written texts, was chosen to be the reference corpus.

3.5 Research Design

A combination of the research approaches of CL and CDA is more productive than the mere utilisation of a single method (Baker, 2006a). By analysing frequent lexical and semantic patterns and interpreting them in the broad historical, social and ideological context, the study reveals the media representations concerning Macau's gaming industry in 2014 in three news article corpora.

Two corpus tools Wordsmith 7.0 (Scott, 2016) and Wmatrix (Rayson, 2008) were employed to provide the linguistic evidence for data analysis.

As a first step, the Wordlist function in the Wordsmith Tool 7.0 (Scott, 2016) was utilised to generate single lexical word frequency lists and the lists of trigrams in three news article corpora (i.e., *XH&CDC*, *SCMPC* and *MPDC*). The Wordlist function of Wordsmith (Scott, 2016) not only produces the wordlist of a single word but also automatically identifies 2-word n-grams, 3-word n-grams and 4-word n-grams. The stop list was applied to discard 50 grammatical words, including determiner, conjunctions, prepositions etc. (e.g. *the*, *of*, *and*, *to*, *in*, *a*) in the frequency lists. Grammatical words always occur at the top of the frequency list (Cheng, 2012). The function of stop list can reduce the size of the list and generate lexically-rich word lists. Numerous grammatical words can reveal the style of data and grammatical patterns (Brindle, 2016a), which are not the focus of the present study.

The top 20 lexical words in each news article corpus were examined and compared with each other in terms of the relative frequency due to the different sizes of the three corpora. The frequency of the lexical words can then reveal the topics and ideas most frequently presented in each corpus, showing "the ideological position of the writer whose texts were utilised to compile the data" (Brindle, 2016a, p. 44) related to Macau's gaming industry in 2014. Apart from comparing frequencies of occurrence, the co-selection patterns of the shared single lexical words and top unique words in each corpus were examined.

In the second step, the Concord function of Wordsmith Tool 7.0 (Scott, 2016) was used to generate the collocates and concordance lines of the most frequent 20 single lexical words. Each lexical word was then analysed manually in terms of the extended units of meaning (Sinclair, 2004) through the expanded concordance lines. The word span for the collocates was set at five words to the left and to the right of the node to identify words which have a relationship with each other (Baker et al., 2013).

As a final step, Wmatrix (Rayson, 2008) was utilized to obtain the top 20 key semantic fields in each news article corpus, compared with the same reference corpus BNC Sampler (Written). The top key 20 semantic fields with the largest LL values in each of the three news article corpora were investigated and then compared with each other in order to identify similarities and differences, if any, among the three corpora at the semantic level.

CDA was then used to interpret and explain the findings, taking the historical, socio-cultural, economic and political context of each region into account.

3.6 Summary

The topics of the news articles collected from four English newspapers are related to Macau's gaming in 2014. Therefore, the examination and comparison of the frequent single lexical words and their co-selections, trigrams and key semantic fields among the three news article corpora provide comprehensive findings of the respective reporting focuses, preferences and attitudes of newspapers published in 2014 in the three territories towards Macau's gaming industry.

References

Archer, D., Wilson, A., & Rayson, P. (2002). Introduction to the USAS Category System. Benedict Project Report. Retrieved, from ucrel.lancs.ac.uk/usas/usas%20guide.pdf.

Baker, P. (2006). *Using corpora in discourse analysis.* London: Continuum.

Baker, P. (2017). *American and British english: Divided by a common language?* Cambridge: Cambridge University Press.

Baker, P., Gabrielatos, C., & McEnery, T. (2013). *Discourse analysis and media attitudes: The representation of Islam in the British press.* Cambridge: Cambridge University Press. https://doi.org/10.1017/CBO9780511920103

Baker, P., & McEnery, T. (2015). Introduction. In P. Baker & T. McEnery (Eds.), *Corpora and discourse studies: Integrating discourse and corpora* (pp. 1–20). London: Palgrave.

Biber, D. (2006). *University language: A corpus-based study of spoken and written registers.* The Netherlands: John Benjamins Publishing.

Brindle, A. (2016). *The language of hate: A corpus linguistic analysis of white supremacist language.* London: Routledge.

Chan, Y. Y. (2000). The English-language media in Hong Kong. *World Englishes, 19*(3), 323–335.

Cheng, W. (2012). *Exploring corpus linguistics: Language in action.* New York: Routledge.

Cheng, W., & Lam, P. W. Y. (2010). Media discourses in Hong Kong: Change in representation of human rights. *Text & Talk, 30*(5), 507–527.

Cheng, W., & Lam, P. W. Y. (2013). Western perceptions of Hong Kong ten years on: A corpus-driven critical discourse study. *Applied Linguistics, 34*(2), 173–190.

Evison, J. (2010). What are the basics of analysing a corpus? In A. O'Keeffe & M. Michael (Eds.), *The Routledge handbook of corpus linguistics* (pp. 122–135). London: Routledge.

Flowerdew, J., Li, D. C., & Tran, S. (2002). Discriminatory news discourse: Some Hong Kong data. *Discourse & Society, 13*(3), 319–345.
Freake, R., Gentil, G., & Sheyholislami, J. (2011). A bilingual corpus-assisted discourse study of the construction of nationhood and belonging in Quebec. *Discourse & Society, 22*(1), 21–47.
Frisch, N., BelairGagnon, V., & Agur, C. (2018). Media capture with Chinese characteristics: Changing patterns in Hong Kong's news media system. *Journalism, 19*(8), 1165–1181.
Gabrielatos, C., & Baker, P. (2008). Fleeing, sneaking, flooding: A corpus analysis of discursive constructions of refugees and asylum seekers in the UK press, 1996–2005. *Journal of English Linguistics, 36*(1), 5–38.
Government Information Bureau of the MSAR. (n.d.). Retrieved, from https://www.gcs.gov.mo/index.php?PageLang=E&PassType=PUB&PageCode=PUB
Li, J. (2009). Intertextuality and national identity: Discourse of national conflicts in daily newspapers in the United States and China. *Discourse & Society, 20*(1), 85–121.
Liu, M. (2017). Contesting the cynicism of neoliberalism. *Journal of Language and Politics, 16*(2), 242–263.
McArthur, T. (1981). *Longman lexicon of contemporary English*. London: Longman.
McCartney, G. (2015). *When the eggs in one basket all cracked: Addressing the downturn in Macau's casino and VIP junket system*. Gaming Law Review and Economics, *19*(7), 527-537.
McEnery, T., & Xiao, R. (2011). What corpora can offer in language teaching and learning. In E. Hinkel (Ed.), *Handbook of research in second language teaching and learning* (pp. 364–380). London: Routledge.
McEnery, T., Xiao, R., & Tono, Y. (2006). *Corpus-based language studies: An advanced resource book*. London: Routledge.
Moody, A. (2008). *Macau English: Status, functions and forms*. English today, *24*(3), 3-15.
O'Halloran, K. (2017). *Posthumanism and deconstructing arguments: Corpora and digitally-driven critical analysis*. New York: Taylor & Francis.
Potts, A. (2016). Semantic annotation. In P. Baker & J. Egbert (Eds.), *Triangulating methodological approaches in corpus linguistic research* (pp. 57–72). London: Routledge.
Rayson, P. (2008). From key words to key semantic domains. *International Journal of Corpus Linguistics, 13*(4), 519–549.
Rayson, P., Archer, D., Piao, S., & McEnery, A. M. (2004). The UCREL semantic analysis system.
Scollon, R. (2000). Generic variability in news stories in Chinese and English: A contrastive discourse study of five days' newspapers. *Journal of Pragmatics, 32*(6), 761–791.
Scott, M. (2016). *WordSmith Tools (Version 7) [Computer software]*. Stroud: Lexical Analysis Software.
Sinclair, J. (1991). *Corpus, concordance, collocation*. Oxford: Oxford University Press.
Sinclair, J. (2004). *Trust the text: Language, corpus and discourse*. London and New York: Routledge.
The Macau Post Daily. (n.d.). *Introduction*. Retrieved, from http://www.macaupostdaily.com
Xin, X. (2012). *How the market is changing China's news: The case of Xinhua news agency*. Maryland: Lexington Books.
Xinhuanet. (n.d.). *Brief Introduction to Xinhuanet*. Retrieved, from http://www.xinhuanet.com/english/special/2015-09/06/c_134594253.htm

Chapter 4
Outlining Discursive Representations on Macau's Gaming Industry at the Lexical Level

This chapter outlines the discursive representations of Macau's Gaming Industry at the Lexical Level by describing top frequent single lexical words, patterns of co-selections of lexical items, and trigrams.

4.1 Introduction

This chapter focuses on analysing the most frequent twenty single lexical words in each of the *XH&CDC*, the *SCMPC*, and the *MPDC*, which does not only contribute to obtaining the most frequently mentioned themes and topics in each news article corpus but also presents an in-depth analysis of patterns of co-selection of frequent lexical items. In the analysis of single lexical word co-selection patterns, the semantic preference and prosody associated with the lexical items are presented and illustrated with examples of concordance lines. This is followed by presenting the findings regarding the phraseological patterns in each news article corpus by examining the top 20 trigrams to understand better how the news articles represented Macau's gaming in 2014.

The findings are described in terms of frequencies of single lexical words, patterns of co-selections of lexical items, trigrams, and key semantic fields. The findings are then discussed with reference to the previous literature. The purpose is to address the research question:

How do English-language newspapers published in Mainland China, Hong Kong SAR, and Macau SAR compare regarding their representations of Macau's gaming industry?

This chapter starts with analysing the most frequent twenty single lexical words in each of the *XH&CDC*, the *SCMPC*, and the *MPDC* (4.2), which does not only contribute to obtaining the most frequently mentioned themes and topics in each news article corpus but also presenting an in-depth analysis of patterns of co-selection of frequent lexical items. In analyzing patterns of single lexical word co-selection, the semantic preference and semantic prosody associated with the lexical items under

Y. Wu, *Media Representations of Macau's Gaming Industry in Greater China*,
https://doi.org/10.1007/978-981-19-7724-4_4

study are presented and illustrated with examples of concordance lines (4.3). This is followed by presenting the findings regarding the phraseological patterns in each news article corpus by examining the top 20 trigrams (4.4) to gain a deeper understanding of how the news articles represented Macau's gaming in 2014. The following section presents the findings of the key semantic field analysis (4.5) to compare the three news article corpora at the semantic level. The final Sect. (4.5) discusses findings related to the literature reviewed in Chap. 2.

4.2 Quantitative Analysis: Frequency Analysis

Table 4.1 shows the most frequent 20 single lexical words, except for the two-word unit *Hong Kong* which is a proper noun, from the wordlist of each of the three news article corpora (i.e., *XH&CDC*, *SCMPC*, and *MPDC*) according to rank, raw frequencies and percentages.

Table 4.1 shows the most frequent 20 single lexical words, except for the two-word unit Hong Kong which is a proper noun, from the wordlist of each of the three news article corpora (i.e., *XH&CDC*, *SCMPC*, and *MPDC*) according to rank, raw frequencies, and percentages.

For comparative purposes, the top 20 lexical words in each news article corpus in Table 4.1 are classified into three categories according to their occurrences in each wordlist of three news article corpora. The lexical words shared in three news article corpora are highlighted in yellow. The lexical words shared in any of the two news article corpora are highlighted in blue. The unique words which can only be found in one corpus are highlighted in purple.

It is found that five single lexical words *Macao/Macau, gaming, government, said*, and *year* are shared among the three news article corpora. *Said* is a reporting verb, commonly used in the news article to indirectly quote speech, reflecting the neutral voice of the media (Bednarek & Caple, 2012). The high frequency of words, such as *Macau/Macao* and *gaming*, is predictable as these words very much represent the themes of the news articles retrieved and examined. The word *year* is quite abstract, which cannot readily demonstrate the topics without referring to the contextual information.

Six lexical words (N = 6; 14.63%), namely China, mainland, Hong Kong, revenue, billion, and one, are shared between the *XH&CDC* and the *SCMPC*. By comparison, only two words, casino, and city, are shared between the *SCMPC* and the *MPDC*, implying that Hong Kong and Mainland Chinese news articles show a higher degree of similarity in terms of topics and themes than those of Hong Kong and Macau. Only one lexical word percent is shared between the *XH&CDC* and the *MPDC*, except for the five shared words (i.e., Macao/Macau, gaming, government, said, and year). This indicates that only a few themes and topics in the *SCMP* and the *XH&CDC* were reported in the *MPDC*.

In the *XH&CDC*, eight lexical words (N = 8; 19.51%), namely *development, Chinese, economic, Macao's, SAR, growth, years*, and *tourism*, are unique, and

Table 4.1 Top 20 single lexical words from each wordlist of the news article corpora (i.e., *XH&CDC*, *SCMPC*, and *MPDC*)

R	Top 20 lexical words in *XH&CDC*	Raw freq./ %	Top 20 lexical words in *SCMP*	Raw freq./ %	Top 20 lexical words in *MPDC*	Raw freq./ %
1	Macao	632; 2.02%	Macau	646; 1.17%	Said	1433; 1.28%
2	Said	220; 0.70%	Said	363; 0.65%	Macau	927; 0.82%
3	Percent	196; 0.63%	China	357; 0.64%	Gaming	801; 0.71%
4	Hong Kong	165; 0.53%	Hong Kong	329; 0.59%	Government	605; 0.54%
5	China	156; 0.50%	Per	314; 0.57%	Year	585; 0.52%
6	Gaming	151; 0.48%	Year	313; 0.57%	Percent	555; 0.49%
7	Government	136; 0.44%	Cent	303; 0.55%	Yesterday	368; 0.33%
8	Development	131; 0.42%	Gaming	283; 0.51%	Local	355; 0.32%
9	Year	130; 0.42%	Casino	241; 0.44%	Last	310; 0.28%
10	Mainland	119; 0.38%	Revenue	159; 0.29%	According	296; 0.26%
11	Economic	111; 0.36%	HK	146; 0.26%	City	288; 0.26%
12	Revenue	99; 0.32%	City	140; 0.25%	Public	286; 0.25%
13	Billion	92; 0.29%	New	133; 0.24%	Employees	254; 0.23%
14	Growth	92; 0.29%	Billion	132; 0.24%	Casino	252; 0.22%
15	Chinese	89; 0.28%	One	126; 0.23%	Patacas	248; 0.22%
16	Macao's	83; 0.27%	Mainland	125; 0.23%	Smoking	230; 0.20%
17	SAR	82; 0.26%	US	119; 0.21%	Casinos	229; 0.20%
18	Years	78; 0.25%	Government	117; 0.21%	Staff	206; 0.18%
19	Tourism	73; 0.23%	Month	108; 0.19%	Two	195; 0.17%
20	One	71; 0.23%	Business	99; 0.18%	Company	192; 0.17%

all of them are not semantically directly connected with the gaming industry. The predominant use of *development* and *economic* in the *XH&CD* demonstrates that the related topics concerning the development and the economic perspective of Macau are constantly mentioned by only the Mainland Chinese media, which deserves further examination. In addition, the *XH&CD* shows the reporting preferences of the *XH&CD*[1] for promoting the China's national identity and emphasizing Macau's administrative status by employing *Chinese* (ranked 15th) and *SAR* (ranked 17th).

In the *SCMPC*, the unique lexical words *per*, *cent*, *HK*, *new*, *US*, *month*, and *business* are all closely related to the gaming industry. For instance, *billion* is used to describe financial statistics, especially for casino revenues. Both *US* and *HK* represent the currency units rather than the geographical location. The majority of the unique lexical words is found to do with money, implying that the *SCMP* focuses on the financial performance in Macau's gaming industry.

[1] *XH&CD* refers to *Xinhua news* and *China Daily*.

As shown in Table 4.1, the *MPDC* has the most significant number of unique words (N = 12; 29.27%) in the three news report corpora, suggesting that themes presented in the newspaper have a significant diversity in contrast to the other two corpora. Specifically, the *MPD* expresses its reporting preferences for local social perspectives regarding gaming issues of Macau as the lexical words *local, smoking, employees, staff*, and *public* cannot be found in the other two news corpora. *Employees* and *staff* here refer to people working in Macau casinos. *Smoking* is closely connected with gaming, about the rule[2] launched by the Macau SAR government in April 2014, where they stated that smoking is banned in the public areas of casinos. Together with the above unique lexical words, the *MPD* is found to show its reporting preferences on social issues. The word *according* is likely to be indicative of general press reporting language, customarily used for indirect quotes in the news articles. *Patacas* refers to MOP, which is Macau's official currency unit. *Hong Kong* does not appear in the *MPDC*, suggesting that Macau's local newspaper does not emphasise this geographical location too much compared with the other two corpora.

4.3 Qualitative Concordance Analysis: Patterns of Single Lexical Word Co-selection: Collocation, Semantic Preference, and Semantic Prosody

The above findings have provided a general picture of the major themes expressed in the three news article corpora. This section conducted a detailed analysis of lexical words to examine their co-selection patterns (Sinclair, 2004), supported by expanded concordance lines. Related contextual information explains how these words are frequently co-selected in each news article corpus.

4.3.1 Shared Single Lexical Words Among Three Corpora

This section starts by describing and comparing the patterns of co-selection of four shared lexical words *Macau, gaming, government*, and *year* among three news article corpora, based on Sinclair's (2004) descriptive model of five categories of co-selection of a lexical item.

In Table 4.2, the top 20 most frequent lexical collocates of *Macau* (*Macao*) in the three news article corpora are listed and ranked by frequency and percentage.

In Table 4.2, we can find that some of the collocates of *Macao* in the *XH&CDC* are also among the top 20 lexical words (see Table 4.1) such as *gaming, development, economic,* and *SAR*. The most frequent collocate of *Macao* is *SAR*, which represents *Special Administrative Region*. The full name of the SAR (i.e., collocates such *as special, administrative, and region*) also appear in the top 20 lexical collocate lists of

[2] The legal document of the Chief Executive No. 141/2014.

Table 4.2 The 20 most frequent lexical collocates of Macau (Macao)

Rank	*XH&CDC* (Freq.; %)	*SCMPC* (Freq.; %)	*MPDC* (Freq.; %)
1	SAR (58; 10.02)	Gaming (69; 11.26)	Gaming (106; 16.61)
2	Government (52; 8.98)	Kong (53; 8.65)	Said (54; 8.46)
3	Kong (37; 6.39)	Hong (52; 8.48)	Industry (44; 6.90)
4	Said (34; 5.87)	Casino (52; 8.48)	Hong (38; 5.96)
5	Hong (33; 5.70)	Casinos (39; 6.36)	Kong (33; 5.17)
6	Development (31; 5.35)	Wynn (34; 5.55)	Workers (33; 5.17)
7	People (31; 5.35)	Said (31; 5.06)	Association (33; 5.17)
8	Region (29; 5.01)	Revenue (30; 4.89)	Frontline (30; 4.70)
9	Gaming (29; 5.01)	Junket (27; 4.40)	Forefront (26; 4.08)
10	Economic (27; 4.6)6	Government (26; 4.24)	University (26; 4.08)
11	Administrative (26; 4.49)	China (25; 4.08)	Last (26; 4.08)
12	Casino (25; 4.32)	Chief (23; 3.75)	Government (24; 3.76)
13	Executive (25; 4.32)	Gambling (22; 3.59)	Yesterday (23; 3.61)
14	Revenue (25; 4.32)	Executive (22; 3.59)	Trade (22; 3.45)
15	Special (25; 4.32)	Operator (19; 3.10)	Delta (21; 3.29)
16	Mainland (22; 3.80)	Per (19; 3.10)	New (21; 3.29)
17	Chief (20; 3.45)	Operators (18; 2.94)	Union (20; 3.13)
18	Tourism (18; 3.11)	One (18; 2.94)	FMG (20; 3.13)
19	Term (16; 2.76)	Mainland (17; 2.77)	First (19; 2.98)
20	Percent (16; 2.76)	Xi (17; 2.77)	Unions (19; 2.98)

Macao in the *XH&CDC*. The repetitive co-occurrences of *Macau* and *SAR* reveal that Macau's administrative status is highlighted by the *XH&CD*, indicating that Macau is one of the SARs of the PRC, underlining its official relationship with Chinese Mainland that "the Macau SAR shall be a local Special Administrative Region of the PRC" (The Basic Law of the Macau Special Administrative Region of the People's Republic of China, Art 12, 1993).

Apart from the top collocate *SAR*, it is noted that the other top collocates of *Macao* (i.e., *chief*, *government*, and *executive*) in the *XH&CDC* are also semantically related to administrative and legal aspects of Macau. Specifically, "*Chief Executive*" of the Macau Special Administrative Region shall the head of the Macao SAR government" (The Basic Law of the Macau Special Administrative Region of the People's Republic of China, Art 45, 1993) suggests that the mainland press is likely to pay special attention to the political structure and governing system of Macau. *Tourism* (N = 18, 3.11%), ranked 18th, is currently another vital industry in Macau and the relatively frequent use of *tourism* in the *XH&CDC* indicates that mainland press regards tourism industry as an essential hallmark of Macau.

In Table 4.2, the most frequent collocate of *Macau* is *gaming* in the *SCMPC* (N = 69; 11.26%) and the *MPDC* (N = 106; 16.61%). By contrast, *gaming* (N = 29;

Table 4.3 Unique collocates of Macau in three news article corpora

XH&CDC	*SCMPC*	*MPDC*
SAR	Wynn	Industry
Development	Junket	Workers
People	China	Association
Economic	Gambling	Frontline
Region	Operator	Forefront
Administrative	Per	University
Special	Operators	Yesterday
Tourism	One	Trade
Term	Xi	Last
Percent	Casinos	New
		Union
		University
		Delta
		FMG
		First
		Unions

5.01%) is only ranked 9th in the *XH&CDC*, indicating that the mainland Chinese press seems reluctant to put *Macau* and *gaming* together in order not to focus too much on business regarding Macau's gaming industry.

Conversely, the *SCMPC* contains the largest number of collocates (N = 9; 45%) of *Macau*, which are found to be closely connected with the theme of gaming, namely *gaming* (N = 69, 11.26%), *casino* (N = 52; 8.48%), *casinos* (N = 39; 6.36%), *Wynn*[3] (N = 34; 5.55%), *revenue* (N = 30; 4.90%), *junket* (N = 27; 4.40%), *gambling* (N = 22; 3.59%), *operator* (N = 19; 2.94%), and *operators* (N = 18; 2.94%), implying the relevant themes regarding gaming industry are connected with *Macau*. In comparison, only one collocate (N = 1; 5%) of *Macau* in the *MPDC* is semantically relevant to the gaming industry, namely *gaming* (N = 106; 16.49%) at the 1st rank. Similarly, a small number of collocates (N = 3; 15%) of *Macau* in the *XH&CDC* are related to gaming, namely *gaming* (N = 29; 5.01%) ranked 9th, *casino* (N = 25; 4.32%) ranked 12th, and *revenue* (N = 25; 4.32%) ranked 14th.

Table 4.3 illustrates the unique collocates of Macau in each news article corpus. To better understand these unique collocates in each corpus, they are grouped into several categories according to their meanings.

Specifically, the types of unique collocates of *Macau* are diverse in the *XH&CDC*, which can be classified into five groups: (1) political organization: *SAR*, *special*, *administrative*, and *region*; (2) industry: *tourism;* (3) the participants of Macau society: *people;* (4) the process and state of Macau: *development* and *economic*; and (5) figures used to describe gaming revenue: *percent*. Specifically, *development*

[3] Wynn: One of the famous casinos in Macau. see also: http://www.wynnmacau.com/en/.

connotes that the mainland's press attempts to portray positive aspects of Macau, suggesting that the concept of development plays a significant role in the news articles of the *XH&CDC*, and *economic* reveals a specific focus on the state of the economy in Macau within the discourse of Chinese mainland news coverage.

By contrast, the categories of unique collocates of *Macau* in the *SCMPC* are different, which can be classified into four groups: (1) companies and participants involved in the gaming business in Macau: *Wynn*, *operator*, *operators*, *junket*, and *gambling*; (2) geographical location: *China;* (3) figures used to describe gaming revenue: *one* and *per;* and (4) the powerful political figure: *Xi*; this refers to the Chinese President Xi Jinping, implying that the *SCMP* tends to associate this political figure closely with Macau, which is worthy of further concordance analysis in order to obtain contextual information. The majority of collocates of *Macau* is found to be closely related to gaming, as evidenced by the categories (1) and (3).

In the *MPDC*, unique collocates are different from those in the other two news article corpora. They can be divided into four categories: (1) companies and participants involved in the gaming business in Macau: *workers*; Specifically, *workers* denotes the employees working in the casinos; (2) organizations and associations in Macau: *new*, *union*, *unions university*, *association*, *frontline*, *forefront*, and *FMG*; (3) time: *last* and *yesterday;* and (4) industry: *industry*. The word *industry* here does not only refer to Macau's gaming industry but also includes other industries, such as hospitality, tourism, creative, entertainment, and even the illegal industries. Besides, collocates such as *workers, trade, union,* and *association* can only be found in the *MPDC,* showing that Macau's local press tends to report the themes to do with employment concerning Macau's gaming sector. Specifically, *union* refers to the trade union of Macau's gaming industry while *association* refers to various organized groups concerning Macau's gaming. It can be inferred that the *MPD*, as the regional newspaper, placed emphasis on the social perspectives of gaming industry in Macau.

The word Macau was qualitatively examined through detailed line-by-line concordance analyses with the aim of figuring out its semantic preference and semantic prosody in the three news article corpora. An interesting finding is noted: Mainland Chinese press is accustomed to spelling Macau as Macao, whereas in the *SCMPC* and the *MPDC*, the term Macau is employed in most news articles. Macau is the Portuguese spelling, while Macao is the English spelling. Both Macau and Macao are adopted in both Portuguese and English documents. After Macau reverted to the Chinese sovereignty in 1999, the English spelling *Macao* became the preferred version for most government institutions (Moody, 2008). In the *XH&CDC*, the proper noun *Macau* is found to be used as a living entity in most cases (e.g., *Macau will brace its second mass-construction period; Macau is embracing a "new normal" situation; Macao pursues an open economic policy*). Besides, *Macau* is used as the geographical name (e.g., *descendants of Portuguese living in Macao used to have many advantages)* or as part of an organization's name (e.g., *Macao International Music Festival, Macau International Airport).*

Concordance analysis of the lexical item *Macau* in the *XH&CDC* shows that the first semantic preference is 'economic situation and economic development of

Macau' (43 out of 114, 37.72%) as *Macau* co-selects with words and phrases to do with economy, such as *Economic Partnership, economic development, economic structure, economic policy, GDP (gross domestic product), economic adjustment, gaming revenue, economic story*, and *budget*, implying that Macau's economic state is one of the major focuses for the Chinese mainland newspapers.

As for the semantic prosody regarding 'economic situation and economic development of Macau', *Macau* co-occurs with phrases and clauses with a positive semantic prosody, such as *great progress and achievements, open economic, tourism 'golden', notable economic and social progress, sustained prosperity, bright, rapid economic and social process, harmonious, steady, leapfrog development, successful social and economic progress, Macau has written a successful economic story, recent strong economic growth, fast economic growth, Macao has made impressive stride since the handover*, and *brilliant chapter in the story of Macau*. All the co-occurring phrases and clauses with *Macau* are employed in the *XH&CDC* to highlight Macau's success from the economic development perspective; therefore, the semantic prosody is "good and promising" (19 out of 43, 42.85%). This suggests that the economic situation of Macau has been portrayed positively by the Chinese media.

The following examples are sentence concordance lines extracted from the XH&CDC to demonstrate that the Chinese press specifically foregrounded Macau's success after its handover to the PRC in 1999 through employing languages with positive meanings, such as notable economic and social progress in example 1, impressive economic growth in example 2, the use of doing very well and outstanding achievements in example 3, and rapidly developing economy, fastest growing in example 4.

1. Dec. 8 (*Xinhua*) – China's central government has always been a strong support behind **Macao**'s notable economic and social progress over the past 15 years, and will continue to back up **Macao**'s development, said Li Gang, director of the Liaison Office of the central government in Macao.
2. Syed said **Macao**'s impressive economic growth has a lot to do with the sound macroeconomic management of the Macao authorities, including prudent fiscal policy, large fiscal reserves, flexible labour markets and a stable financial system.
3. **Macao**'s economy is "doing very well" and has made "amazing" achievements in the in the past 15 years.
4. The past 15 years since Macao' s return to the motherland is the fastest-growing period in **Macao**, he said, citing a rapidly developing economy, ever-improving livelihood, and a harmonious and stable society in the region.

The second semantic preference in regards to *Macau* in the *XH&CDC* is related to the 'political affairs and policy', representing 62.28% (71 out of 114), with its surrounding words and phrases, such as *Basic Law, One Country, Two Systems, central government, government, SAR government, Chief Executive, Liaison Office, sovereignty, motherland*, and *visa rules*. The corresponding semantic prosody is 'supportive and positive' as *Macau* co-occurs with words and phrases to do with support and words and clauses with a positive meaning, such as *continue to back up Macao's development, support Macau, Law has guaranteed that Macau people, strong supporter, give firm support, help Macau, boost development, strong support, Macao will progress steadily on the right track, guided by the "One Country, Two Systems", "One Country, two systems" will make steady and continuous progress along the right track and Macao will have a better future, the positive results produced by the "One Country, Two Systems" policy, great success of "One Country, Two Systems"*, amounting to 16.90% (12 out of 71). This prosody reveals the positive and praising attitude of the Chinese press towards Macau. Specifically, Mainland Chinese media tend to highlight Macau's success and achievements being owed to the support of the Chinese central government.

Representative concordance lines are shown in the following extracts taken from the *XH&CDC*. For example, Macau's *"leapfrog development"* benefits from the "*full central gov's support*" as seen in example 5. Examples 6 and 7 show that the Chinese mainland media select the very words with the strong meanings, *highlight* and *great vitality* to foreground the importance of the principle of "One Country, Two Systems" for Macau.

5. **Macao** achieves "leapfrog development" with full central gov's support.
6. The achievements in **Macao** have highlighted the great vitality of the "One country, Two systems" policy, Chui told.
7. The 15 years of development in **Macao** also proved a great success for the "One country, Two systems" policy.

In addition to highlighting the economic achievements of Macau, the examination of concordance lines reveals that the Chinese mainland press also discuss Macau's future economic development direction. The third semantic preference of *Macau* in the *XH&CDC* is 'Macau's future economic development direction' as *Macau* co-occurs with such phrases and clauses as *a major move to help Macau readjust its economic structure, promote appropriately diversified and sustainable economic development, economic transformation,* and *an opportunity for Macau to develop a diversified economy,* amounting to 26.32% (30 out 114). The corresponding semantic prosody is 'Macau's economic structure needs to be diversified", representing 100% (30 out of 30).

The findings from analysing concordance lines demonstrate that Macau's present gaming-dominant economy needs diversification to sustain its future development of Macau. Specifically, Mainland Chinese media have adopted an encouraging attitude to persuade Macau to diversify its economy; for example, example 8 shows the future development direction of Macau aims to be the "*Centre of Tourism and Leisure*" in support of the Chinese central government rather than its gaming industry. Examples 9–11 illustrate that the *XH&CD* highlights the positive influence of economic divarication on Macau's future development. It is noted that the Chinese mainland media attempt to downplay the reasons why Macau should promote economic diversification, instead they attempt to illuminate the benefits to economic diversity, stating that it will bring more opportunities and also provide solutions to diversity the economic structure of Macau; for instance, Macau could shift its emphasis from gaming to become a centre of tourism.

8. The central government supports **Macao** in developing itself into a center of tourism and leisure.
9. Chinese mainland's economic rebalancing in the next few years could also provide opportunities for **Macao**'s economic diversification.
10. The regional cooperation between Guangdong province, Hong Kong and Macao will be an opportunity for **Macao** to develop a diversified economy.
11. Have expressed confidence in a more diversified future for **Macao.**

As for *Macau* in the *SCMPC*, *Macau* is often used as part of the casino operators' name (N = 55) (e.g., *Wynn Macau* and *Galaxy Macau*). It is not surprising that the semantic preference of *Macau* is closely related to "gaming", such as *casinos, gaming revenues, gambling house,* and *casino operator*, all of which concern Macau's gaming industry, amounting to 65.38% (N = 221 out of 338). The semantic prosody of *Macau* in the gaming domain is 'tough and struggling', which refers to the present situation of the gaming industry of Macau. Its neighbouring phrases and clauses, such as *crack down, dropped, fell the most, decline, battered, hit, slowdown, rein, gloom, flagging gaming industry, tumbled, tumble,* and *plunging,* indicate that the gaming industry is going through a difficult period, representing 29.86% (66 out 221). The following examples are representative sentence concordance lines:

12. Xi headed China's advisory team on Hong Kong and **Macau** affairs for four years. His corruption crackdown - coupled with an economic slowdown on the mainland - has hit Macau's casino revenues hard.
13. as overall gaming revenue in **Macau** slowed since May following the mainland's crackdown on illegal money transfer
14. More gloom expected for **Macau** casinos in the first half after negative year from anti-graft drive, Union Pay rule changes and smoking ban Macau's gaming industry is expected to remain depressed until at least the second half of next year when new resorts launch
15. All Macau casino stocks dropped in trading yesterday in the wake of news of the crackdown, which comes just 48 h before President Xi Jinping arrives in **Macau** to lead ceremonies marking the 15th anniversary of the former Portuguese enclaves return to Chinese sovereignty.
16. A clampdown on liquidity has also hurt Macau badly. On Wednesday, a senior Beijing official issued the sternest warning yet that **Macau**'s overreliance on casino revenue was not only against the interest of the city, but also the whole nation.

As shown from the above sentence concordance examples, the selection of language used in the *SCMPC* concerning Macau tends to be more negative, expressing the concern towards the future of Macau's gaming industry by using a series of evaluative language, such as *hit the economy hard* in example 12, *crackdown* in example 13, *depressed* in example 14, *dropped* in example 15, and *sternest* and *badly* in example 16, together to create a negative connotation of Macau's economic situation. In addition, the metaphorical expression "*groom*" in example 14 makes a negative implication towards the economic performance of Macau.

Moreover, in the *SCMPC*, 34.62% of *Macau* (N = 117 out of 338 concordance lines) is found to co-occur with words such as *Basic Law, government, chief executive, political system, pro-democracy,* and *government liaison office*, suggesting the semantic preference is 'politics'. The semantic prosody concerning 'politics' in the *SCMPC* is 'adjustment'. Specifically, in 34 of 117 concordance lines (29.06%), through co-occurring with such phrases and clauses as *needs stronger leadership, move away from its over-reliance, create another Macau, diversify, tight, going to have to change, position Macau,* and *create another Macau,* the media representation is that Macau needs to adjust its current economic structure from the monotony of the gaming industry to a more diverse selection of industries.

There are 970 concordance lines involving *Macau* in the *MPDC* and the number of concordance lines is much higher than the other two corpora. Therefore, the randomized concordance entries function of the Wordsmith tool is adopted to reduce concordance lines to 191 entries in total. As for the semantic preference of *Macau* in the *MPDC*, the noticeable feature is the 'Macau's local institution, organization and association' as *Macau* constitutes part of them, such as *Macau Youth Dynamics (MYD), organization, Macau Pensioners and Retirees Association, Macau Monetary Authority (AMCM), Macau Media Advancement Association, Macau Journalist Advance Association, Macau Jiangmen Communal Society, Macau Federation of Trade Unions, Forefront of Macau Gaming (FMG), City University of Macau, Macau Polytechnic Institution, UM (University of Macau), New Macau Association, Macau Civil Servants Association, Macau General Union of Neighbourhood,* and *Macau University of Science and Technology.* These account for 17.27% (33 out of 191). However, it is noted that this semantic prosody of Macau related to "institution, organization and association" in the *MPDC* is relatively neutral without containing the same evaluative language used by the other two corpora.

Gaming

Gaming is a lexical word shared by the three news article corpora. The percentage of *gaming* in the *XH&CDC* is smaller (N = 151; 0.48%) than those in the *SCMPC* (N = 283; 0.51%) and the *MPDC* (N = 801; 0.71%).

Table 4.4 shows the top 20 lexical collocates of *gaming* in each news article corpus, ranked by frequency and percentage.

As shown in Table 4.4, four collocates of *gaming* (*Macao, industry, revenue,* and *said*) are found in the three news article corpora. These co-occurrences of *gaming* are predictable because the gaming industry was the pillar industry in Macau in 2014, as described in Chap. 1. Besides, gaming revenue is considered an essential indicator for gaming industry of Macau in 2014.

In the *XH&CDC*, when *gaming* co-occurs with Macau, it shows several uses. First, it is primarily used as a part of some specific organizations related to Macau's gaming industry, such as *The Gaming Inspection and Coordination Bureau, Macao Gaming Industry Frontline Workers' union,* and *The Institute for the Study of Commercial Gaming* and *commercial gaming at the University of Macau.* By contrast, when *Macau* co-occurs with *gaming* in the *SCMPC,* it covers several uses. In most cases, it co-occurs with words semantically related to the gaming market, referring to Macau's

Table 4.4 Collocates of gaming among three news article corpora

Rank	*XH&CDC* (Freq.; %)	*SCMP* (Freq.; %)	*MPDC* (Freq.; %)
1	Macao (29; 11.55)	Macau (69; 17.47)	Macau (123; 10.87)
2	Revenue (29; 11.55)	Revenue (62; 15.70)	Operators (119; 10.51)
3	Industry (28; 11.16)	Industry (32; 8.10)	Industry (116; 10.25)
4	Bureau (15; 5.98)	Said (29; 7.34)	Venues (88; 7.77)
5	Percent (13; 5.18)	Gross (26; 6.58)	Employees (76; 6.71)
6	Gross (13; 5.18)	Per (20; 5.06)	Said (66; 5.83)
7	Coordination (13; 5.18)	Cent (18; 4.56)	City (62; 5.48)
8	Macao's (12; 4.78)	Casino (14; 3.54)	Smoking (58; 5.12)
9	Inspection (12; 4.78)	Fell (14; 3.54)	Workers (53; 4.68)
10	Revenues (11; 4.38)	Non (13; 3.29)	Revenue (45; 3.98)
11	According (11; 4.38)	Revenues (13; 3.29)	Operator (45; 3.98)
12	Casino (8; 3.19)	Year (10; 2.53)	Frontline (38; 3.36)
13	Sector (8; 3.19)	Macau's (10; 2.53)	Sector (34; 3.00)
14	Non (8; 3.19)	VIP (10; 2.53)	Local (34; 3.00)
15	Las Vegas (7; 2.79)	Stocks (10; 2.53)	Chips (34; 3.00)
16	Said (7; 2.79)	City (9; 2.28)	Forefront (33; 2.92)
17	Month (7; 2.79)	China (9; 2.28)	Casinos (30; 2.65)
18	Dependence (7; 2.79)	Analysts (9; 2.28)	Six (28; 2.47)
19	Billion (7; 2.79)	Month (9; 2.28)	Set (25; 2.21)
20	Growth (6; 2.39)	Online (9; 2.28)	FMG (25; 2.21)

gaming revenue, stocks, and taxes. Second, it denotes Macau's gaming industry and it is adopted as part of the specific organizations relevant to gaming, such as the *Forefront of Macau Gaming union, Macau's Gaming Inspection and Coordination Bureau*. Finally, it also co-occurs with *tables*, indicating the employment policies held by Macau, where only Macau permanent residents can be allowed to operate gaming tables in casinos.

In the *MPDC*, when *gaming* co-occurs with *Macau*, it also displays several uses. First, it is primarily used to cover a wide variety of local associations or organizations related to gaming in Macau, such as *Macau Gaming Industry Frontline Workers, Macau Responsible Gaming Association, Macau Gaming Enterprises Staff Association, Macau Gaming Industry Laborers Association,* and *Gaming Employees Club*. Second, it refers to the gaming revenue and financial aspects of Macau's gaming market. It is also used to report employment in Macau's gaming industry. It is noted that only 1 collocate (i.e., *city*) is shared between the *SCMPC* and the *MPDC*, reflecting that the topics concerning gaming in Macau's local news media are covered less compared to the other two corpora. By contrast, 5 collocates *percent, Macau's, revenues, casino,* and *non* are shared between the *SCMPC* and the *XH&CDC*,

Table 4.5 Unique collocates of gaming in three news article corpora

XH&CDC	*SCMPC*	*MPDC*
Coordination	Year	Venues
Inspection	VIP	Employees
According	Stocks	Workers
Sector	China	Operator
Las Vegas	Analyst	Frontline
Month	Month	Sector
Billion	Online	Local
Growth	Fell	Chips
Dependence		Forefront
		Casinos
		Six
		Set
		FMG
		Smoking

implying a higher degree of similarity in terms of their representations of gaming in Macau in 2014, with a focus on its financial aspect.

Table 4.5 illustrates the unique collocates of *gam*ing in the three news article corpora in order to highlight the differences in the ideological positions of the different media towards gaming in Macau in 2014.

In the *XH&CDC*, *bureau*, *coordination* and *inspection* are the combinations of a particular organization in Macau, namely the *Gaming Inspection and Coordination Bureau.*[4] In addition, an American city *Las Vegas* (N = 7; 2.79%) has also been repeatedly associated with *gaming* because of its similar economic background to Macau, which is also famous for its gaming industry. This correlation implies that the mainland's media prefer to take Las Vegas as a reference in order to highlight the fact that the current gaming scale of Macau has surpassed this American city, with a focus on Macau's significant economic developments in the post-handover era, as shown in the following concordance lines in examples 17–19:

17. In 1998, it was relative smaller economy and its gaming sector was not well developed. But now Macao has overtaken **Las Vegas** as the largest gaming center in the world and become a big economy.
18. The former Portuguese colony has overtaken **Las Vegas** to become the world's gaming industry with its state of heart of casinos, hotels and resorts.
19. The Chinese region overtook **Las Vegas** in terms of gaming revenues almost decade ago.

---

4 . The Gaming Inspection and Coordination Bureau (hereafter called as the DICJ), provides guidance and assistance to the Chief Executive of Macao SAR on the definition and execution of the economic policies for the operations of the casino games of fortune or other ways of gaming, Pari-Mutuels and gaming activities offered to the public.

Dependence (N = 7; 2.79%) denotes Macau's present economic structure and how it is heavily dependent on gaming. The unique use of *dependence* in the *XH&CDC* suggests that the Mainland Chinese media, serving as the "mouthpiece" of the Chinese authorities, tell Macau that its heavy dependence on gaming is not a perfect option for its economy and needs to be adjusted. For example, example 20 demonstrates that diversification is the only way for Macau's future development by citing the speech made by an influential political figure, the director Li Gang from the Liaison Office of the Central People's Government. Example 21 is similar to example 20, showing *XH&CDC's* opinion that the overwhelming dependence on the gaming industry is very dangerous for Macao's economy. Example 22 demonstrates that Macau should develop other sectors instead of simply relying heavily on gaming.

20. Li said is a major move to help Macao readjust its economic structure and lessen its heavy **dependence** on the casinos gaming "only by diversifying the economy could Macao prevent from economic crisis", he said.
21. To lessen the overwhelming **dependence** on gaming which is especially risky for micro economy like Macau
22. By lessening the SAR's heavy **dependence** on the casinos and development other industries of cultural creativity, convention and exhibition.

In the *SCMPC*, *China* (N = 9; 2.28%) is the unique collocate of *gaming*, containing two uses. First, *China* is used as a possessive, referring to *China's gaming capital.* Second, it is used as part of the organization, denoting *China Union Gaming*. *VIP* (N = 10; 2.53%) is used to denote VIP gaming revenue, reflecting that the *SCMP* shows special attention to the unpromising outlook in terms of *VIP* revenue, as illustrated in the following sentence concordance lines in examples 23 to 24.

23. the anti-corruption drive the has caused decelerating VIP **gaming** volumes, pushing the gaming hub into a six consecutive mouths.
24. VIP **gaming** revenue segment remained weak and was not expected to recover this year.

Stocks (N = 10; 2.53%) co-occurs with *gaming*, denoting gaming stocks with the above collocates, including *VIP*, implying that the *SCMP* focuses on the financial performance in Macau's gaming industry. *Online* (N = 9; 2.28%) co-occurs with *gaming*, referring to online gaming sites.

As shown in Table 4.5, two words with the opposite meanings are observed. Specially, *fell* is the collocate of *gaming*, which is exclusively found in the *SCMPC* vis-à-vis *growth* is the unique collocate of gaming in the *XH&CDC*. The word *fell* in the *SCMPC* co-occurs with the words that have to do with money (e.g., *revenue*, *revenues*, and *stocks*), implying that the topics related to the decline of Macau's gaming revenue or stocks in 2014 are constantly referred to in the *SCMPC*. By contrast, the *XH&CD* tends to focus on reporting the *growth* situation of Macau. As discussed in the above section, *growth* is also the top lexical single word in the *XH&CDC*, reflecting the economic growth that Macau has obtained in the past 15 years since its handover to China. This reflects that the media in Hong Kong and Mainland China select their respective report interests in their news articles.

In the *MPDC, gaming* collocates with *venues* (N = 88; 7.77%), co-occurring with words such as *smoking, anti-Tabaco, air quality*, and *law*, revolving around the discussion about the set-up of smoking rooms in the gaming venues and the failed quality assessment in those venues, as shown in examples 25 to 29:

25. According to current anti-tobacco legislation, all **gaming** venues are allowed to set up smoking areas.
26. In reducing smoking in the city's **gaming** venues.
27. The reasons for why the air quality in **gaming** venues has not improved include gambler ignoring the law, insufficient ventilation equipment.
28. The regulation on smoking areas in the city's **gaming** venues took effect on January 1 last year.
29. She wondered aloud why 14 **gaming** venues failed their second air quality assessment tests.

The word *employees* (N = 76; 6.71%) refers specifically to staff who work for casinos. Examples 30–32 demonstrate an unsatisfactory working environment for gaming employees. Examples 33–34 imply that the government of Macau should adopt measures to protect employees' health, showing that the *MPC* not only focuses on gaming revenues but also expresses concerns for the gaming employees' benefits and work environment.

30. The gaming **employees** still suffer a great deal from the inhalation of second-hand smoke.
31. Many gaming **employees** suffered from low morale due to their difficult working environment
32. Both Choi and Lei expressed concerns that the gaming **employees** working in VIP rooms will be exposed to even more second hand smoke.
33. They also said that the government should be more concerned with the health of the city's gaming **employees**, not just the benefits of the gaming operators.
34. Protest today such as Macau Gaming Industry Frontline Workers (Forefront of Macau Gaming, FMG) and Gaming **Employees** Club demand the government amend the law immediately and implements a full-smoking ban.

Smoking (N = 58; 5.12%) here refers to the smoking ban and to smoking rooms. *Set* (N = 25; 2.21%) revolves around establishing smoking areas and a full smoking ban in the casinos. *Chips* (N = 34; 3.00%) co-occurs with *gaming* at N + 1 to indicate gaming chips, which refers to the tokens used instead of cash in the casinos. The co-occurring words of *gaming chips*, such as *fake, bogus*, and *counterfeit*, demonstrate some gaming-related criminal activities, such as using fake gaming chips in the casinos, as shown in the following two examples:

35. The Judiciary Police (PJ) announced yesterday the arrest of a Hong Kong man for using bogus gaming and being a key figure of gaming whose members used the **chips** to cheat local casinos.

36. According to the spokesperson, Shi and Zhou are cross-border gaming which has been operating since 2011 and is mainly involved in using fake gaming **chips**.

Frontline, *Forefront*, and *FMG* denote the organization of *Macau Gaming Industry Frontline* and *Forefront of the Macau Gaming* (FMG). *Sector* (N = 34; 3.00%) refers to the gaming sector, and its surrounding words are semantically related to the employment situation in Macau, such as *the health of gaming sector employees*, *vacancies*, *recruitment*, *people*, *staff*, *local employees*, *recruitment prerequisites*, *workforce*, and *job vacancy*, proving that the *MPD* shows its special interests in reporting on the employment situation in Macau's gaming sector as shown in the following examples:

37. In the quarter of last year, 3503 new employees were hired by the gaming **sector**.
38. At the end of last year, the gaming **sector** had 1996 vacancies, down by 158 year-by-year.
39. In the second quarter, the gaming **sector** employed about the 15 percent of the city's total workforce.
40. Three social activists who claim to be fighting for the rights of gaming **sector** employees protested yesterday.
41. Lei said the health of gaming **sector** employees should not be sacrificed for the development of industry.

Examples 37, 38, and 39 demonstrate the employment figures of the gaming sectors. Examples 40 and 41 show the protest activities and comments regarding the fight for the gaming employees' rights, implying that the *MPDC* attached importance to the employment status in the gaming sector rather than the economic aspect of gaming. *Local* (N = 34; 3.00%) and *city's* (N = 62; 5.48%) co-occurs with *gaming*, denoting Macau's gaming industry, enterprises, and operators.

Among 125 instances of *gaming* in the *XH&CDC*, this lexical item has two semantic preferences and semantic prosodies. First, the word *gaming* co-occurs with words and phrases to do with business and financial figures, such as *revenue*, *revenues*, *stocks*, *gross*, *percent*, *data*, *income*, *shares*, and *billion*. The semantic preference of *gaming* is 'The financial performance of Macau's gaming industry', accounting for 51.25% (64 out of 125), and its corresponding semantic prosody is 'neural', whose news focuses on financial statistics reports, business reports by the casinos' operators as well as information from official government departments.

Second, *gaming* is often used in association with words and phrases such as *industry*, *gambling-dominated economy*, *Macao's economy*, *the entire economy*, *a big economy*, *other industries of cultural creativity*, *hi-tech industries*, and *economic diversification*, with the amount to 48.8% (61 out of 125), reflecting that the semantic preference is 'the economic structure of Macau'. As for the prosody of *gaming* in the *XH&CDC*, it manifests that the economy of Macau cannot only heavily depend on the gaming industry but also needs to be adjusted. Discussion of the development of other industries in the future co-occurs with phrases and clauses including *healthy adjustment*, *adjusting*, *dominance of gaming industry*, *developing other industries such as cultural creativity, diversifying the economy, economic diversification, overwhelming dependence on gaming, heavy dependence, overreliance on gaming, diversify its economy away from gaming, seek diversified development, nurture new growth areas for its economy, economic transformation, appropriately diversified*, and *healthy adjustment,* amounting to 29.51% (18 out of 61), suggesting that Macau needs to diversify its economy and thus revealing that the semantic prosody represented by the mainland newspaper is 'lacking and needs to be developed and diversified'.

In the *SCMPC*, three semantic preferences and semantic prosodies of *gaming* have been identified. The first semantic preference of *gaming* is 'economy and industry of Macau' in association with words and phrases such as *industry, Macau's flagging gaming industry*, amounting to 25.17% (32 out of 127). As for the prosody of Macau's gaming industry in the *SCMPC*, it is 'negative and challenging' being put towards the gaming industry of Macau as evidenced by the use of the words, phrases, and clauses, such as *Macau's gaming industry is expected to remain depressed, heaps pressure, nervous, threatened, fears*, and *brunt,* accounting for 50% (16 out of 32).

The following examples show concordance lines that present the unfavourable economic situation of Macau. Examples 42–43 show that the *SCMP* employs two metaphors (i.e., *perfect storm, death with a thousand cut*) to describe the unfavourable circumstance of Macau's casino industry.

42. The mainland's crackdown on graft, protests in Hong Kong and a ban on smoking indoors combined last month to create **a perfect storm** for Macau's casino industry.
43. The number of negative factors that converged over the past year prompted one gaming analyst to describe it as "**death by a thousand cuts**"

Examples 44–49 show that the *SCMP* represents Macau's gaming dominant economy, and the financial position, to be bleak, through employing words and phrases that carry a negative meaning, such as *depressed, rocked, under pressure, fear, concerns,* and *worst contraction.*

44. Union Pay rule changes and smoking ban Macau's gaming industry is expected to remain **depressed.**
45. Beijing inspired dirty-money crackdown that has **rocked** the city's under the **pressure** casino sector.
46. Steve Wynn has dismissed **fears** that Macau's gaming industry is threatened by the mainland's crackdown on corruption and extravagance.
47. Macau's already battered gaming stocks fell sharply following Li's comments, amid concerns the **worst** contraction of city's economy since 2009 will not reversed any time soon.
48. The financial position in a gaming market facing increasing **challenges**.
49. Macau's gaming industry is expected to remain **depressed.**

Example 50 reveals that Hong Kong's press reports the opinions about economic diversification for Macau, showing the *SCMP*'s reporting perspectives and attitudes different from the mainland press. The *SCMP* tends to adopt a stronger tone of voice (i.e., *it has no option but to diversify*) to describe Macau's economic dilemma. Example 51 indicates the use of metaphorical language *cracks the whip* together with the use of robust language *The most blunt warning* to suggest that the Chinese central government (Beijing)'s urgent appeal for the change in terms of Macau's economic structure. In example 52, it is also stated that the use of *the blunt warning* evidences Beijing's attitudes towards Macau's economic diversification of its gaming-dominant economy. Besides, the *SCMP* also expresses its concern that Macau may lose the support of the Chinese government (see example 53); for instance, the *SCMP* cites a question raised by Nomura[5] *whether the Chinese authority might withdraw its support for Macau as a gaming enclave*, demonstrating that the *SCMP* expresses its doubt whether Macau's gaming industry is losing the support from the Chinese government and the potential unfavourable effect on Macau's future development.

50. But Macau is going to have to change, it has no option but to diversify and come up with a plan with more vision. Gaming is facing **a perfect storm**, and while it will continue to be vital, its challenges are many."
51. Beijing **cracks the whip**, telling city its reliance on casinos affects 'whole nation' Macau has been told to address its overreliance on casino revenues "in the interests of the whole nation" in the **most blunt warning** yet about the need for economic diversification.
52. And with Macau set to record its first full-year decline in casino revenue, there have been **blunt warnings** from Beijing about diversifying into areas other than gaming
53. A Nomura report on December 11 raised questions over whether Beijing might **withdraw its support** for Macau as a gaming enclave.

Second, *gaming* co-occurs with *revenue*, *revenues*, *capital*, *stocks*, and *gross* and is combined with *percen*t and *figures*, demonstrating that the semantic preference is 'Macau's financial performance in the gaming industry', accounting for 69.29% (88 out 127). The semantic prosodies of *gaming* associated with the semantic preference of 'Macau's financial performance in gaming industry' are mixed. The first is 'neutral', which is related to reports that cover the gaming statistics without adopting any attitudinal or evaluative language, which amounts to 86.36% (76 out 88). In addition, the co-selections of *gaming* with, for example, *reel, weak, plunge, slump tumble, sharp decline, economic contraction, hit hard*, and *prolonged decline,* create the semantic prosody 'gloomy', accounting for 13.64% (12 out of 88), reflecting that Macau's financial performance in the gaming industry in 2014 was not optimistic.

The following examples, 54–59 demonstrate that the *SCMP* employed words with negative meanings, such as *slump, sharp, hit, sharply, battered, prolonged decline,* and *heavily*, to depict Macau's bad financial performance in the gaming industry in 2014.

54. A slump in **gaming** revenue, the mainland crackdown on corruption and competition from Hengqing Island in Zhuhai have combined to drive down prices in Macau down 10 per cent.

[5] Nomura is a Japanese financial holding company, and a principal member of the Nomura Group.

55. Macau recorded a sharp 23.2 per cent decline in gross **gaming** revenue.
56. An economic slowdown on the mainland has hit Macau's casino revenues hard.
57. Macau's already battered **gaming** stocks fell sharply following Li's comments.
58. Macau's gross **gaming** revenues have fallen for three consecutive months, the first such prolonged decline in five years.
59. **Gaming** industry analysts bet heavily against the house last month and got it right, with gross revenues at Macau's casinos plunging 23.2 percent year-on-year.

Third, *gaming* also co-occurs with words and phrases that share a semantic feature related to criminal and illegal activities, such as *organized crime*, *illegal online gaming sites*, *vast flows of illicit money*, *illegal money*, *illicit funds*, *money laundering*, *washing machine for proceeds of crime*, *criminal groups*, and *criminal money*, revealing that the semantic preference of *gaming* is 'gaming-related economic crimes', with the amount of 12.70% (10 out of 127). As for the semantic prosody of *gaming* in the context of 'gaming related economic crimes', it is 'problematic and under the control', accounting for 90% (9 out 10), in association with words and phrases such as *much of the problem*, *greed of money*, *arrested*, *evasion of taxes*, *crackdown*, *exerting greater control*, and *rein*, as exemplified in the following examples 60–63:

60. Following the mainland's crackdown on illegal money transfer and corruption.
61. Beijing is to launch a major crackdown on the multibillion-dollar flow of illicit funds through Macau casinos in a coordinated security drive that will see the country's power Ministry of Public security play a leading role.
62. President tells new government to exert more control over the industry as Beijing looks to stem the flow of illicit funds through the city.
63. Government authorities will be given access to all Union Pay transaction to crack down on money laundering.

All examples 60–63 demonstrate that the *SCMP* selected to report on more stringent measures adopted by the Chinese authorities and the local government of Macau to crack down the gaming-related criminal activities in Macau, such as money laundering and illicit financial outflow, in 2014.

In the *MPDC*, by investigating the concordance lines of *gaming*, the study has identified three semantic preferences and semantic prosodies. First, *gaming* co-occurs with words and phrases to do with stakeholders regarding the gaming industry of Macau, such as *employees*, *workers*, *operators* and *enterprises*, together with phrases and clauses such as *health of gaming employees*, *working in VIP rooms*, *fighting for the rights*, *protect the city's frontline gaming sector employees*, *pay their employees more*, *improve their salaries*, *protection of interests of frontline gaming employees*, *better benefits and protection*, *safe working environment*, *working under pressure*, *major salary increase*, and *workings in such a bad environment*, revealing the semantic preference of 'welfare', amounting to 64.97% (293 out of 451). These concordance lines focus on how gaming operators should improve the quality of their work environment, as well as how they should focus on improving their employees' benefits and well-being. In terms of semantic preference 'welfare', the semantic prosody of 'unsatisfied and controversial', amounts to 24.22% (71 out of 292). Specifically, *gaming* was found to co-select with phrases and clauses that carry negative meanings, such as *employees protested, problems such as illegal worker, suffer a great deal of second-hand smoke, low morale, strike, difficult work environment abuse, failure to protect employees, useless, concerns, ineffectiveness, not caring about gaming employees, tackling the smoking issue,* and *unfair*, regarding the controversial issue of whether or not to implement the smoking ban policy in all casinos in Macau in order to improve the work environment. Some critical comments related to the gaming employees' benefits are presented in the following examples:

64. "Why does the government continue be coerced by **gaming** operators into allowing them to keep their employees working in such bad environment."
65. FMG executive board member Kelvin Leong said that **gaming** operators had abused the system of assistant jobs.
66. "We hope our action will push other **gaming** operators to improve their employees' salaries."
67. "**Gaming** operators have the duty to protect croupier, they should not downplay or neglect instances where they get assaulted."
68. The Reason for why the air quality in **Gaming** venues has not improved include gamblers ignoring the law, insufficient ventilation
69. Lei said that the health of **gaming** sector employees should not be sacrificed for the development of the industry
70. Choi also said the three unions were aware of cases where **gaming** operators violated their employees' right by unilaterally changing the terms of their contracts
71. Asked by reporters as to why the government apparently hasn't doing anything to ensure that the 14 **gaming** venues have reduced their smoking areas by 10 percent.
72. She also criticized the government for not caring about **gaming** employees and not providing a safe working environment for them when a full-smoking ban is implemented.
73. Several members of the audience slammed the government for lacking the determination to slap a full smoking ban on all **gaming** venues. They also said the government should be more concerned with the health of the city's gaming employees, not just the benefits of the gaming operators.

Examples 64–73 show that the *MPD* has cited various voices that are critical towards Macau's casino operators and the government of Macau about a series of arguments about gaming employees' benefits and their working environment.

Second, when *gaming* co-occurs with *industry* or *sector*, it reflects another semantic preference 'socio-economic aspect of Macau', with co-selected phrases and clauses such as *tourism-related industry, dominant economic force, local and non-local labour, employed 25,250 croupiers, gaming operators' social responsibility, government's gradual approach, workforce, croupiers working,* and *local people's livelihoods*, accounting for 33.26% (150 out of 451). The semantic prosody associated with 'socioeconomic aspect' is 'strict', evident in the co-occurrences of phrases and clauses with *gaming*, such as *more measures to oversee gaming industry, constantly monitoring all economic activities, dominance of gaming industry was not good for Macau's society, strengthen supervision of gaming industry, scrutinize, imposing tough measures, stricter measures, keeping a close eye, tackling, tough measure, gradual approach, prohibited, more vigilant about tackling such illegal activities, reduced use of China Union debits cards on local gaming industry, improving regulations, and oversee*, accounting for 13.33% (20 out of 150). This reveals that more stringent measures will be implemented by the MSAR government to regulate the gaming industry.

The third semantic preference associated with *gaming* is 'economic situation and politics'; co-occurring words and phrases include *development*, *local economy, political stability, future growth, diversify city's economy, dominant role,* and *local economy,* only representing 3.77% (17 out of 451). The semantic prosody of 'economic situation and politics' is 'needs to be adjusted', amounting to 64.71% (11 out of 17), with such co-occurring phrases and clauses as *diversification is needed, adequate economic diversification is the evitable choice, the importance of economic diversification,* and *the dominance of gaming industry was not good for Macau's society,* revealing that Macau's current economic structure, which mainly depends on the gaming industry, needs to be adjusted and diversified.

In summary, the semantic preferences and prosodies of *gaming* in each news article corpus suggest the diverse topical and ideological concerns and attitudes adopted by different newspapers in the three regions. Specifically, the *XH&CD* is primarily concerned with reporting the financial performance in Macau's gaming industry with a neutral attitude, and in the meantime stressing that Macau's economic dependence on gaming industry in 2014 needs to be adjusted, diversified and developed with non-gaming elements. By contrast, the *SCMP* held a mixed ideological position and attitude towards the financial performance of Macau's gaming industry. In addition to holding a neutral attitude towards the financial figures, the *SCMP* also expresses its negative attitude towards the dismal financial performance in Macau's gaming industry in 2014. Besides, the *SCMP* emphasises Macau's gaming industry's negative side, mentioning some illegal gaming-related activities. By contrast, the *MPD*, as a news press based on Macau society, shows a reporting preference towards local social issues in relation to gaming industry of Macau in 2014, such as the gaming employees' benefits, their work environment, and the ban on smoking policy in the casinos.

Government

In the *XH&CDC*, *government* (N = 140; 0.44%), ranked 7th, primarily co-occurs with *Macao* (N = 49; 35%), *SAR* (N = 26; 18.57%), and *central* (N = 49; 35%), representing Macau SAR government and Chinese central government (i.e., Central People's Government).

The high frequency of Macau SAR government is expected as the news discourse is based on Macau. The repeated occurrences of *central government* in the *XH&CDC*

show the tendency to mention the Chinese central government in their news articles constantly. After examining 140 concordance lines, the study finds that co-selections of *government* have to do with the economic and social situation of Macau society; for instance, *economic, socio-economic, economy, livelihood, people, public housing, low employment rate, quality of life, economic and social development*, and *people's lives*. The semantic preference is 'socio-economic aspect of Macau', amounting to 19.29% (27 out 140). The semantic prosody is 'support and corporation' as evidenced by such co-occurring words, phrases, and clauses as *improve, support, strong support, strong supporter, strong backing, firm support, cooperation, joint efforts, upload relations, cherishes, healthy development of relations between the central government the Macao SAR, pins high hope, strong backing, vigorous support, politics, rule of law, legitimacy, law, policy implementation, One Country, Two Systems*, amounting to 81.48% (22 out of 27). This suggests that the Mainland Chinese media adopt very strong language, such as *vigorous, firm*, and *strong*, to highlight the supportive role of the Chinese central government for its positive influence on Macau's socio-economic development. In the meantime, the significance of implementing related policies such as 'One country, Two Systems' in Macau is also emphasised in their news articles.

Besides, two instances are marked, which are found to refer to the former British Hong Kong government rather than the Portugal colonial government, as shown in example 74:

74. Another cause of Hong Kong's problem is today the socio-political elites in the city that ere nurtured by the **former colonial government**. This was done to maintain Britain's influence of Hong Kong. These British and United States-educated political operators have caused considerable unrest over the past 17 years.

The use of *the former colonial government* here demonstrates that the *XH&CD* especially emphasises its negative influence on Hong Kong that *cause the considerable unrest*.

In the *SCMPC*, the lexical word *government* (N = 117; 0.21%), ranked 17th, primarily co-occurs with *Macau* (N = 26; 22.22%), mainly indicating Macau government, with two lines referring to the Liaison Office of the Central People's Government in Macau. *Government* is followed by the verb *said* (N = 15; 13.27%), which is commonly employed in the news article, suggesting the use of indirect quotes to represent information or proposition concerning the government. *Government* also co-occurs with *central* (N = 11; 9.40%), representing the Chinese central government.

The dominant semantic preference of the lexical item *government* in the *SCMPC* is 'the economic structure of Macau', which is manifested by co-occurring with words and phrases, such as *economic, city's economy, industry, casino revenue, gaming industry, casino industry, economic slowdown, gross domestic product, economic model*, and *market revenue*, accounting for 18.80% (22 out of 117). The corresponding semantic prosody is 'stricter regulation and diversification', manifested by surrounding phrases and clauses such as *a diverse economy is an important mission and a requirement the central government has for Macau, ramps up its austerity drive, diversify its economy, cracks down Macau Gaming, impact, undertake a review, wide diversity, push for the government to up its game on economic diversification, greater courage and wisdom to strengthen and improve regulation, piles up more pressure on the Macau government to come up with a plan to diversify, exert more control, move to tighten rules,* and *rolls out stricter enforcement,* representing 68.18% (15 out of 22). This suggests that the MSAR[6] government came up with stricter rules to control the gaming industry of Macau in 2014. In addition, the *SCMP* suggests the fact that the economy of Macau heavily relies on its gaming industry began to be aware of the Chinese authorities and other subsidiary bodies of institutions like the National People's Congress Standing Committee the government liaison office in Macau. Therefore, diversification is needed for its casino-reliant economy.

In the *MPDC*, *government* (N = 559, 0.88%), ranked 4th, is much higher than the rankings in *XH&CDC* (rank 7) and the *SCMPC* (Rank 18). It co-occurs with the reporting verb *said* (N = 128; 22.90%) and adjective *local* (N = 73; 13.06%). The high presence of these two words implies that the journalists in the *MPDC* use many quotations to report government-related topics or themes in their news articles. Besides, the local issues are closely associated with *government* in the context of the *MPDC*. The second most frequent collocate of *government* is *central* (N = 73; 13.05%) at N-1, denoting the repetitive occurrences of *Central Government* in the news articles of the *MPD.*

Through examining concordance lines, the study finds that the semantic preference of *government* is 'social issues in Macau', especially in the sense of the Macau government as the lexical item *government* is co-selected by such phrases and clauses *as subsidy for low income workers, problem gamblers, petitions, salary, public housing unit, heavily overcrowded tourist spots, local's view, local residents' livelihood, building public housing flats, medical insurance, increasing cost of consumer goods, cross-emotional poverty, full smoking ban, employment opportunities, gaming workers, remove slot-machine parlours from residential neighbourhoods, casino worker's, traffic problems, employees' health, safety and wellbeing, tourism capacity, subsidize customers,* and *electricity supply facilities,* accounting for 55.64% (311 out 559), suggesting that the topical concerns of the *MPD* regarding the Macau government in 2014 were closely associated with the social issues in the context of Macau society, ranging from the residents' livelihood, living environment, housing problems, employment, traffic problems to the gaming workers working environment and benefits. The semantic prosody is 'lacking', as evidenced by the co-selected words and modal verbs *should, urged, stop, deal with,* and *establish,* representing 90.03% (290 out of 311), suggesting that the MSAR government is urged to come up with more measures to address the above social issues in order to improve the livelihood of the people. On the other hand, the MSAR government is working and planning to implement some measures to address those social issues.

Besides, when the government refers to the Chinese *central government* (N = 70; 12.52%), its semantic preference is 'politics', as *government* co-occurs with phrases

[6] MSAR represents Macau Special Administrative Region.

and clauses to do with political issues, such as *political reform, political stability, elections, re-selection, policy secretaries' appointment, clean governance, anti-corruption campaigns, crackdown on graft, Chinese People's Consultative, local government, frugality, launch the scheme, clamp down on prodigality,* and *imposing tough measures,* amounting to 31.43% (22 out of 70). Its corresponding prosody is 'affected', indicating that Macau's casino economy and politics are affected by the related policies lunched by the Chinese central government, as evidenced by co-selected phrases and clauses, such as *imposed, affects, had an impact, promote, impact, affected, cooled, has the authority to start, warned, affect, putting pressure, some regulations are being breached,* and *hit,* accounting for 72.72% (17 out of 22). This suggests that the *MPD* is concerned about the impact of the anti-corruption campaign launched by the Chinese central government on Macau's gaming industry in 2014. It is noted that the *MPD* has constantly mentioned the central government to highlight the Chinese authorities initiated the anti-corruption campaign.

To summarize, the *XH&CD* emphasises the Central Government's support for the development of Macau, especially its economic development at the macro-level. The *SCMP* highlights the regulation made by the government on Macau's gaming industry. In comparison to the two above news article corpora, the *MPD* is preoccupied with local issues and Macau government's implementation of related policies, strategies, and measures concerning the livelihood issues.

Year

In the *XH&CDC*, *year* co-occurs with words to do with financial figures such as *percent, billion, Patacas,* and *revenue,* suggesting the semantic preference of *year* is 'financial performance in Macau's gaming industry', amounting to 53.85% (70 out of 130) and the corresponding semantic prosody is 'neutral', as manifested by co-occurring with clauses, such as *at the end of the third quarter of 2014, up 2.6 percent year-on-year, official figures showed on Thursday* and *with their average earning growing 8.4 percent year-on-year.* In addition, *year* is used to refer to China's national policy *12*th *Five-year plan* (N = 4; 3.10%), implying that Macau should be guided by this national policy for its socio-economic development.

In the *SCMPC*, *year* co-occurs with words related to money, such as *per, cent, billion, HK,* and *revenue,* implying the semantic preference is 'the financial performance of Macau's industry' amounting to 64.86% (203 out of 313) and the semantic prosody concerning financial performance of Macau's gaming industry is found to be mixed. The first semantic is 'neutral', representing 66% (134 out of 203) as evidenced by co-occurring with clauses, such as *casino revenue figures for this month will not be release until the new year* and *revenue for the first nine months of this year was up 5.9 percent year on year at 275. 94 billion Patacas.* The second semantic prosody is negative as evidenced by co-selecting with words and phrases carrying with negative meanings, such as *more groom, negative, depressed, sharpest and most prolonged declines, economic contradiction, warning, turbulent,* gloomy, amounting to 33.99% (69 out of 203). This implies the *SCMP* holds a negative attitude towards the financial performance of Macau's gaming industry.

In the *MPDC*, the patterns of co-selection of *year* are similar to the other two corpora. *Year* primarily co-occurs with words to do with money, such as *percent*, *billion*, and *Patacas*, implying the semantic preference is 'financial performance of Macau', representing 55.72% (326 out of 585), and the semantic prosody expressed by these financial figures is 'neutral' as evidenced by co-occurring with clauses, such as *up 7.4 percent in real terms*, *amounted to 361.9 billion patacas last year*, and *11.9 percent growth year-on-year*, representing 96.01% (313 out 325). The *MPD* is found to cover several financial indicators in its news articles, implying the reporting focuses of the *MPD* are not limited to the gaming revenue of Macau, but financial performance in other areas, like *Macau' s retail sales*, *GDP*, *high-end residential rent*, *employment*, etc.

4.3.2 *Shared Single Lexical Words Between Any of Two Corpora*

In this section, the most frequently occurring shared single lexical words between any two of news article corpora in each word frequency lists are analysed and compared in terms of their patterns of co-selection. However, it is noted that those lexical words used to describe the financial statistics, such as *percent*, *revenue*, and *billion*, are not analysed as the financial figures are the objective data without conveying any stances or ideological positions. Three lexical words *Hong Kong*, *China*, and *city* are examined for the co-selection patterns.

Hong Kong

The proper name *Hong Kong* can be found in both the *XH&CDC* and the *SCMPC*. In the *XH&CDC, Hong Kong* (N = 167; 0.53%) co-occurs with *Macao* (N = 33; 19.76%), showing that Hong Kong and Macao are reported as being two Special Administrative Regions of the PRC. For example, the *XH&CD* puts Hong Kong and Macau together, underlining that the Chinese central government treats these two regions equally, as shown in examples 75, 76, and 77.

75. We must continue to govern **Hong Kong** and **Macao** and uphold the practice of "one country, two systems"
76. The central government cherishes both **Hong Kong** and **Macao**.
77. Both give play to the role of the mainland as the staunch supporter of **Hong Kong** and **Macao**.

When *Hong Kong* co-selects with *Macau*, it is found to co-occur with words to do with government and politics, such as *One Country, Two Systems*, *central government*, *regional cooperation*, *constitutional development*, *chief executive*, *SAR government*, *uphold the practice of One country, Two systems*, *the development*, *policy*, *independent political*, *entity*, *autonomy in the SARs*, and *democracy*. This indicates that the semantic preference is 'politics', amounting to 39.39% (13 out 33), and the corresponding semantic prosody is 'restrictive' with co-occurring words, such as *fully* and *must*.

Another semantic preference is 'Hong Kong's situations', such as *Hong Kong's problem, Hong Kong's economy, Hong Kong has to ensure street violence, Hong Kong's fell,* and *setbacks* amounting to 2.99% (5 out of 167). Regarding semantic prosody, 100% (5 out of 5) of instances carry negative meaning, as evident in co-occurring clauses such as *Hong Kong has not been doing well, suffered terrible social and religious upheaval,* and *has not lived up to people's expectations.* The semantic prosody of *Hong Kong* implies that the Chinese Mainland press tends to be related to Hong Kong's unfavourable situation. The following examples 78–79 show that the Mainland Chinese media express their concerns about the negative influence on Hong Kong exerted by a foreign force.

78. The first cause of **Hong Kong**'s problems is the political reforms instigated by C which suffered terrible social and religious upheaval after Britain left in 1947.
79. Another cause of **Hong Kong**'s problems in the socio-political elites in the city that were nurtured by the former colonial government. Chris Patten, the las British colonial governor.

In addition to putting Hong Kong and Macau together to underline the importance for these two SARs to uphold the practice of One Country, Two Systems in these two regions, the *XH&CD* is found to contrast Hong Kong with Macau, as exemplified below:

80. Contrary to Macao, **Hong Kong** continues to sputter in economic transformation and territory's industrial structure has retained the status quo.
81. Benefiting from 'One country, two systems' policy like Macao, **Hong Kong** has not doing as well in terms of economic growth since return over.
82. More than 750,000 tourists from the mainland have poured into the world's largest gambling center since the National Day holidays known as Golden Week began Oct 1, with growth accelerating to 17 percent over last year. The surge came as the Occupy Central protests pushed **Hong Kong** into worst chaos in decades and cut its rise in Golden Weeks visitors.
83. Those data show that Macao has surpassed **Hong Kong** in many ways.
84. Macao has set an excellent example for **Hong Kong** in this regard.
85. Macao is a great success of 'One Country, Two Systems'. **Hong Kong** should learn from Macao.
86. What Macao tells us in **Hong Kong** are as follows. First, the SAR should upload relations with the central government.

Examples 80–86 show that the *XH&CD* draws a comparison between Hong Kong and Macau, in which Macau is set as a good model of the successful implementation of the national principle of "One Country, Two Systems", whereas Hong Kong's situation is not satisfactory after its return to the Chinese sovereignty in 1997. Specifically, examples 80–81 demonstrate unfavourable economic situation of Hong Kong. Example 82 shows that the *XH&CD* employs very strong language, using the phrase *worst chaos* to describe Hong Kong's negative circumstance, owing to how it was affected by the Occupy Central protest. Examples 83, 84, and 85 show that the *XH&CD* constructs Macau as a *successful* and *excellent* role model for Hong Kong to learn. Examples 85–86 show that the *XH&CD* adopts the modal verb *should* to advise Hong Kong to learn from Macau to uphold the practice of "One Country, Two Systems".

In the *SCMPC, Macau* (N = 52; 18.77%) is also the top collocate of *Hong Kong* (N = 250; 0.59%), implying that the co-occurrences of these two regions are presented in news articles published in Chinese Mainland and Hong Kong, 2014. The semantic preferences and prosodies are identified via the detailed concordance analysis of *Hong Kong*. The first semantic preference of *Hong Kong* is 'politics' together with phrases to do with the law, government, political figures, and political movements like *Basic Law, Chief Executive, Xi, policy stance, national interests, law enforcement authorities in Beijing, politically engagement, political risks, political system, body politic, government, law enforcement scrutiny, Hong Kong Law, political development, political storm, mini-constitution, political power, political risk, administration*, etc., amounting to 8.40% (21 out of 250). The semantic prosody in the field of 'politics' is 'uncertainty' towards the political development of Hong Kong, shown by such words as *wonder, uncertainty*, and *concern,* accounting for 47.62% (10 out 21).

87. we wonder whether Beijing has started to re-examine its overall policy stance towards, Taiwan, **Hong Kong** and Macau, chief executive replaces all top officials in move seen as a response to growing crises
88. Political developments in have so far added uncertainty to earning prospects in the city.
89. The reshuffle and the appointment of two officials closely involved in recent moves to stymie the city's nascent pro-democracy movement also sparked speculation that Beijing was sending a message to **Hong Kong** that it was running out of patience over the Occupy turmoil.
90. Concerns over prolonged policy paralysis in the Legislative Council will underpin an increased political risk premium for **Hong Kong** market

Examples 87–90 reveal that the *SCMP* shows concern towards Hong Kong's future, due to the uncertainty of the political development of Hong Kong but also doubts whether the Chinese central government's stances and attitudes towards Hong Kong have been changed.

The second semantic preference is 'the comparison between Hong Kong and Macau', manifested by co-occurring words and phrases such as *contrast, Macau and Hong Kong versions*, and *two cities*, representing 4% (10 out 250), and its corresponding semantic prosody is 'different', accounting for 100% (10 out 10), as evidenced by co-selected words and phrases such as *stark contrast, vastly different, different ways*, and *unlike*. This implies that the *SCMP* constantly accentuates the diversity between Hong Kong and Macau. The following examples are the comparison between Hong Kong and Macau:

91. Stark contrast between the body politic of the former Portuguese Enclave and that of **Hong Kong**
92. Lou added: "Even so, it understands well that this system is not applicable to **Hong Kong**. The two cities have vastly different conditions."
93. Turning back to the Basic Law, Valente points out that although the Macau and **Hong Kong** versions are fundamentally the same, they interpreted and used in a different way "while Macau's Basic Law makes no direct mention of universal suffrage.
94. Unlike **Hong Kong**'s basic law, Macau's mini-construction makes no mention of universal suffrage. But calls for democracy have been growing.
95. China has more social and economic influence in Macau than in **Hong Kong**. This is one of the factors that explain a less politically engaged society.
96. They don't have the power or backing to mobilize [like in **Hong Kong**]

Examples 91–96 show that the *SCMP* underlines the existing diversity in terms of economic, political, legal systems and societies between Hong Kong and Macau. The *SCMP* seems to respond to the comment made by the *XH&CDC* that '*Macau has surpassed Hong Kong in many ways*' in example 83. In example 91, the *SCMP* states that the politics between Hong Kong and Macau is totally different from each other by employing the evaluative adjective *stark* to describe the vast diversities between these two regions. In example 92, the *SCMP* uses the adverb *vastly* with *Hong Kong* to modify the adjective *different*, accentuating the huge difference in conditions between these two cities. Examples 93 and line 94 stress the diversity in the versions of Basic Laws between the two regions, specifically universal suffrage is not mentioned in the Basic Law of Macau. Examples 95 and 96 explain why Macau's political environment differs from that in Hong Kong, indicating that these regions cannot be compared with each other directly, as they vary significantly.

97. Macau lacks **Hong Kong**'s level of political engagement, but there are signs that may be changing. Li was likening Hong Kong to the wayward older sibling who could learn a thing or two from its more compliant and respectful junior.
98. Neighbouring city of protest-hit **Hong Kong** is praised by top officials for its compliance, possibly to pre-empt copycat Occupy activities.
99. National and local officials in charge of Macau have praised the world's gambling capital for fully adhering to its Basic Law and the principle of "one country, two systems", in an apparently veiled warning against any activities modelled after the Occupy Central civil disobedience protests. Li's words on Macau contrasted with Chief Executive Leung Chun-ying's view of Occupy student protesters in **Hong Kong**, whom he said betrayed their lack of familiarity with the city's Basic Law in pressing for Beijing's withdrawal of conditions on the 2017 vote for Leung's successor.
100. As Xi spoke, nearly 100 young Macau protesters took to the streets to demand an open and fair political system. Some said they had been inspired by **Hong Kong**'s "umbrella movement" The president urged the Macau government to strengthen education for younger generation to ensure that the cause of "one country, two systems" could be advanced and a sense of national pride grown.

In addition to highlighting the diversity of the two versions of Basic Law, the *SCMP* mentions that Macau's political environment could be changing (examples 97–98). Example 97 addresses two issues: the first expresses the notion of the Chinese authorities, stating that Macau is a successful example of practising the policy of "One Country, Two Systems", and the other issue is that the *SCMP* contrasts Macau and Hong Kong's political situations through adopting a metaphor *veiled warning,* to imply that Hong Kong has received an implicit warning from the Chinese Central Government because of the Occupy Central protest (i.e., Umbrella Movement) that took place in Hong Kong in 2014.

Previously, Macau has been seen as the "*more compliant and respectful junior*" (example 97) in the view of Director Li Gang from the Liaison Office of the Central People's Government of Hong Kong, but the *SCMP* points out that Macau could not serve as the role model of practising the policy of "One Country, Two Systems" any more. This is because Macau's political and social environment could be changing as some pro-democratic protests against the local political systems happened in Macau during Chinese President Xi's visit under the inspiration of Umbrella Movement in Hong Kong (example 99). The *SCMP* also mentions the content of Xi's speech that the Macau government should enhance its related education towards teenagers concerning the national education in order to enhance the Chinese ethnic consciousness to prevent the recurrence of similar affairs in Hong Kong from happening in Macau (example 100).

Overall, the above examples of concordance lines reveal that the stances and attitudes expressed in the *SCMPC* are different from those in the *XH&CDC*. The *XH&CD* expresses its attitude towards Hong Kong with a particular emphasis on its unfavourable political environment, wherein it infers that Hong Kong should learn from Macau as it is regarded as a successful example of practising the national policy 'One Country, Two Systems'. Conversely, the *SCMP* shows its concern towards the future of Hong Kong's political development and also claims the difference between Hong Kong and Macau. In terms of politics, these regions differ in body politics and versions of Basic Law (examples 91, 93 and 94). As for the socio-economic aspect, the social conditions of these two cities are different as Macau is under more economic and social influence of Mainland China compared with Hong Kong (example 95). The above-mentioned diversities between these two regions explain that it is very difficult for Hong Kong to follow Macau's example. The *SCMP* also provides the news coverage of Macau's democracy movements, which are not mentioned in the *XH&CDC*. This reveals that the *SCMP* emphasises that there are existing democracy activities in Macau similar to Hong Kong, instead of it being the 'perfect model' that the central government likes to refer to.

The third semantic preference of *Hong Kong* is 'business and economy of Macau', as the word *Hong Kong* co-occurs with phrases to do with money and business, such as *economy, casino capital, economic diversification, revenue, per cent, dollar, billion, stocks, junket figure, company, gaming revenues, and protest*, amounting to 12% (30 out of 250). The semantic prosody associated with 'business and economy' is 'affected and negative', accounting for 83.33% (25 out of 30), evident in co-occurring words, phrases and clauses such as *downturn, warned, unexpected, take their toll, negative bits, weakened tourists numbers, affect the number of mainlanders, frozen the assets, remained week, impact, cut ties, increasing scrutiny from Beijing, stricter enforcement, combat money laundering activities, reflecting a build-up of pressures on Macau casinos, monitoring, track, ramps up its austerity drive,* and *street protest,* as well as the use of the metaphor *twist of the knife for an industry,* as shown in example 101, *'perfect storm' for Macau's casinos industry* is used to describe the economic downturn of Macau, primarily referring to the gaming and tourism industry of Macau. This unfavourable situation is influenced by several factors such as the Occupy Central Protest in Hong Kong, the anti-corruption campaign in Chinese Mainland, the casino's smoking ban, and sticker money control, which are believed to have led to the significant decrease in the number of mainland visitors, revealing that the *SCMP* held a negative attitude towards economy and business in Macau.

101. The downtown in mainland tourism to **Hong Kong** and Macau attributed to pro-democracy street protests in Hong Kong was **a twist of the knife** for an industry already reeling from other disincentives of gambling.

China

The proper noun *China* is shared between the *XH&CDC* and the *SCMPC*. In the *XH&CDC*, *China* (N = 156; 0.50%) is ranked 5th. The high presence of *China* is expected as *Xinhua News* and *China Daily* are both China-based presses. The most frequent collocate of *China* is *Daily* (N = 40; 25.64%), namely *China Daily Information Company*, indicating one of the sources of the news articles of the *XH&CDC*. These 40 instances are removed and they are not analysed in the present study. The other 25 instances of *China* are also excluded as they are used as part of the name of an organization, such as *Sands China Ltd* (N = 10), *MGM China* (N = 2), and *China Mobile* (N = 2). Apart from these proper names, *China* is used as the geographical location, preceded by a preposition *between* (N = 13; 14.29%), co-occurring with such phrases and clauses as *Portuguese speaking countries, cooperation,* and *Macao as a platform has played an irritable role in China's cooperation with these countries,* highlighting the service role that Macau performs in the economic and trade cooperation between China and Portuguese-speaking countries, rather than placing emphasis on its gaming industry by quoting a high-ranking Chinese official, "*the dominance of gaming industry is not good for overall interest of Macau*" and "*That would make 2014 one of worst year in Macao's economy*". This implies that Macau's gaming industry is positioned as hindered by the Chinese authorities that might not be good for Macau's further development.

China is followed by the adverb *where* (N = 5; 5.95%), suggesting that the *XH&CD* expressly underlines that Macau is the only place in China where casinos are legal, as gambling is prohibited in China. *China* also co-occurs with *return* (N = 13; 14.29%) and *handed over to China,* referring to the 15th anniversary of Macau's return to China in 1999. The XH&CDC repeatedly covers this event.

The semantic preference of *China* is identified as the 'socio-economic development and further development direction of Macau', especially in the context of Macau's handover to China, as evidenced by co-occurring words, phrases and clauses, such as *economic and social progress, economic development, achievements, economic and trade cooperation, commercial and trade cooperation*, and *a bridge-head for relations*, accounting for 21.98% (20 out of 91). The semantic prosody is 'favourable', representing 100%, as manifested by words and phrases with the a positive meaning, such as *progress, grown, nothing rapid economic and social progress, irreplaceable role, achievement obvious development, unique charm*, and *Macau has transformed into an international city*, suggesting that the *XH&CD* portrays Macau from a positive perspective to the audience; for example, the rapid growing pace of economy, and the fast developing society of Macau since its handover to China are highlighted in the news articles of the *XH&CDC*.

Another semantic preference is 'promoting Chinese image', representing 13.19% (12 out of 91) with the semantic prosody 'positive' as evidenced by co-occurring words and phrases such as *great country, time-honoured history and rich civilization, tremendous achievement, richness of civilization, glorious journey, strong country, prosperous, strong, culturally advanced, largest trading partner, success*, and *pride*, accounting for 100% (12 out of 12), reflecting that the *China Daily* and *Xinhua News* as the state-run new media attempts to convey the readers the positive images about China as well as to foster in people a national sense of pride.

By contrast, the extended units of meaning associated with the lexical item *China* in the *SCMPC* are different from those in the *XH&CDC*. *China* (N = 357, 0.64%) ranked 3rd, primarily co-occurs with *south* (N = 217; 60.78%), referring to the news publisher *South China Morning Post*, which is the news source of the *SCMPC* and these instances are not included in the analysis. The other 50 instances used as part of the name of an organization, such as *Sands China, MGM China, Bank of China*, and *China Mobile*, are also removed.

China co-occurs with the proposition *through* (N = 12; 12.90%) in association with phrases to do with money, such as *illicit money flows, suspicious transactions, economic crimes, funds, fake or fraudulent transactions, transfers, massive wealth, the multibillion-dollar illicit funds*, and *capital fight problem*, referring to the suspicious funds or money into Macau through China. This shows a semantic preference of 'control of gaming-related economic crime', accounting for 15.56% (14 out of 90) and its corresponding prosody is 'increasing', evident in co-selected words and phrases such as *action taken, identify, investigation, concerns at the highest levels, major crackdown, increasing law enforcement*, and *serious*, representing 92.86% (13 out of 14 instances), suggesting the illegal or suspicious funds through China to Macau are under the more stringent supervision.

City

City is a shared lexical word between the *SCMPC* (12th; N = 140; 0.25%) and the *MPDC* (11th; N = 288; 0.26%). In the *SCMPC*, *city* mainly refers to Macau, which has no strong patterns of collocation or colligation. The dominant semantic preference of *city* is about 'the general situation of Macau', including its political, economic, and social aspects, which are all closely connected with its gaming industry as it is associated with such words and phrases as *average wage, employment, income, casino industry, casino revenue, economy, gaming, political, economic future*, and *One Country, Two Systems*, representing 28.57% (40 out of 140). The semantic prosody is 'changing', manifested by co-occurring words and phrases such as *affected, greatest political shake-up, most significant political shake-up, sweeping changes*, and *diversification*, implying that both the economic and political situations of Macau have changed and Macau's financial circumstance is unfavourable, with co-occurring words and phrases carrying negative meanings, such as *grim economic figures, worst contracting of the city's economy, a danger, most prolonged decline, sank the city into recession, slump, economic contradiction*, and *turbulent*, accounting for 57.5% (23 out of 40).

As shown in example 102, the modal verb *must* is employed to express the vital necessity of the Chinese authorities and the MSAR government to diversify Macau's economy instead of simply developing its gaming-reliant economy. Example103 also shows the opinion made by the Chinese officials that Macau's present economic situation is dangerous, which is not only harmful to Macau's local economy, but also the interest of the whole nation.

102. Both central and local governments have made it clear that the **city** must diversify into areas other than gaming. That refrain has grown louder…
103. The mainland figures that the situation poses a danger not only to the **city**'s economic situation, but to the national interest of the name "as a whole'

In the *MPDC*, *city* is primarily used as the geographical location. 47 instances are employed as the part of a film's name (i.e., *Roulette City*) and the casinos' name (e.g., *City of Dreams, Studio City*, and *City U*), which are not analysed in the present study. *City* co-occurs with words and phrases, such as *gaming, property, housing, operator, venue*, and *receiving capacity*, suggesting the reporting focus of the *MPD* covers a lot of aspects of this city, ranging from its gaming industry to people's livelihood. Specifically, *City* (N = 233) co-occurs with *gaming venues* (N = 16; 6.87%), *gaming operators* (N = 25; 10.73%), together with *smoking rooms, set up designated smoking areas, the regulation of smoking areas, impose a full smoking ban, install smoking rooms, reducing smoking*, and *the regulation on smoking areas*, revolving the discussion concerning the implementation of the anti-smoking law, reflecting that the semantic preference is 'the introduction of anti-smoking law in casinos of Macau', accounting for 20.17% (47 out of 233). The semantic prosody is 'measures implemented' as evidenced by co-occurring with clauses, such as *come up with measures, a joint proposal submitted by the city's six gaming operators suggesting that their casinos should include airport-like smoking rooms, a joint proposal from the city's gaming operators which suggests that a smoking room*. This suggests that the gaming operators in Macau are making the joint proposals to make improvements towards the set of smoking rooms in the casinos of Macau.

Besides, *city* co-occurs with words and phrases to do with social issues, such as *housing problem, housing woes, shortage of affable housing*, and *housing shortage*, indicating that the topics related to the housing problem in Macau society is the focus of news articles of Macau's local press. This shows that the semantic preference is 'the housing problem in Macau', amounting to 8.58%, (20 out of 233), the corresponding semantic prosody is 'insufficient', representing 80% (16 out 20) as *city* is co-selected with phrases and clauses such as *was not doing enough to solve the city's shortage of affordable housing, worries, its failure to tackle the city's housing problem, slam, not building enough public housing unit*, and *protests*, implying that the *MPD* presents public opinions to criticize the government's ineffective measures to tackle the housing problems. And four instances (5%) are quoting the government official's speech that the Macau government plans to place housing problems as a priority.

4.3.3 Top 2 Unique Single Lexical Words

In this section, the most frequent two unique single lexical words in each news article corpus, *development*, *economic*, *business*, and *local* are analysed for their co-selection patterns.

Development

In the *XH&CDC, development* (N = 131; 0.42%), ranked 8th, co-occurs with *economic* (N = 35; 26.72%), indicating that topics concerning economic development are frequently referred to only in the news articles published by *XH* and *CDC*. *Development* co-occurs with *Macao* (N = 31; 23.31%) and *Macao's* (N = 13; 9.77%) to specify the development regarding Macau. Besides, several collocates of *development*, such as *diversified* (N = 13; 9.77%), *sustainable* (N = 13; 9.77%), and *appropriately* (N = 10; 7.52%), are related to the future development direction of *Macau*. Examination of concordance lines shows that *development* has two uses semantically: the Chinese mainland press does not only focus on reporting on the state of the development of Macau, using co-selected phrases and clauses with a positive meaning, such as *achieves leapfrog development, golden year for Macao's substantial development, great success,* and *the rapid developments,* but also pays attention to the long-term development direction of this region, with the use of phrases and clauses such as *promote sound economic and social development, adjustment of economic structure, consolidate Macao's economic and social development*, and *blue prints for its development.* Two semantic preferences of *development* are found. The first semantic preference is labelled as 'economy and society in Macau', with co-selected phrases having to do with the economic state of Macau, such as *economic development, economic structure, socio-economic development, Macao's economy, business, tourism industry,* and *social development and well-being of the people,* implying that the *XH&CDC* gives a great reporting priority to the economic and social development of Macau. The semantic prosody in the sense of 'economy and society in Macau' is 'diversified and cooperative', as shown in co-selected phrases and clauses such as *appropriately diversified, adjustment of economic structure, adequate economic diversification, diversifying the economy, regional cooperation, deepen its cooperation, expand the development*, and *the cooperation between Macau and Guangdong, cooperation with the mainland,* indicating that the attitudes and ideological positions of the *XH&CD* towards Macau's future development directions, especially economic structure, are that Macau's future development directions should be adjusted and diversified and also Macau can deepen their regional cooperation with Chinese Mainland.

The second semantic preference is 'law and policy', evident in the implementation of the *"One Country, Two Systems" policy, socio-political stability, the law, constitutional reform, political* and *constitutional, relations between central government and the Macao SAR,* and *political development.* The prosody is 'strict implementation', due to co-selected phrases *compressive implementation, in accordance with law,* and *policy implementation,* indicating that adherence to law and policy can secure and support the development of Macau.

Economic

The unique word *economic* (N = 113, 0.36%) ranked 11th in the top 20 lexical word frequency list of the *XH&CDC.* The most frequent word co-selected with *economic* is *development,* followed by *growth,* reflecting Macau's economic development and growth. Other co-selected expressions of *economic* are *social development* (N = 11; 9.73%) and *social progress* (N = 3; 2.66%), co-occurring with words carrying positive meanings, such as *sound, notable,* and *rapid,* suggesting that the *XH&CD* speaks highly of Macau's social and economic development.

Besides, *economic* also co-occurs with *diversified, sustainable, cooperation, promote, China, trade, appropriately, diversification,* and *adjustment,* accounting for 32.74% (37 out 113), and the use of these words indicate Macau's further development direction, namely Macau needs to adjust its economic structure to promote its diversified and sustainable economic development, and thus serving as a platform for the cooperation with the Portuguese-speaking countries.

Business

In the *SCMPC,* most unique lexical words are to do with money, such as *per, cent, HK, US,* and *month,* that are employed to describe the financial figures. These words are not examined in the present study. Thus, the lexical word *business* (N = 99; 0.18%) is further discussed in terms of its extended units of meaning. The first semantic preference of *business* is to do with 'gaming-related crime' associated with words and phrases such as *organized crime, unlicensed betting, illegal bets,* and *gangland,* accounting for 12.12% (12 out of 99), referring to the illicit online gambling business. The corresponding semantic prosody of *business* is 'worrying and regulated' as manifested by words and phrases such as *worrying, deep and worrying link, concern, growing fears, stifle,* and *block access,* representing 100% (12 out 12), implying that the concern about online gambling business is increasing and that online gambling business is increasingly regulated.

The second semantic preference is about 'Chui family's business and his family background', representing 8.08% (8 out of 99). The examination of concordance lines shows that several family members of Chui family are mentioned, not only the Chief Executive of Macau Chui Sai-On, but also his family members, such as Tak-seng, Chui Sai-chong, and Chui Sai-peng. The *SCMP* is found to have given a complete account of the Chui family in the business field, as demonstrated in the examples below:

104. Chui Sai-cheong become a lawmaker representing the **business** community
105. Ties between Chui family and Macau's **business** elite grow stronger
106. His only sibling, Lawmaker Chui Sai-cheong, 60, inherited a property and **business** portfolio from their father

Examples 104–109 demonstrate that the *SCMP* has illustrated some examples related to Chui Sai-on and his family members' financial circumstances such as their respective financial interests in the commercial world, and also his older brother Chui Sai-cheong's duty in the government of Macau as a lawmaker in the Legislative Assembly of Macau SAR. This indicates that the *SCMP* seems to convey a message to the audience that the Chui family has a strong and deep connection with business and political fields in Macau society (examples 107–109).

107. As the brother's careers indicate, the ties between **business**, politics and government can be tight in Macau.
108. Ties between Chui family and Macau's **business** elite grow stronger.
109. Chui family's entrepreneurial imperative has not diminished. Its **business** interests have included construction, real estate, pharmaceuticals, oil……

Local

Local (N = 355; 0.32%) is the unique word in the *MPDC*. It primarily co-selects with *government* (N = 41; 11.55%) to refer to the Macau government. When *local* co-occurs with *government*, the semantic preference is 'Macau citizens' livelihoods' by being surrounded words and phrases such as *livelihood*, *protect local employees*, *local tap water's salinity issue*, and *local's views*, representing 73.17% (30 out of 41) and semantic prosody is "lacking and improvement needed' implying that the local residents' livelihoods need to be improved, such as *can be controlled*, *tackle*, and *should be improved*, amounting to 64.52%.

4.4 Phraseological Analysis: Analyzing Trigrams

This section discusses the findings of the frequent trigrams in each news article corpus, as n-grams cannot only reveal the phraseology used in different contexts (Cheng, 2012) but also can provide an "information related to meaning correlates in that they reveal representative ways of saying things" (Brindle, 2016, p. 43). The trigrams analyses are considered as the further phraseological analysis in order to complement the single lexical wordlists in the last section.

4.4.1 Top 20 Trigrams in the XH&CDC

Table 4.6 demonstrates the Top 20 trigrams in the *XH&CDC*, ranked by the frequency and percentage.

As demonstrated in Table 4.6, we can find that some trigrams are fixed titles, which are related to administration and politics categories, for example, *the central government*, *Special Administrative Region*, *The Chinese Mainland*, *The Basic Law*, *The Macau SAR*, and *[One] country two systems*. This implies that those legal and political terms are constantly used in the news articles of the *XH&CDC*.

Specifically, the trigram *the central government* (N = 37; 0.12%), ranked 2nd, is found primarily to be co-selected with *Macao* (N = 13), suggesting the *XH&CD* tends to put the central government and Macau together with an accent on their close relationship with each other. The following examples 110, 111 and 112 show that the *XH&CD* underlines that Macau has constantly been receiving the support in terms of related policies provided by the central government, and it has played a crucial role in the development of Macau in many aspects since the unification of Macau with China in 1999. Example 113 shows that the *XH&CD* emphasised that the governing power of the Central Government is exercised well in Macau

Table 4.6 Top 20 trigrams in the *XH&CDC*

N	Word	Freq	%
1	Of the Macao	50	0.16
2	The cental government	37	0.12
3	Country two systems	36	0.12
4	In Hong Kong	33	0.11
5	The Macao sar	33	0.11
6	One country two	28	0.09
7	Special administrative region	28	0.09
8	As well as	23	0.07
9	Hong Kong and	23	0.07
10	Of Hong Kong	21	0.07
11	The Chinese mainland	21	0.07
12	To the motherland	21	0.07
13	Macao special administrative	20	0.06
14	The gaming industry	19	0.06
15	In the world	18	0.06
16	The basic law	18	0.06
17	The Macao special	17	0.05
18	According to the	16	0.05
19	Of one country	16	0.05
20	The fourth term	16	0.05

and similarly, example 114 implies that the *XH&CD* mentioned the speech made by the Chief Executive of Macau about one of the reasons to accelerate Macau's rapid development is keeping the healthy relationship between the central government and Macao SAR for the purpose of highlighting the significance of the Central Government to Macau's progress. By comparison, example 115 shows the *XH&CD* illustrated an opposite example about Hong Kong SAR. Hong Kong is described as a living entity, the victim who has to *endure violent street politics,* where some people deliberately spoil the central government's sovereign rule over Hong Kong, implying that the exercise of governing power of the central government does not work very smoothly and has been challenged in Hong Kong by some people's behaviour by using the verb *sabotage*, implying their destructive and violent acts. This is another example illustrated by the XH&CDC for the purpose of making the comparison between Hong Kong and Macau, with the accent on Macau's better performance for its understanding and accurate implementation of the "One Country, Two Systems" political framework. In contrast, the violent street protests undermined the rule of law in Hong Kong.

110. **the central government** gave firm support for Macao to build a world tourism and leisure center and a platform for economic and trade cooperation with Portuguese-speaking countries
111. Over the past 15 years, with the strong support of **the central government** and the mainland and under the leadership of the Chief Executive and government of the SAR, people from various sectors in Macao have united as one, made vigorous efforts to implement the principle of "one country, two systems" and achieved fruitful results.
112. It needs to make good use of the policies and measures put forward by **the central government** to support Macao's development and deepen its cooperation with the mainland, particularly with Guangdong province and the Pan-Pearl River Delta region.
113. **The Central Government**'s overall governing power is effectively exercised while the high degree autonomy enjoyed by the SAR is fully guaranteed.
114. The chief executive attributed the rapid development in Macao to an accurate understanding and comprehensive implementation of the "One country, Two systems" policy, and the healthy development of relations between **the central government** and the Macao SAR.
115. Consequently, this year Hong Kong had to endure violent street politics aimed at undermining the rule of law and the legitimacy of the SAR government. The people behind these destructive acts aim to sabotage **the central government's** sovereign rule over Hong Kong.

Besides, the trigram *in Hong Kong* (N = 33; 0.11%), is marked ranked 4th in the top 20 list since the news articles were all collected related to Macau's gaming, implying that the Chinese press seems to exemplify some affairs or events happening in Hong Kong, and this trigram deserves further examination. The following are representative concordance lines:

116. It's because of London's and Washington's interferences that the One country, Two systems **in Hong Kong** is arriving at a critical crossroad.
117. The younger generation **in Hong Kong** is frustrated by employment, career and housing problems so that many of them support the so-called "genuine universal suffrage", and some of them even joined in the "Occupy Central movement".

Both examples 116 and 117 show that the *XH&CD* is likely to convey the information to the readers that Hong Kong's situation was not optimistic in terms of its social as well as political environment. Specifically, example 116 demonstrates that the *XH&CD* adopted a metaphor to describe the unfavourable present political situation of Hong Kong, which is situated at the *crossroad* and illustrates the negative influence of foreign interfaces on Hong Kong's affairs. Example 117 shows that the *XH&CD* specifically attributed the Hong Kong Occupy Central Protest to Hong Kong's younger generation's frustration with the social environment of Hong Kong, such as *employment*, *housing problem*, and *career*.

118. Macao has played an irreplaceable role in China's cooperation with these countries. On the contrary, the United Kingdom has consistently meddled **in Hong Kong** affairs with a dream of resuming its role over the territory.
119. Another cause of Hong Kong's problems today is the socio-political elites in the city that were nurtured by the former colonial government. This was done to maintain Britain's influence **in Hong Kong** after the handover.
120. Xi's remarks come shortly after police **in Hong Kong** cleared the final site of the Occupy Central protest.
121. The number of mainland tourists arriving in Macao climbed to 846,000. The 17.1-percent increase was attributed to the protests **in Hong Kong** which have continued since Sept 28.
122. Macao is a great success of "One Country, Two Systems". Hong Kong should learn from Macao. What Macao tells us **in Hong Kong** are as follows.

Besides, the *XH&CD* draws a comparison between Macau and Hong Kong. On the one hand, the Chinese mainland press underlines the critical role of Macau in connecting China and other Portuguese-speaking countries. On the other hand, it criticizes that some foreign countries such as the former colonizer Britain invoked Hong Kong's affairs, as shown in examples 118–119. Example 120 demonstrates Hong Kong's situation after Xi's remark. Example 121 shows that the *XH&CD* specifically mentioned the positive tourism statistics about the growing number of tourists visiting Macau and believed this situation was caused by the Occupy Central Protest in Hong Kong, indicating that the Mainland Chinese press contrasted implicitly between Hong Kong and Macau. Example 122 is another example illustrating that the *XH&CDC* made a contrast between Macau and Hong Kong, suggesting the principle of "One Country, Two Systems" worked much better in Macau than in Hong Kong. The *XH&CD* employs the modal verb *should* in order to express the strong wish that Hong Kong should learn from Macau in terms of upholding the policy of "One Country, Two systems".

The third most frequent trigram *country two systems* (N = 41) refers to the policy of "One Country, Two Systems" and its surrounding words are strong adjectives, such as *fully, correctly, continuously, vigorous, fully,* and *firmly*, as well as the employment of the modal verb *must* with the absolute attitude as shown in examples 123–127, implying the stance held by the *XH&CDC* is to highlight the significance of implementing this policy in Macau as "the use of adjectives is probably the most obvious way to express evaluation in language" (Caro, 2014, p. 330) and the "use of modal verb can indicate the writer's attitude towards that which she or he is reporting" (ibid., p. 332). This trigram also co-selects with words and phrases with a positive meaning, such as *great vitality, achievements, fruitful results, good, beautiful,* and *success*, suggesting that the *XH&CDC* tries to underline the contribution and the significance of this policy to Macau. For instance, examples 123 and 125 show that the *XH&CD* attached the importance of the policy of 'One Country, Two Systems' for Macau through quoting the speech made by the powerful political figure, the Chief Executive of Macau Chui Sai On.

123. The achievements in Macao have highlighted the great vitality of the **'one country, two systems'** policy, " Chui told Xinhua
124. achievements to the full and correct implementation of the principle of **'one country, two systems'** and the Basic Law.
125. He pledged to fully devote himself to implementing the principle of **" one country, two systems, "** while improving Macao people 's livelihood.
126. It must also be in accordance with the **one country, two systems** principle and the Basic Law.
127. made vigorous efforts to implement the principle of **"one country, two systems"**

To the motherland (N = 21; 0.07%), ranked 7th, indicating this trigram repeatedly occurs in the *XH&CDC*, which co-occurs with *return* (N = 13; 61.90%) and *returned* (N = 7; 33.33%), implying the high frequency of themes and topics related to the Macau's reunification to the motherland in the *XH&CDC* and its surrounded words and phrases such as *great progress, achievements, successful economic story, granted more development opportunities, fastest-growing period, rapid progress, improved,* and *exponentially grown,* demonstrating that the *XH&CD* aims to construct the positive image of Macau and convey the related information to the audience that Macau always has made the great progress and achieved the astonishing success since its return to China (i.e., the Motherland). Besides, by using *motherland* instead of China, the *XH&CDC* attempts to strengthen the national identity about China as well as boost Macau residents' the patriotism.

4.4.2 Top 20 Trigrams in the SCMPC

Table 4.7 demonstrates the top 20 trigrams in the SCMPC ranked by frequency and percentage.

Table 4.7 Top 20 trigrams in the *SCMPC*

N	Word	Freq	%
1	In Hong Kong	56	0.10
2	Year on year	52	0.09
3	The City's	39	0.07
4	Cent year on	35	0.06
5	Per cent to	35	0.06
6	Per cent Year	35	0.06
7	The former Portuguese	35	0.06
8	One of the	33	0.06
9	The Hong Kong	29	0.05
10	Hong Kong and	28	0.05
11	Former Portuguese enclave	26	0.05
12	Gross gaming revenue	25	0.05
13	The number of	25	0.05
14	To Hong Kong	24	0.04
15	In the world	23	0.04
16	President Xi Jinping	23	0.04
17	The world's	22	0.04
18	Chamber of commerce	21	0.04
19	Chui Sai on	20	0.04
20	Fernando Chuisai	20	0.04

As shown in Table 4.7, four trigrams are related to *Hong Kong,* occupying 20%, namely *in Hong Kong, The Hong Kong, Hong Kong and,* and *to Hong Kong*. This suggests that the *SCMP* puts its focus on reporting topics and themes relevant to Hong Kong. The trigram *in Hong Kong* (N = 56; 0.10%) ranked 1st in the top 20 list. The significant occurrence of this trigram in the *XH&CDC* is marked as the themes and topics of news corpora related to Macau's gaming industry, in which the trigram such as *in Macao SAR* should have been mentioned more frequently rather than *in Hong Kong*. However, it cannot be found in the top 20 words in the wordlist. By examining the corresponding concordance lines, the study finds that the *SCMP* is likely to associate some of Macau's related political affairs with the relevant political issues happening in Hong Kong; for instance, example 128 demonstrates that the *SCMP* made the sharp contrast between Hong Kong and Macau, showing the positive favourable situation that Macau was praised for its implementation of the model "One Country, Two Systems", whereas Hong Kong was given a warning about the protesters in Hong Kong. Example 129 quoted the remark made by one of the power figures Li Gang, the director of the Chinese Liaison office in Macau. He can be regarded as the Chinese government's representative, criticizing Hong

Kong's issues for its Occupy Central protest by conveying the message to Macau's teenagers.

128. While praising Macau, which is marking the 15th anniversary of its return to China, for its implementation of the model devised by paramount leader Deng Xiaoping, Xi warned against "external infiltration and interference", in what an analyst described as remarks aimed at protesters **in Hong Kong**.
129. Macau-based observer Larry So Man-yum saw Li's remarks as related to Occupy. "He has delivered a very clear message for Macau's youngsters, telling them not to do anything that departs from the Basic Law, like what is happening **in Hong Kong**."

Other concordance lines related to *Hong Kong* are examined in the previous section. The *SCMPC* seems to make the comparison between Hong Kong and Macau with the aim of highlighting the differences between these two Special Administrative Regions.

The following trigram *year on year* ranked 2nd, primarily co-occurring with financial figures and money, such as *per cent, revenue, billion, Patacas,* is used to describe the financial data, reflecting that the financial performance of Macau is frequently mentioned by the *SCMPC* and other co-occurrences of *year on year* including *fell, decline, contraction, drop, suffered*, reflect the unpromising economic performance of Macau in 2014 according to the news coverage of the *SCMP* as shown in example 130. Other top 20 trigrams like *cent year on* (N = 35; 0.06%), *per cent to* (N = 35; 0.06%), *per cent year* (N = 35; 0.06%), *gross gaming revenue* (N = 25; 0.05%) are all related to the financial figure, showing the financial performance in gaming of Macau is one of reporting preferences for the *SCMP*, which is consistent with the previous single lexical word analysis.

130. 2014 saw the largest **year-on-year** revenue drop on record, and, significantly, in October? usually a peak season. Overall, Macau is poised to record its first full-year casino revenue decline.

The former Portuguese (N = 35; 0.06%) ranked 7th, refers to Macau. The *former Portuguese enclave* and the *former Portuguese colony* indicate the colonial history of Macau. It is noted that this usage is exclusively found in the *SCMPC*, suggesting that this way of addressing Macau is frequently adopted by the Hong Kong press in order to connote its previous historical connection with Portugal. By examing concordance lines, the *SCMP* seems to relate the term with negative issues in Macau, when this former enclave has faced many economic and political challenges since its reunification with China. Specifically, example 131 demonstrates that the *SCMP* employed the phrase *the significant political shake-up* to describe Macau's unfavourable political circumstance. Examples 132–133 show that the *SCMP* points the Macau's economy is experiencing some difficulties under the influence of China's anti-corruption campaign. Line 134 shows that the *SCMP* mentioned a controversial social issue in Macau's society. Example 135 shows *SCMP*'s concerns towards some legal problems concerning the Macau's Basic Law.

131. On Monday, Chui named an all-new team of top officials for his crucial second term as city leader in what is being seen as the most significant political shake-up since **the former Portuguese** enclave returned to Chinese sovereignty.
132. Economically, **the former Portuguese** enclave is grappling with shirking casino revenues, partly due to China's crackdown on corruption and extravagance.
133. Expectations are low for the fourth quarter, especially for VIP players given the central government's announcement of a new anti-corruption office and preparations for President Xi Jinping's visit to **the former Portuguese** colony next month to celebrate the 15th anniversary of the handover.
134. **The former Portuguese** colony's taxi issue has a lot to do with the failings of the public transport system.
135. Macau's Basic Law states residents have freedom to demonstrate, strike, and organise trade unions. However, **the former Portuguese** colony does not have a collective bargaining law.

The trigrams *the number of* (N = 25; 0.05%) ranked 7th, co-occurs with *tourists* (N = 6), *visitors* (N = 6), and *mainland* (N = 7), referring to reports on the number of tourists. Another n-gram *gross casino revenue* (N = 25; 0.05%) ranked 12th, reflecting that the topics related to gross casino revenue are one of the major concerns in the *SCMPC*.

To Hong Kong (N = 24; 0.04%) ranked 14th with concordances showing that this n-gram mainly has two uses in the *SCMPC*. First, Hong Kong is used individually as the participant, who has received the warning message from the Chinese authorities, and Beijing's top representative Li, for Hong Kong's previous Occupy Central protest as seen in examples 136–139. Secondly, Hong Kong and Macau, these two Special Administrative Regions, are considered as a whole, which can be found in examples 140 and 141.

136. Beijing was sending a message **to Hong Kong** that it was running out of patience over the Occupy turmoil. The central government has the final say on all appointments.
137. This is a landmark moment for Macau as the 15th anniversary approaches, but it also sends a clear message **to Hong Kong**."
138. Chief executive replaces all top officials in move seen as a response to growing crises in Macau-and as a message from Beijing **to Hong Kong**.
139. Li, the director of the liaison office, is Beijing's top representative in Macau. He delivered the rodent-laced rhetoric as he praised the city for its adherence to its mini-constitution, a similar if not identical document to that of Hong Kong. But the overwhelming view in Macau is that Li was talking directly **to Hong Kong**.
140. Draft legislation allowing Singaporean authorities to block access to unlicensed betting websites was introduced this month to tackle a global business that according to a Sunday Morning Post investigation has significant ties **to Hong Kong** and Macau.

141. Occupy Central protests that began in Hong Kong on September 28, ahead of the National Day holiday week which is usually one of the strongest tourist seasons of the year, have weakened mainland tourist numbers because visitors have increasingly been combining visits **to Hong Kong** and Macau in one trip.

In addition, two trigrams about two persons' names are found in the top 20 list. Specifically, the n-gram *President Xi Jinping* (N = 23; 0.04%), ranked 17th, which is exclusively be found in the *SCMPC*, suggesting that the relevant news articles revolved around the powerful figure are frequently mentioned. It is co-selected with *corruption* (N = 7; 30.43%), *lead* (N = 5; 21.74%), *drive* (N = 3; 13.04%), implying that the *SCMP* seems to lay an emphasis on the agent, Xi Jinping, who leads the anti-corruption campaign. Concordance analysis shows that this n-gram *President Xi Jingping* is always associated with *anti-corruption campaign, anti-graft drive,* and *crackdown,* indicating that some measures proposed by President Xi co-occur with words and phrases with negative meanings, such as *starkest warnings, hit, stem, tighter, piles more pressure, downward trend, slowdown*, and *worse*, suggesting that the *SCMP* holds a negative attitude towards Macau's economy and gaming industry as it is affected by a series of measures such as the anti-corruption campaign, increasing law enforcement scrutiny. Specifically, examples 142–145 all demonstrate the causes that lead to the economic decline of Macau's economy, highlighting the agent President Xi to initiate and drive this anti-corruption campaign, and example 146 demonstrates that the *SCMP* emphasised that Chinese President Xi Jinping required gaming industry of Macau to be controlled. Example 147 shows the pessimistic attitude held by the *SCMP* about the Macau's casino revenue, as this worse situation is attributed to the more stringent visa control to visitors' entry to Macau, in preparation for the important upcoming event, President Xi's visit to Macau.

142. The chief executive also appointed a new anti-corruption chief, just 18 days before **President Xi Jinping** is expected to arrive to lead celebrations for the 15th anniversary of the handover. **Xi**'s "tigers and flies" anti-graft drive has been seen as key to the slowdown in Macau's casino-driven economy.
143. turns up the heat on controversial VIP junket operators who generate the bulk of Macau gaming revenues as they come under increasing law enforcement scrutiny amid the "tigers and flies" anti-corruption drive ordered by **President Xi Jinping.**
144. **President Xi Jinping's** crackdown on corruption and over-the-top official lifestyles, and a smoking ban on gaming floors. Administrative measures to strengthen the mainland's campaign to root out and deter graft also do nothing to raise spirits in Macau.
145. Analysts attributed the fall to **President Xi Jinping**'s campaign against corruption, which has dented spending by high rollers in Macau, the only place in China where casinos are legal.
146. President tells new government to exert more control over the industry as Beijing looks to stem the flow of illicit funds through the city. **President Xi Jinping** has urged Macau to put its gambling house in order by exerting

greater control over the casino industry which has turned the city into the world's biggest gaming location.

147. Casino revenue figures for this month will not be released until the new year. However, Barclays is forecasting a decline worse than last month's because of tighter checks on travellers on transit in the lead-up to **President Xi Jinping'**s visit to mark the 15th anniversary of Macau's handover.

Another political figure *Chui Sai on* (N = 20; 0.04%) and *Fernando Chui Sai* (N = 20; 0.04%), ranked 19th and 20th, both refer to the Chief Executive of Macau, Fernando Chui Sai On. Concordance analysis shows that this n-gram co-occurs with phrases and clauses such as *budget, economic model, economically, political position, reshape, greater cooperation, rely on less economically on its gaming, announced sweeping changes,* and *pledges diversification away from gambling,* implying that Macau's future in terms of economic and political perspective could be changed.

4.4.3 *Top 20 Trigrams in the* MPDC

Table 4.8 demonstrates the top 20 trigrams in the MPDC ranked by frequency and percentage.

As demonstrated in Table 4.8, the trigram *the number of* (N = 96; 0.09%), ranked 5th in the *MPDC*, can also be found in the *SCMPC,* primarily co-occurring with *visitors* (N = 12) and *growth* (N = 8), referring to the tourism statistics including the report of number of visitor arrivals to Macau as well as the prediction of the number of tourists. Examples 148 to 150 show that the *MPD* held a positive attitude toward the growth in the number of visitors to Macau. It is noted that example 150 describes some measures adopted by the government and external factors, such as infectious diseases, which lead to a decrease in the number of visitors to Macau, with a relatively conservative attitude through listing some vague causes. The *SCMP* has mentioned that the two major causes of the decline in the number of tourists is about Chinese President Xi's visit and his drive for anti-corruption in the Chinese Mainland and the Occupy Central protest in Hong Kong. The corresponding part cannot be found in the *MPDC.*

148. The MGTO director also said she believes the city's tourism carrying capacity can cope with the expected growth in **the number of** visitors in the next few years.
149. Liu attributed the drop to recent government measures that shortens **the number of** days that transit visitors from the mainland can stay in Macau and limits the transactions on Union Pay terminals in retail shops in casinos.
150. There are many external factors affecting [local] tourism such as infectious diseases however, we are prudently optimistic about growth in **the number of** visitors]," she said,

Table 4.8 Top 20 trigrams in the *MPDC*

N	Word	Freq	%
1	The city's	174	0.15
2	Also said that	154	0.14
3	According to the	141	0.13
4	Said that the	137	0.12
5	The number of	96	0.09
6	Year on Year	77	0.07
7	The central government	70	0.06
8	Percent of the	69	0.06
9	Slot machine parlours	65	0.06
10	The government's	63	0.06
11	That the government	60	0.05
12	Percent year on	57	0.05
13	He also said	55	0.05
14	In the first	55	0.05
15	One of the	53	0.05
16	The spokesperson said	51	0.05
17	Pointed out that	50	0.04
18	The government to	50	0.04
19	Said adding that	48	0.04
20	The chief executive	47	0.04

In addition, with the concordance examination of the trigram *the number of* implying that the *MPD*, as the regional newspaper of Macau, does not only focus on reporting the tourism statistics like the *SCMP*, but also puts its focus on the wide variety of local social affairs happening in the society of Macau, for example, the number of the problem gamblers or gambling addicts in Macau society is constantly mentioned in the *MPDC* as shown in examples 151–153. Example 154 shows that the *MPD* also focused on the transportation benefits of employees working in the gaming industry. Example 155 focuses on the housing market in Macau and 156 on the local labour market, reflecting that social issues are the primary concern in the *MPDC*.

151. We also found that there has been no significant increase in **the number of** registered problem gamblers or gamblers addicts and there have been more residents seeking help from the centre in the early stages of their condition when they realized gambling could become a problem
152. Wu also said that **the number of** officially registered problem gamblers might, however, not show the true situation. She pledged that the government will continue to work with civic associations to improve awareness of the harm problem gamblers can bring to themselves and others.

153. According to statistics from the Social Welfare Bureau (IAS), **the number of** gambling addicts who asked for help from counselling centres in Macau stood at just 134 last year, compared to 149 in 2012 and 144 in 2011.
154. Chiang also said the government was negotiating with gaming operators about the possibility of them providing transport for imported workers employed on their construction sites, adding that the operators were open to this idea. He also said the government was still in talks with them about increasing **the number of** shuttle bus routes.
155. For the whole year, **the number of** property sales is going to be below 10,000, which is a 17-percent drop from last year's 12,046 transactions.
156. **The number of** workers imported from the mainland was 99,781, or 64.2 percent of the total number of imported labor. The number of workers imported from the Philippines reached 20,141, including 9,948 domestic helpers. A total of 12,780 workers were imported from Vietnam and 8,612 from Hong Kong.

The trigram *the central government* (N = 70; 0.06%) ranked 7th, which is shared in the *XH&CDC* and the *MPDC*. Through concordance analysis, the study finds that the use of this trigram *the central government* in the *MPDC* is different from that in the *XH&CDC*. Specifically, as mentioned above, the *XH&CDC* underlines the positive influence of the Chinese Central Government on Macau's development. By contrast, the *MPD* not only highlights the positive perspective about the support provided by the Central Government, but also reports some negative aspects.

Firstly, the *MPD* demonstrates that the central government had conducted several measures and regulations to regulate the gaming industry, which was considered to have an impact on the gaming industry as seen in examples 157–160. It is noted that the *MPD* tends to accentuate the anti-corruption campaign implemented by the central government rather than highlight the initiator of this campaign, Chinese President Xi Jinping in the *SCMPC* (examples 142–144).

157. Monica Leong Chairman and Chief Executive Officer of Wynn Resorts Steve Wynn said yesterday that **the central government**'s anti-corruption campaign was for the benefit of the nation and Macau, and his company's huge investment in Cotai was its vote of confidence.
158. the newspaper also said that Macau had been hit by the slowdown of the mainland economy in addition to austerity and anti-graft campaigns by **the central government**.
159. Siu pointed out that as capital flow into the market remained low due to frugality measures imposed by **the central government**, which also affects investors' confidence in the market, gaming revenue for May and June would remain low.
160. He said with **the central government** imposing tough measures to combat corruption, it would affect Macau's gaming industry and in turn the city's housing market, where prices might not increase as much as in the past few years.

Secondly, the *MPD* also mentions some local social opinions about the adverse effects arising from the related preferential policies provided by the Chinese central government. For example, individual Visit Scheme[7] was introduced by the central government in 2003, which is seen as a benefit to Hong Kong and Macau's economy. However, examples 161, 162, and 163 show the negative social impact on the local society brought by the Individual Visit Scheme (See details in Chap. 1); for example, the overload of tourists had an impact on the daily life of local residents of Macau (example 162).

161. I am argued that the scheme only benefits Macau's tourism industry while local residents suffer. He said his party was urging the government to tell **the central government** about local people's predicament.
162. Staff Reporter The radical Labour Party urged the government in a press conference yesterday to speak to **the central government** about what is sees as the adverse impact of the Individual Visit Scheme on Macau, in the hope that Beijing will set a cap on the number of mainlanders allowed to visit Macau using the scheme.
163. Li, who took up his new post earlier this month, also said that he and other Liaison Office staff would often visit the local community to listen to residents and then reflect their opinions to **the central government.**

Thirdly, it highlights the central government's authority in terms of Macau's political reform. For example, the *MPD* quoted the Chief Executive Chui's speech in which the modal verb *must* is employed to emphasise the importance of being in accordance with the Basic Law as seen in example 164, and underlined the authority of the central government through the indirect quotation of Chui, the Chief Executive of Macau (example 165).

164. "In Macau it must be in line with the Basic Law and Chief Executive Election Law, if opinions are collected [about the democratic reform process], being the chief executive I would be pleased to pass them on to **the central government**," Chui said.
165. Staff Reporters Chief Executive Fernando Chui Sai On said yesterday he was willing to convey locals' opinions on the city's political reform to the central government in Beijing, stressing that only **the central government** has the authority to start any political reform process in Macau.

Other trigrams, such as *year on year, percent of the, percent year on,* and *in the first,* co-occur with words and phrases to do with numbers and figures, implying the gaming statistics is frequently mentioned in the news articles of the *MPD.*

The trigram *slot-machine parlours* (N = 65; 0.06%) ranked 9th, is one form of gambling in the casinos of Macau, which cannot be found in the other two news

[7] The Individual Visit Scheme was launched by Beijing in July 2003 in the wake of the SARS crisis that had resulted in a sharp decline in the number of mainland and foreign visitors to Macau and Hong Kong. The scheme allows mainlanders to visit Hong Kong and Macau on an individual basis. Prior to the scheme, mainlanders could only visit the two cities on business visas or in group tours.

corpora. It is noted that the n-gram *the gaming industry* can only be found in the top 20 list of the *XH&CDC*, implying that the Chinese mainland newspapers showed their reporting preferences to the overall development of the gaming industry in Macau. In contrast, the *MPD* showed its interest in detailed parts concerning gaming industry. This trigram co-occurs with *casinos* (N = 20), *areas* (N = 12), *residential* (N = 12), *law* (N = 10), *outside* (N = 7) and *venues* (N = 10), with the examination of concordances lines revealing that the *slot-machine parlours* is related to one of the social problems in Macau, mainly revolving around the heated debate concerning the removal of slot-machine parlours out of the residential areas in order to reduce its potential bad influence on Macau's local residents. Both examples 174 and 175 show that *MPC* quoted different persons' voices including the Chief Executive Chui Sai-on (example 166), and the government official The Secretary for Economy and Finance Mr Tam (examples 167–168). Examples 169–170 show the locaresidents' opposition to the set of slot-machine parlous in the residential areas, which shows that the *MPD* emphasized local gaming issues.

166. "Obviously, this shows there is loophole in the by-law which allows slot-machine parlours to be set up in commercial buildings within 500 m from existing casino-hotels. Under this rule, the slot-machine parlous are still allowed to be set up in residential areas, even though one aim of the by-law is to move all **slot-machine parlours** out of residential areas to reduce the possible impact of gambling [on the community]," Chui said, adding that the government should review the by-law at once.
167. "I think I need to make this clear, the government's ultimate goal is to completely get rid of the [stand-alone] **slot machine parlours** that there won't be any outside casinos", said Tam.
168. Tam also revealed yesterday that the government's ultimate goal was to get rid of all **slot-machine parlours** located outside casinos.
169. Kai Fong collects 10,000 signatures against **slot-machine parlous** in residential areas.
170. Collected about 10,000 signatures from residents expressing their opposition against **slot-machine parlous** operating in residential areas.

References

Bednarek, M., & Caple, H. (2012). *News discourse*. Continuum.

Caro, E. M. (2014). The expression of evaluation in weekly news magazines in English. In G. Thompson & L. Alba-Juez (Eds.), *Evaluation in context* (pp. 321–344). John Benjamins Publishing.

Cheng, W. (2012). *Exploring corpus linguistics: Language in action*. Routledge.

Moody, A. (2008). Macau English: Status, functions and forms. *English Today, 24*(3), 3–15.

Sinclair, J. (2004). *Trust the text: Language, corpus and discourse*. Routledge.

Chapter 5
Macroscopic Analysis on Macau's Gaming Industry at the Semantic Level

This chapter moves from the lexical analysis to a microscopic level, presenting the findings of the key semantic field analysis at the semantic level. Semantic differences were found among three news article corpora, indicating the diversity of predominant themes or topics in Chinese Mainland, Hong Kong, and Macau news media.

5.1 Outlining Key Semantic Fields Among Three Corpora

The key semantic field analysis was conducted to examine and compare the respective semantic saliency of the three corpora (i.e., *XH&CDC, SCMPC*, and *MPDC*). Each news article corpus is compared with the same reference corpus British National Corpus (BNC) Written Sampler in order to obtain the general tendencies of each news article corpus.

Table 5.1 provides an overview of each news article corpus's top 20 key semantic fields (with the most significant LL values). For the comparative purpose, three types of key semantic fields are highlighted with different colours in Table 5.1. Specifically, Type I (N = 8; 22.22%), highlighted in yellow, refers to the key semantic fields shared among the three news corpora. Type II (N = 8; 22.22%), highlighted in blue, denotes the key semantic fields found in any of the two news article corpora. Type III (N = 20; 56.56%), highlighted in purple, accounts for the largest percentage and represents the unique key semantic fields, indicating that these key semantic fields can only be found in one corpus. Table 5.2 demonstrates the respective percentage of three types of key semantic fields.

In Table 5.1, key semantic fields "GAMES", "GOVERNMENT", "BUSINESS: GENERALLY", "DANGER", "QUALITIES", "SPEECH COMMUNICATIVE", and "NUMBERS" are shared among three news article corpora, showing that the above themes or topics all appear in each new article corpus. There is a considerable overlap in terms of the number of shared key semantic fields between the *SCMPC*

Y. Wu, *Media Representations of Macau's Gaming Industry in Greater China*,
https://doi.org/10.1007/978-981-19-7724-4_5

Table 5.1 Top twenty key semantic fields of *XH&CDC*, *SCMPC* and *MPDC* ranked by LL value

Rank	*XH&CDC*	*SCMPC*	*MPDC*
1	Geographical names	Games	Games
2	Games	Geographical names	Speech: Communicative
3	Government	Government	Government
4	Places	Time: Period	Money generally
5	Business: Generally	Money generally	Work and employment: Generally
6	Money generally	Law and order	Smoking and non-medical drugs
7	Size: Big +	Unmatched	Speech acts
8	Cheap	Business: Generally	Belonging to a group
9	Change	Crime	Telecommunications
10	Danger	Money and pay	Law and order
11	Time: Period	Telecommunications	Numbers
12	Industry	Danger	Time: Past
13	Geographical terms	Information technology and computing	Quantities: many/ much
14	Helping	Speech: Communicative	Danger
15	Size: Big+++	Quantities: little	The Media: Newpapers etc.
16	Quantities: many/much	Numbers	Measurement: General
17	Quantities	Paper documents and writing	Unmatched
18	Comparing: Similar/different	Quantities	Business: Generally
19	Speech: Communicative	Size: Big+++	Quantities
20	Numbers	Work and employment Professionalism	Places

Table 5.2 Three types of key semantic fields and their respective percentages

THREE TYPES OF SEMANTIC FIELDS

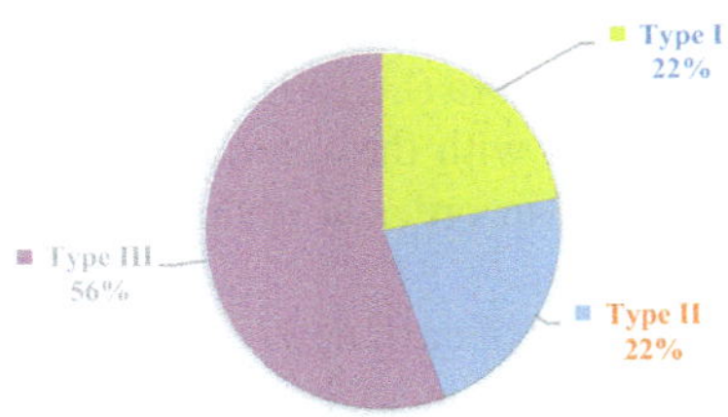

and the *MPDC* (N = 11; 30.56%), between the *XH&CDC* and the *SCMPC* (N = 10; 27.78%), and between the *XH&CDC* and the *MPDC* (N = 9; 25%).

When the *XH&CDC* was compared with the *SCMPC*, 36.67% (11 out of 30) of the key semantic fields were the same; for example, key semantic fields "SIZE: BIG+++", "TIME PERIOD", and "GEOGRAPHICAL NAMES" were only shared between these two corpora. Some unique key semantic fields, such as "SIZE BIG+", "CHEAP", "CHANGE", and "HELPING", in the *XH&CDC* were quite abstract and needed further examination. Apart from the semantic field "GEOGRAPHICAL NAMES" shared between the two corpora, the *XH&CDC* covers more key semantic fields relevant to location or places, namely "PLACES" and "GEOGRAPHICAL

TERMS", than the other two news article corpus. By contrast, the *SCMPC* covers more semantic fields related to the areas of finance and business, including the shared key semantic fields: "MONEY GENERALLY" and "BUSINESS: GENERALLY", and a unique semantic field "MONEY AND PAY", suggesting that themes or topics concerning "MONEY" are salient in this corpus. The exclusive use of the key semantic field "CRIME" in the *SCMPC* shows that related news coverage is likely to encompass topics relevant to criminal activities, which needs to be examined in detail. The contrasting occurrence of the key semantic field "QUANTITIES: MANY/MUCH" in the *XH&CDC* and the *MPDC* and "QUANTITIES: LITTLE" in the *SCMPC* indicate that these two opposite key semantic fields deserve further examination.

According to Culpeper (2009), "the notion of a semantic field is obviously more abstract than that of a lexical item" (p. 47). Thus, in the following section, three types of key semantic fields are analysed and discussed to uncover semantic meanings and other language patterns. They include four Type I semantic tags ("GAMES", "GOVERNMENT", "MONEY: GENERALLY", and "NUMBERS"), three Type II key semantic fields ("GEOGRAPHICAL NAMES", "LAW AND ORDER", and "TELECOMMUNICATION"), and all Type III key semantic fields.

5.2 Analysis of Shared Key Semantic Fields Among Three Corpora

K5.2. GAMES

Table 5.3 shows the LL value, the raw and relative frequencies of words, and the rank in the key semantic field "GAMES" in each corpus.

As demonstrated in Table 5.3, the most frequent key semantic field shared by the *MPDC* and the *SCMPC* is "K5.2, GAMES", ranked 1st with the highest LL value, indicating that gaming-related topics are given greater attention in these two news article corpora. This is consistent with the findings in the above wordlist analysis that the most significant lexical words in above two corpora is *gaming* and that the overrepresentation of semantic tag K5.2, "GAMES" is expected as the topics of news articles collected in the *SCMPC* all related to the gaming industry of Macau. By contrast, the key semantic field with the highest LL (i.e., 1226.19) value in the *XH&CDC* is "Z2, GEOGRAPHICAL NAMES", suggesting this semantic field is the most significantly overused, while the field "K5.2, GAME" is ranked 2nd with an LL value of 741.63, suggesting themes related to gaming in the *XH&CDC* were not predominant in comparison to the other two corpora.

The words in the semantic field "GAMES" (see Table 5.3), which occur more than 10 times in the *XH&CDC* and the *SCMPC*, are the same (i.e., *casino, casinos,* and *gamblers*). By contrast, the *MPDC* contains a unique item to do with the gaming occupation, namely *croupiers*, referring to a person working in the casino whose job is to collect and pay out money at the gambling tables. Its occurrence demonstrates

Table 5.3 The semantic field K5.2, "Games"

Semantic field	LL value XH&CDC	Word (raw and relative frequency)	Rank	LL value SCMPC	Word (raw and relative frequency)	Rank	LL value MPDC	Word (raw and relative frequency)	Rank
K5.2 GAMES	764.61	Casino (N = 62;0.22%) casinos (N = 57; 0.20%) gamblers (N = 19;0.07%)	2	1743.51	Casino (N = 202;0.42%) casinos (N = 90;0.19%) gamblers (N = 31;0.06%)	1	2856.87	Casino (N = 184; 0.23%) casinos (N = 167; 0.22%) gamblers (N = 106; 0.12%) cropiers (N = 84; 0.08%) gambler (N = 10; 0.01%)	1

that this particular occupation is specific to the context of Macau's local newspaper (i.e., *Macau Post Daily*).

In K5.2, *casino* and *casinos* are the most frequent items in the three corpora. In the *XH&CDC, casino* (N = 62; 0.22%) co-occurs with words relevant to the financial statistics, namely *revenue* (N = 27; 38.71%), *revenues* (N = 10; 16.13%), *percent* (N = 20; 32.26%), *billion* (N = 18; 29.03%) and *patacas* (N = 9; 14.52%), indicating that themes concerning the profitability of Macau's casinos are the focus of the news coverage. *Casinos* (N = 57) primarily co-occurs with *revenue* (N = 12; 21.05%), denoting the salience of Macau's gaming revenues in the news articles.

In the *SCMPC*, the relative frequency of *casino* is nearly twice higher than that in the *XH&CDC*. Similar to the *XH&CDC*, the singular form *casino* (N = 202; 0.42%) mainly co-occurs with *revenue* (N = 43; 21.29%) and *per cent* (N = 22; 10.89%), describing the financial figures in gaming industry of Macau. Besides, it also co-occurs with *operators* (N = 31; 15.35%), and *operator* (N = 21; 10.40%), referring the casino operators, which are companies that participate in the gaming industry and also do business. By contrast, the concordances of *casinos* display another picture compared to its singular form. Its plural form co-occurs with words and phrases closely related to illegal activities associated with casinos. For example, *casinos* (N = 90; 0.19%) primarily co-occurs with the preposition *from* (N = 22; 24.44%), showing the sources of the suspicious funds as shown in the following examples:

1. From suspicious funds channelled **from** China through Macau casinos by junket operators
2. Macau's casinos are a major conduit for capital flight **from** the mainland.
3. Macau's gaming stocks are under pressure as casinos reel **from** the mainland's anti-corruption campaign
4. Distance himself **from** the rampant organised crime within his casinos and remains very much in the game.

By comparison, in the *MPDC, casino* (N = 184; 0.23%) co-occurs with words related to persons (rather than economic areas as in the other two corpora), such as *workers* (N = 54; 54.34%), *staff* (N = 27; 14.67%), *employees* (N = 24; 13.04%), and *croupiers* (N = 14; 7.61%), demonstrating that references relating to employment are more salient in the *MPDC* and that reporting focus is given to these groups of people who work in the casinos, thereby affirming the findings of frequency. Instead, *casino* only co-occurs with *revenue* (N = 18; 9.78%), representing a relatively small percentage; the plural form *casinos* (N = 167) co-occurs with *smoking* (N = 57; 34.13%), discussing the related smoking ban policy in Macau's casinos.

The next item, *gamblers*, is found in all the three corpora and its singular form *gambler* can only be found in the *MPDC*. The co-occurrences of *gamblers* in the *XH&CDC* and the *SCMPC* are similar. In the *XH&CDC, gamblers* (N = 19; 0.07%) is mainly used to refer to *high-stakes gamblers* (N = 6; 31.58%), *VIP gamblers* (N = 2; 10.53%), and *high-spending gamblers* (N = 1; 5.26%) from mainland China, implying that the *XH&CDC* puts its emphasis on mentioning the impact of the Chinese anti-corruption campaign on these high-end gamblers. In the *SCMPC, gamblers* (N = 31; 0.06%) mainly co-occurs with *Chinese* (N = 10; 32.26%), *mainland* (N = 9; 29.03%), and *drop* (N = 4; 12.90%), specially mentioning that the majority of high-end gamblers is from Chinese mainland, for instance, the drop of high-end gamblers from Chinese Mainland leads to the decline of Macau's gaming revenue.

By contrast, the reference to *gamblers* (N = 106; 0.12%) in the context of the *MPDC* is different from that in the other two news article corpora. Specifically, the frequency of *gambler* is still very small (N = 10; 0.01%). Its plural form *gamblers* (N = 106; 0.12%) co-selects with *problem* (N = 33; 31.13%) at the N-1 to the left, denoting another type of gamblers, namely *problem gamblers*. These people normally have compulsive gambling and pathological gambling behaviours. It also co-occurs with *secret* (N = 26; 24.52%), specifically referring to gamblers working in the casinos, who try to keep their gambling activity secret from family and friends. The exclusive use of these two groups of gamblers suggests that the *MPD*, as the regional press, tends to draw the attention to the social impact of the gaming industry on Macau society; this focus is associated with the introduction of the policy proposed by the Macau SAR government in 2008 of 'responsible gambling' (DICJ, n.d.), aiming to reduce societal harm related to gambling. This reflects that the *MPD* is more aware of social issues rather than the economic performance of Macau as related references to high-rollers or high-end gamblers from the Chinese mainland are seldom mentioned in the *MPDC*.

G.1.1. GOVERNMENT

Table 5.4 shows the LL value, words' raw and relative frequencies, and the rank in the key semantic field "GOVERNMENT" in each corpus.

The shared semantic field G.1.1, GOVERNMENT (N = 495; LL = 728.38) ranked 3rd in the *XH&CDC* (Table 5.4). In this key semantic field, *revenue* (N = 99; 0.34%) is the most frequent component, along with its plural form *revenues* (N = 34; 0.12%). Concordance analysis shows that *revenue* mainly refers to gross gaming or casino revenue in Macau; its overrepresentation indicates that the financial performance in Macau's gaming industry is one of the focuses of the news coverage towards the gaming industry of Macau. As mentioned in the introductory chapter, the gaming industry is a very important contributor for Macau's fiscal revenue and is the largest source of direct tax revenues in Macau. Specifically, the local gaming industry's gross revenue contributes the largest proportion of gaming taxes to government coffers. This can explain why *revenues* is significantly overused in related news articles. The second most frequent word, *government* (N = 98; 0.34%), is primarily used to refer to the governments of the three territories, namely the MSAR government, the Chinese government and, the HKSAR government. The majority of concordance lines for *government* refers to the MSAR government (N = 82; 85.4%), and the term is also used as the part of organisation's name, e.g. the *Macao Government Tourist Office* (N = 2; 2.04%). The rest of the concordance lines consist of *central government* (N = 7; 7.14%), *Chinese government* (N = 1), and *central people's government* (N = 2; 2.24%), all of which refer to the Chinese government. To be more specific, their full name is the *Central People's Government of the People's Republic of China*, which is

Table 5.4 The semantic field G1.1, "Government"

Semantic field	LL value XH&CDC	Word (raw and relative frequency)	Rank	LL value SCMPC	Word (raw and relative frequency)	Rank	LL value MPDC	Word (raw and relative frequency)	Rank
G.1. Government	728.38	Revenue (N = 99; 0.34%) Government (N = 96; 0.34%) Country (N = 53; 0.19%) Central_government (N = 37; 0.13%) President (N = 34; 0.12%) Revenues (N = 34; 0.12%) Bureau (N = 18; 0.07%) Nation (N = 16; 0.0.6%) Governments (N = 13; 0.05%) Governance (N = 10; 0.04%)	3	636.35	Revenue (N = 155; 0.32%) Government (N = 106; 0.22%) President (N = 39; 0.08%) Revenues (N = 39; 0.08%) Officials (N = 39; 0.08%) Country (N = 24; 0.05) Bureau (N = 24; 0.05%) Authorities (N = 19; 0.04%) Ministry (N = 18; 0.04%) Nation (N = 16; 0.03%) Official (N = 14; 0.03%) Authority (N = 13; 0.03%) Central_government (N = 11; 0.02%)	3	2856.87	Government (N = 445; 0.44%) Bureau (N = 15; 0.15%) Revenue (N = 113; 0.11%) Governments (N = 93; 0.09%) Officials (N = 79; 0.08%) Official (N = 71; 0.07%) Central_government (N = 62; 0.06%) President (N = 47; 0.05%) Legislature (N = 33; 0.03%) Govt (N = 31; 0.03%) Country (N = 30; 0.03%) Revenues (N = 27; 0.03%) p.m. (N = 26; 0.02%) mp (N = 24; 0.02%) Legislatures (N = 22; 0.02%) Census (N = 21; 0.02%) Civil_servants (N = 20; 0.02%) Civic (N = 16; 0.02%) Officially (N = 16; 0.02%) Vice-president (N = 15; 0.01%) Authority (N = 15; 0.01%) Citizens (N = 15; 0.01%) Bureaus (N = 13; 0.01%) Council (N = 12; 0.01%) Passport (N = 12; 0.01%)	3

the administrative branch of the state's government. The *HKASAR government* and *HK government* only occur twice.

It is noted that *central government* (N = 37; 0.13%) is tagged as a separate lexical item in this semantic field, ranked 4th, which co-occurs with *support* (N = 10; 27.03%), illustrating that the central government offers support to Macau. Specifically, the occurrences of *president* (N = 33; 0.12%) concentrate mainly on the news coverage published in December and the news articles, revolving around Chinese President Xi Jinping's official visit to Macau for the 15th anniversary of its handover to China. The high relative frequency of *president* indicates the *XH&CD* devoted extensive news coverage of his official visit to Macau.

Country (N = 53; 0.19%) is ranked 3rd in this key semantic field. It is noteworthy that this term does not only indicate a particular area, but also primarily co-occur with *one* (N = 37; 68.5%) at the N-1 position, signifying that the policy of "One Country, Two Systems" is overused in the semantic field of "GOVERNMENT". By manually checking its corresponding concordance lines, we can find that 37 of the entries in the XH&CDC quoted examples regarding the successful implementation of the government policy in Macau society, with the aim of advocating and underlining the significant status of this principle in the Macau SAR.

In the *SCMPC*, the word occurring as frequently as in the *XH&CDC* is *revenue* (N = 155; 0.31%), predominately co-occurring with *gaming* (N = 73; 47.10%), *cent* (N = 76; 49.03%), *per* (N = 75; 48.39%), *billion* (N = 45; 29.03%), and *casino* (N = 42; 27.10%), indicating the financial performance in gaming of Macau is the priority for the *SCMP*. *President* (N = 39; 0.08%) ranked 3rd, primarily co-occurs with *Xi* (N = 28; 70%), denoting that the Chinese President Xi Jinping also received massive attention in the news coverage of the *SCMPC*. However, concordance analysis reflects that the major reporting focus regarding President *Xi Jinping* is associated with *anti-corruption* (N = 10; 50%), referring to the "tigers and flies" anti-corruption campaign drive launched by the Chinese President Xi Jinping in 2012, and here is mentioned by the *SCMP* in order to explain the reasons for the sudden drop in Macau's casino revenue. Apart from this, his official presence in Macau, such as *anniversary* (N = 9; 37.5%) has been minimally covered by the *SCMP*. *Country* (N = 24; 0.05%) mainly co-occurs with *two* (N = 12; 50%), referring to the "One Country, Two Systems" model; its occurrence concentrates in news articles in relation to Chinese President Xi Jinping's visit to Macau in December 2014. The concordance analysis reveals that the way of illustrating this policy in many cases is through citing the speech made by Xi to assert the importance of Hong Kong and Macau to stick to this principle. Specifically, a metaphor (i.e., *veiled swipes*) is used by the *SCMP* to colour Xi's insistence that Hong Kong should stick to the principle of "One Country, Two Systems", as shown in example 5:

5. Xi Jinping tells Macau to stick to '**one country, two systems**' in veiled swipe at Hong Kong.

Moreover, the *SCMP* also quoted Xi's speech '*stressing Macau's younger generations to understand the true meaning of this policy*' in association with Hong Kong's situation to make a comment as shown in the following examples:

6. President ends Macau visit by stressing his desire for young people to understand 'true meaning' of "**one country, two systems**" model
7. President Xi Jinping pushed national education and his desire for young people to understand "the true meaning" of the "**one country, two systems**" model to the forefront yesterday as he ended his two-day visit to Macau.

Additionally, the *SCMP* also provided background information about this model for the target audience as shown in example 8:

8. The celebration comes at a time the "**one country, two systems**" model devised by paramount leader Deng Xiaoping to take the two cities through the early post-colonial years is entering a new phase.

In the *MPDC,* the key semantic field G1.1 "GOVERNMENT", ranked 3rd (N = 1506; LL = 1656.08) (Table 5.1), contains a wider range of lexical words compared to the other two corpora (i.e., *SCMPC* and *XH&CDC*) (Table 5.3). The *government* (N = 445; 0.44%), ranked 1st, primarily refers to the Macau SAR Government. *The central government* (N = 62; 0.06%) co-occurs with the reporting verb *said* (N = 10; 16.12%), showing that the *MPDC* prefers to adopt a quotation to report on the central government. *Bureau* (N = 153; 15%), ranked 2nd, represents various local government institutions and departments in the Macau SAR, such as the *Social Welfare Bureau, Labour Affairs Bureau,* and *Statistics and Census Bureau.*

Another lexical item is *president*, occurring in the *MPDC* (N = 47; 0.05%), *XH&CDC* (N = 34; 0.12%), and *SCMPC* (N = 43; 0.08%). The use of *president* in the *XH&CDC* is the highest. Manual concordance examination reveals that the meaning of *president* differs among the three news article corpora. In the *MPDC,* only two concordance lines of *president* are found to refer to the Chinese President Xi Jinping, only accounting for 4.34%. This indicates that Macau's local press did not give much coverage to this political figure; the major use of *president* in the *MPD* refers to chief officers of Macau's local organisations or institutions. By contrast, the news articles in the other two corpora focus on the president of China and the Chinese Communist Party Xi Jinping.

N1. NUMBERS

Table 5.5 shows the LL value, the raw and relative frequencies of words, and the rank in the key semantic field "NUMBERS" in each corpus.

From Table 5.5, it can be seen that the semantic field N1 "NUMBERS" is found in each top 20 key semantic field list of the three news articles corpora, namely *XH&CDC* (20th; N = 648; LL = 70.42), *SCMPC* (16th; N = 1159; LL = 132.86) and *MPDC* (11th; N = 258; LL = 426.08).

This semantic field in the above three corpora contains different components as shown in Table 5.5. Particularly, in the *XH&CDC*, the number of word types tagged as N1 is relatively small, with a frequency above the ten compared with the other

Table 5.5 The semantic field N1, "Numbers"

Semantic field	LL value XH&CDC	Word (raw and relative frequency)	Rank	LL value SCMPC	Word (raw and relative frequency)	Rank	LL value MPDC	Word (raw and relative frequency)	Rank
N1 Numbers	70.42	Two (N = 57; 0.20%) One (N = 56; 0.20%) Xi (N = 29; 0.10%) 2014 (N = 25; 0.09%) 2013 (N = 24; 0.09%) 1999 (N = 18; 0.06%) Five (N = 15; 0.05%) Billion (N = 14; 0.05%) Three (N = 12; 0.04%)	20	132.86	Billion (N = 99; 0.20%) 2014 (N = 98; 0.20%) One (N = 87; 0.18%) Million (N = 69; 0.14%) Two (N = 54; 0.11%) Three (N = 42; 0.08%) Xi (N = 39; 0.08%) Five (N = 34; 0.07%) Quarter (N = 28; 0.06%) Six (N = 27; 0.05%) 15 (N = 20; 0.04%) 2009 (N = 8; 0.04%) Triad (N = 17; 0.03%) 2016 (N = 16; 0.03%) 1999 (N = 15; 0.03%) Four (N = 12; 0.02%) 2005 (N = 11; 0.02%) 2017 (N = 11; 0.02%) Third-quarter (N = 10; 0.02%)	16	426.08	Two (N = 151; 0.15) One (N = 96; 0.10) Quarter (N = 82; 0.08%) Three (N = 76; 0.08%) 10 (N = 59; 0.06%) Four (N = 58; 0.06%) Six (N = 51; 0.05%) Million (N = 50; 0.05%) 14 (N = 49; 0.05%) 1 (N = 45; 0.04%) Billion (N = 37; 0.04%) 30 (N = 33; 0.03%) Five (N = 29; 0.03%) 2012 (N = 27; 0.03%) 2013 (N = 24; 0.02%) 500 (N = 22; 0.02%) 16 (N = 21; 0.02%) 22 (N = 18; 0.02%) 2008 (N = 17; 0.02%) 20 (N = 15; 0.01%) 344 (N = 15; 0.01%) Quarters (N = 14; 0.01%) 2011 (N = 14; 0.01%) 2 (N = 14; 0.01%) 50 (N = 13; 0.01%) 1,000 (N = 13; 0.01%) 2017 (N = 13 0.01%) 12 (N = 0.01%) 2010 (N = 12 0.01%) 18 (N = 12; 0.01%) 4 (N = 12; 0.01%) 10,000 (N = 12; 0.01%) 2016 (N = 12; 0.01%) seven (N = 12; 0.01%) 40 (N = 10; 0.01%) 29 (N = 10; 0.01%) 13 (N = 10; 0.01%) 2015 (N = 10; 0.01%) 35 (10 0.01%) 8 (10 0.01%)	11

two corpora. It is noted that *Xi* (N = 29) is tagged wrongly by Wmatix. *Xi* here refers to the Chinese President Xi Jinping rather than numbers. The most significant item *two* (N = 57; 0.20%) in the *XH&CDC*, which has the higher relative frequency than those in the *SCMPC* (N = 48; 0.01%) and the *MPDC* (N = 151; 0.15%). In most cases, *two* does not signify the exact figure and co-selects with *one* (N = 38; 64.91%), representing the policy of "*One Country, Two Systems*". This principle is found to co-select words and phrases with a positive meaning, such as *great success*, *steady*, *continuous*, and *greater success*, showing that the Chinese press underlines the importance of implementing this policy for Macau and presents the positive outcomes this policy has brought to Macau society, as shown in the following examples 9–11:

9. Thanks to implementation of the 'One country, **Two** systems' policy and the Basic law. The situation is very good
10. The 15 years of development in Macao also proved a great success for the 'One country, **Two** systems' policy, Li added
11. Lavagnino said. China's one country, **Two** systems policy has generated more wealth for everybody.

In the *SCMPC*, *billion* (N = 99; 0.20%), ranked 1st, co-occurs with different currency units, namely *HK* (N = 58; 58.59%), *US* (N = 55; 55.56%) and *Patacas* (N = 5; 5.05%), proving that Macau's financial performance in gaming industry is the focus of the *SCMP*. The next number, *2014*, has been deleted as it is not relevant to the contents of the news coverage, instead of denoting the file number of the news source. *Xi* (N = 31; 0.06%) is also incorrectly identified by Wmatrix and here signifies the Chinese President Xi. *Two* (N = 53; 0.10%), ranked 4th, co-occurs with *systems* (N = 11; 20.75%), denoting the national principle of "*One Country, Two Systems*" and the rest of the concordance lines are used to refer to the exact number rather than this policy.

By contrast, the top 1 word in this key semantic field of the *MPDC* is *two* (N = 151; 0.15%), and just as in its counterpart in the *XH&CDC* ranked 1st. However, concordances analysis shows that the use of this word in the context of the *MPD* is different from that in the other two corpora, and is primarily used as an exact number, such as *two years*, *two cheques*, and *two companies*. Only one concordance line (N = 1; 0.662%) is found to relate to the policy of "*One Country, Two Systems*", suggesting that this principle is rarely mentioned in the news articles of the *MPDC*.

Moreover, the timeframes examined in the news article of three corpora are different. The key semantic field "Number" in the *XH&CDC* only contains three periods: *2014* (N = 25; 0.09%), *2013* (N = 24; 0.08%), and *1999* (N = 18; 0.06%). It is noted the ten concordance lines of *2014* are removed and not analysed as this year is used at the end of the news articles to indicate the period of registration of copyrights, functioning as a source of information. By contrast, the time span in the *SCMPC* is wider than that in the *XH&CDC*, covering 5 periods *2009* (N = 18; 0.04%), *2016* (N = 16; 0.03%), *1999* (N = 15; 0.03%), *2005* (N = 11; 0.02%), and *2017* (N = 11; 0.02%). The *MPDC* contains the widest variety of periods concerning Macau's gaming industry, namely *2012* (N = 27; 0.03%), *2013*(N = 24; 0.02%),

2008 (N = 17; 0.02%), *2011* (N = 14; 0.01%), *2017* (N = 13; 0.01%), *2010* (N = 12; 0.01%), *2016* (N = 12; 0.01%) and *2015* (N = 10; 0.01%).

Specifically, in the *XH&CDC, 2013* co-occurs with words related to business, such as *billion* (N = 11; 45.83%), *percent* (N = 10; 41.67%), and *million* (N = 7; 29.17%). *2013* is found to co-select with another period, *1999* (N = 5; 20.83%), indicating that these two periods were put together to make a comparison in terms of Macau's financial performance, highlighting Macau's economic growth has obtained in the post-1999 era. The period *1999*, with a higher relative frequency than that in the *SCMPC*, co-occurs with *return* (N = 7; 36.84%), marking the establishment of the Macau SAR and Macau's handover to the Chinese sovereignty. This year is mainly employed as the reference to differentiate Macau's past history as a Portuguese enclave from the present Special Administrative Region of the PRC for comparative purposes. It is found to co-select with words with a positive meaning, such as *the growth of Macau's average GDP*, *impressive economic growth*, *obvious development*, *full of delight and vitality*, and *brimming with potential*, representing that the *XH&CDC* underlines the positive side of Macau.

In the *SCMPC*, *2009* (N = 17; 0.04%) is a unique period in the 'NUMBER' semantic field, and does not occur in the other two news corpora. It is surrounded by words to do with decline, such as *contraction* (N = 7; 41.18%), *fell* (N = 2; 11.76%), *fall* (N = 1; 5.88%), *shrinkage* (N = 1; 5.88%) and *worst* (N = 2; 11.76%), as well as some words and phrases with a negative meaning, such as *suffered*, *concerns*, *worst*, *a host of problems*, and *negative*, serving as a contrast with Macau's optimistic economic situation in post-2009. *2016* (N = 16; 0.03%) is connected with the scheduled completion of various projects, such as Hong Kong-Zhuhai-Macau Bridge, a light rail project, and the scheduled opening of several casinos in Macau. Words co-occurring with *1999* (N = 14; 0.03%) in the *SCMPC* are expected: they are *returned* (N = 5; 33.33%) and *handover* (N = 6; 40%), both referring to Macau's handover to China in 1999. Additionally, *1999* also co-occurs with *shake-up* (N = 8; 53.33%), revealing Macau's unfavourable political situation in 2014 as it was undergoing the second significant political shake-up since 1999. In 2014, nine of ten leading officials were replaced, as seen in examples 12 and 13; that is not mentioned in the other two news article corpora. It is noted that 1999 is also used as a reference for comparisons to other news events. Example 14 shows that the *SCMP* mentioned a famous kidnapping that happened in 2001 by using 1999 as the reference time as 1999 is a special year historically for Macau, marking the beginning of Macau's post-colonial era.

12. What is being seen as the most significant political shake-up since the former Portuguese enclave returned to Chinese sovereignty in **1999**
13. In what is seen as the biggest political shake-up since the handover in **1999**, nine of the 10 principal officials have been replaced
14. Valente was also the victim of a high-profile kidnapping in 2001, not long after the **1999** Macau handover.

By contrast, in the *MPDC*, the relative frequency of *1999* is the lowest (N = 6; 0.01%) in comparison with the *XH&CDC* (N = 18; 0.06%) and the *SCMPC* (N =

15; 0.03%), showing that this particular year about Macau's return to China did not receive extensive attention in Macau's local news article whereas in the *XH&CD*, the relative frequency of *1999* is the highest, 6 times higher than that in the *MPDC* and 3 times higher than that in the *SCMP*, suggesting the Chinese mainland media mention 1999 a lot in its news article, highlighting Macau's handover to China.

I2.1 Business: Generally

Table 5.6 shows the LL value, the raw and relative frequencies of words, and the rank in the key semantic field "BUSINESS: GENERALLY" in each corpus.

Table 5.6 displays that the tag I2.1, "BUSINESS: GENERALLY", is shared among three news articles corpora. I2.1 is ranked 5th (N = 263; LL = 263.05) in the *XH&CDC* and 8th (N = 395; LL = 303.93) in the *SCMPC*, while it is only ranked 18th (N = 664; LL = 343.11) in the *MPDC*.

As shown in Table 5.6, the key semantic tag I2.1 in the *XH&CDC* includes various components specific to the fields of economy and business. Specifically, the most frequent item is *economy* (N = 68; 0.24%); by contrast, its counterpart ranked 3rd (N = 50; 0.10%) in the *SCMPC*, and 4th (N = 55; 0.05%) in the *MPDC*, implying that the item *economy* in the *XH&CDC* has a higher relative frequency compared to the other two news article corpora. Meanwhile, its adjective form *economic* is exclusively tagged as one of the top lexical words in the *XH&CDC*, together suggesting that the Chinese mainland press is inclined to pay attention to Macau's economic aspects at the macro level, in comparison to the other two corpora; by contrast, *company*, ranked 1st in both the *SCMPC* (N = 75; 0.16%) and the *MPDC* (N = 115; 0.11%). While the occurrence accounts for only 0.05% in the *XH&CDC*, it indicates that the *SCMP* and the *MPD* focus on the business field, which varies from the *XH&CD*. Specifically, news articles published in the Hong Kong SAR and Macau SAR emphasise specific economic entities in society. The diverse news article priorities among the three corpora can be attributed to the different social and political systems in Mainland China, Hong Kong and Macau. Specifically, given the respective past colonial history in Hong Kong and Macau, these two regions still reserve their existing capitalist systems, whereas Mainland China maintains a socialist market economy. Moreover, Hong Kong and Macau are also different from each other in terms of diverse socio-political environments.

In order to better understand the pattern of *economy* in the three corpora, its collocates were categorised by hand. In the *XH&CDC*, the collocates of *economy* can be divided into five groups: (1) the act of change: *diversify* (N = 16; 23.52%); (2) industry: *gaming* (N = 15; 22.06%) and *tourism* (N = 12; 17.65%); (3) the process of growing: *development* (N = 6; 8.82%) and *growth* (N = 5; 7.35%); (4) degree: *appropriately* (N = 9; 13.24%) and *well* (N = 6; 8.82%); (5) geographical names: *Macao* (N = 14; 20.59%), *Macao's* (N = 10; 14.71%), and *mainland* (N = 7; 10.29%). Detailed concordance analysis has revealed that *economy* here primarily refers to Macau's economy, covering several aspects. Firstly, the *XH&CD* states their clear opinions that Macau's future economy should not only depend on its gaming industry, but must also diversify appropriately in the future, such as promoting the tourism industry. Secondly, the *XH&CD* reviews the status of the development of

Table 5.6 The semantic field I2.1 "Business Generally"

Semantic field	LL value XH&CDC	Word (raw and relative frequency)	Rank	LL value SCMPC	Word (raw and relative frequency)	Rank	LL value MPDC	Word (raw and relative frequency)	Rank
I2.1 Business: Generally	263.05	Economy (N = 68; 0.24%) Business (N = 29; 0.10%) ltd (N = 27; 0.10%) Company (N = 15; 0.05%) Commercial (N = 10; 0.04%) Companies (N = 10; 0.04%)	5	303.93	Company (N = 75; 0.16%) Business (N = 60; 0.12%) Economy (N = 50; 0.10%) Office (N = 31; 0.06%) Chamber of commerce (N = 21; 0.04%) Companies (N = 20; 0.04%) Businesses (N = 19; 0.04%) Agents (N = 10; 0.02%) Dealer (N = 10; 0.02%)	8	343.11	Company (N = 115; 0.01%) Office (N = 99; 0.10%) Business (N = 57; 0.06%) Economy (N = 55: 0.05%) Companys (N = 49; 0.05%) Companies (N = 45; 0.04%) Commercial (N = 40; 0.04%) Enterprises (N = 26; 0.03%) Dealers (N = 20; 0.02%) Consultancy (N = 17; 0.02%) Businesses (N = 12; 0.01%) Businessman (N = 12; 0.01%) Dealer (N = 12; 0.01%) Executives (N = 10; 0.01%)	18

Macau in the past years, with focus on economic growth; several examples reflect the positive side of Macau's recent economic situation by employing a series of adjectives and adverbs like *well, rapidly, strong, amazing, harmonious, stable*, and *bright,* as shown in the following examples:

15. Macao's **economy** is doing very well, and the outlook for the next few years is very strong
16. Macao's **economy** "doing very well"; diversification remains crucial
17. Macao's **economy** is doing very well and has made amazing achievements in the past 15 years
18. Citing a rapidly developing **economy**, ever-improving livelihood, and a harmonious and stable society in the region.

In the *SCMPC,* the co-occurrences of *economy* can be mainly categorised into four groups: (1) the act of change: *diversify* (*N* = *9;* 18%); (2) the process of decline: *slowing* (N = 9; 18%), *slump* (N = 6; 12%), and *slowdown* (N = 3; 6%); (3) degree: *reliant* (N = 6; 12%); (4) geographical names: *Macau* (N = 10; 20%) and *mainland* (N = 9; 18%). Examining the above collocates and concordances shows the different use of economy between the *XH&CDC* and the *SCMPC*. The item *economy* in the *SCMPC* not only denotes Macau's economy but also refers to the Mainland Chinese economy. *Slowing* and *slowdown* are primarily used to describe the mainland's economy, e.g., *a general slowdown in the mainland economy* and *slowing mainland economy,* whereas *slump* is used to portray the situation of casinos of Macau, e.g., *a slump in numbers at the casino tables.* That suggests that the *SCMP* has highlighted the slowing mainland economy as one of the factors affecting Macau's gaming industry.

In the *MPDC*, the category of co-occurrence of *economy* can only be classified into 3 groups: (1) the act of change: *diversify* (*N* = *7*; 12.72%); (2) government officials working in the Macau SAR: *the Secretary for Economy and Finance* (N = 15; 27.27%); (3) geographical names: *Macau* (N = 10; 20%). Together with the examples of concordance lines, the findings reveal that the *MPD*, as a regional newspaper of Macau, shows a comprehensive reporting perspective including employment, social responsibility, and livelihoods towards Macau's economy by citing different opinions, ranging from government officials, professionals to the ordinary people, as shown in the following examples 19 to 23.

19. Macau Polytechnic Institute (IPM) Lecturer Leung Kai Yin said that even though the central government has repeatedly been urging Macau to diversify its **economy**, it was unlikely that Macau could achieve this in the near future
20. MEC Chairman Patrick Chui Chuen Man told reporters the main reason why his organisation decided to hold the interview was to convey a message to the public about the importance of economic diversification, arguing that Macau's **economy** will grow when small and medium enterprises grow
21. Several audience members urged the government to come up with more measures to oversee the gaming industry, urging operators to shoulder more social responsibility including doing more to diversify the city's **economy**

22. Choi also said that local labour regulations still need to be improved and local employees' salaries and benefits have not kept up as the **economy** develops
23. Li praised Chui for working hard to develop the local **economy** and improving residents' livelihoods.

I1. Money Generally

Table 5.7 shows the LL value, words' raw and relative frequencies, and the rank in the key semantic field "MONEY GENERALLY" in each corpus.

I1 ranked 6th (N = 292; LL = 223.15) in the *XH&CDC*, 5th (N = 536; LL = 423.17) in the *SCMPC*, and 4th (N = 1277; LL = 1167.04) in the *MPDC*. In terms of this semantic field, the most significant word among the three corpora is the same, *gaming*, which is predictable as the theme pertaining to the gaming industry of Macau (Table 5.7).

In the *XH&CDC*, *gaming* (N = 111; 0.39%) principally co-occurs with *revenue* (N = 50, 44.64%), referring to the financial figures concerning Macau's gaming revenue, and also with *industry* (N = 34; 30.36%), highlighting that Macau is the only legal zone for the gaming industry. Additionally, *gaming* also co-occurs with *growth* (N = 15; 13.19%), including some discussions of further development concerns gaming. In the *SCMPC*, *gaming* (N = 237; 0.48%) mainly co-occurs with *revenue* (N = 79; 33.33%), portraying actual financial figures. The currency unit *dollars* (N = 32), ranked 2nd, refers to the currency of Hong Kong and the U.S.A., and is used to describe gaming revenue. The 2nd top word, *betting* (N = 40; 0.08%), can only be found in the *SCMPC*, mainly connected with illegal gambling-related criminal activities, such as the *illegal World Cup betting scheme*, *illegal soccer betting*, *unlicensed betting websites*, and *illegal betting*, and *money laundering*. Another form, *bets* (N = 17; 0.03%), is also a unique item; similarly, it mainly refers to illicit activities, demonstrating that the reporting angle of the *SCMP* is wider than the other two news article corpora, not only covering reporting financial performance in gaming of Macau, but also including gaming-related activities. Similarly, *Money* (N = 35; 0.07%), ranked 3rd in this semantic field, co-occurs with words concerning gaming-related criminal activities, such as *illegal* (N = 1; 2.86%), *dirty* (N = 3; 8.57%), *criminal* (N = 3; 8.57%), and *illicit* (N = 5; 14.29%). In addition, it also co-occurs with the word *greed* (N = 3; 8.57%), a word carrying negative connotations. By contrast, the word *money* cannot be found in the semantic field of the *XH&CDC*.

In the *MPDC*, the relative frequency of *gaming* (N = 640; 0.63%) is much higher than that in the other two news article corpora. The high frequency of gaming is expected as the MPD is the local news press based on Macau society, where the gaming industry is its pillar industry and the biggest contributor to the government's revenue, and by contrast, the lowest relative frequency of gaming in the *XH&CD* suggests that the topics related to gaming are less mentioned and the Chinese media have weakened the gaming industry of Macau. The next item *money* (N = 70; 0.07%), with the equal relative frequency of that in the *SCMP*. It co-occurs with *account* (N = 9; 12.86%), *lost* (N = 6; 8.57%), and *losing*, portraying the problem gamblers who have lost money and financial fraud made by the owner of junket operators.

Table 5.7 The semantic field I1, "Money Generally"

Semantic field	LL value XH&CDC	Word (raw and relative frequency)	Rank	LL value SCMPC	Word (raw and relative frequency)	Rank	LL value MPDC	Word (raw and relative frequency)	Rank
I1 Money generally	223.15	Gaming (N = 111; 0.39%) Dollars (N = 32; 0.11%) Financial (N = 19; 0.07%) Monetary (N = 10; 0.04%)	6	423.17	Gaming (N = 235; 0.49%) Betting (N = 40; 0.08%) Money (N = 35; 0.07%) Financial (N = 25; 0.05%) Bets (N = 17; 00.4%) Cash (N = 16; 0.03%) Finance (N = 16; 0.03%) Banks (N = 11;0.02%) Bet (N = 11; 0.02%) Liquidity (N = 10; 0.02%) Multibillion-dollar (N = 10; 0.02%) Monetary (N = 10; 0.02%) Cent (N = 10; 0.02%)	5	1167.04	Gaming (N = 640; 0.63%) Money (N = 70; 0.07%) Cash (N = 36; 0.04%) Finance (N = 32; 0.03%) Financial (N = 28; 0.03%) Bank (N = 21; 0.02%) Cheques (N = 20; 0.02%) Gaming sector (N = 19; 0.02%) Sou (N = 14; 0.01%) Cheque (N = 13; 0.01%) Yuan (N = 12; 0.01%) Account (N = 11; 0.01%) Banks (N = 11; 0.01%) Gaming company (N = 10; 0.01%)	4

5.3 Analysis of Shared Key Semantic Fields Between Two Corpora

Z2. Geographical Names

Table 5.8 shows the LL value, words' raw and relative frequencies, and the rank in the key semantic field "GEOGRAPHICAL NAMES" in each corpus.

Z2 is a key shared semantic field between the *XH&CDC* (1st, N = 1319; LL = 1158.29) and the *SCMPC* (2nd; N = 2016; LL = 1371.64), which contains various lexical words with the cut-off point above 10 times (see Table 5.8).

In the *XH&CDC*, the proper noun *Macao* (N = 584; 2.06%) is the most frequent item in this semantic field and its predominant presence is expected as all the news articles in the corpus are based on Macau.

Hong Kong (N = 119; 0.42%), the second most frequent component, indicates that Hong Kong, another special administrative region, is closely related to the news events concerning Macau's gaming. Analysis of the concordance of *Hong Kong* identifies several uses of *Hong Kong*. Firstly, Hong Kong refers to the geographical location and is also the part of the name of organization or institute. The abbreviation of Hong Kong: *HK* (N = 17; 0.06%) co-occurs with *dollar*, signifying the currency of Hong Kong. Another feature is that *Hong Kong* co-occurs with *Macau* (N = 9; 7.56%), indicating that the Chinese Mainland press prefers to report on these two Special Administrative Regions as a unity.

The third most frequent proper noun is *China* (N = 114; 0.42%). Five concordance lines were removed as they are cases where *China* is adopted as one of the corpus sources: *China Daily*. Several concordance lines (N = 12; 10.43%) of *China* are about Macau's handover to China as 2014 marked the fifteenth year of Macau's return of sovereignty to China. Besides, *China* is used in names of a company, namely *Sands China*[1] (N = 11; 9.65%), the US based leading developer, owner and operator of various casinos in Macau. Another form of China: *Chinese* (N = 89; 32%) is ranked 4th, with its concordance lines revealing that *Chinese* co-occurs with *mainland* (N = 24; 25.80%), referring to the PRC. *Chinese* also co-occurs with *dream* (N = 6; 6.74%), suggesting that the Chinese mainland media prefer to incorporate and promote this concept (i.e., Chinese Dream[2]) proposed by the Chinese President Xi Jinping in their news articles.

It is noted that *Patacas* (N = 42) is identified wrongly by the automatic semantic tagger as a geographical name; it actually refers to the local currency of Macau. Besides, the following two places (i.e., *Portuguese* and *Las Vegas*) do not belong to the Great China Region, but they are connected with Macau to some extent. Firstly, *Portuguese* (N = 31; 0.11%), ranked 7th, primarily co-occurs with *speaking* (N = 13; 41.93%), *countries* (N = 12; 38.71%), *cooperation* (N = 10; 32.26%), and *China*

[1] https://www.sandschina.com/the-company/company-information.html.

[2] The "Chinese dream," put forth by Chinese President Xi Jinping, is to build a moderately prosperous society and realize national rejuvenation: http://www.chinadaily.com.cn/china/Chinese-dream.html.

Table 5.8 The semantic field Z2, "Geographical names"

Semantic field	LL value XH&CDC	Word (raw and relative frequency)	Rank	LL value SCMPC	Word (raw and relative frequency)	Rank	LL value MPDC	Word (raw and relative frequency)	Rank
Z2 Geographical names	1158.29	Macao (N = 581; 2.06%) Hong_Kong (N = 119; 0.42%) China (N = 114; 0.40%) Chinese (N = 89; 0.31%) Macaos (N = 54; 0.19%) Patacas (N = 42; 0.15%) Las_Vegas (N = 18; 0.06%) HK (N = 17; 0.06%) Portuguese (N = 15; 0.05%) Kongs (N = 15; 0.05%) Asian (N = 14; 0.05%) Asia (N = 14; 0.05%) Guangdong (N = 11; 0.04%)	1	1371.64	Macau (N = 530; 1.10%) Hong_Kong (N = 277; 0.58%) South_China (N = 196; 0.58%) Macaus (N = 90; 0.17%) China (N = 67; 0.14%) Beijing (N = 56; 0.12%) Chinese (N = 51; 0.11%) Patacas (N = 52; 0.11%) Portuguese (N = 45; 0.09%) Las_Vegas (N = 38; 0.08%) Asia (N = 30; 0.06%) British (N = 21; 0.04%) Asian (N = 17; 0.04%) Singapore (N = 17; 0.04%) Europe (N = 16; 0.03%) Australia (N = 14; 0.03%) HK (N = 14; 0.03%) Kongs (N = 12; 0.02%) Beijings (N = 12; 0.02%) Philippines (N = 12; 0.02%) Malaysian (N = 12; 0.02%) China's (N = 11; 0.02%) Stanley_Ho (N = 11; 0.02%) Japan (N = 10; 0.02%)	2	X	X	X

(N = 11; 35.48%), suggesting that role of Macau is characterized by the *XH&CD* as the service platform for commercial and trade cooperation between China and Portuguese-speaking countries. When it co-occurs with *colony* (N = 2; 13.33%), *enclave* (N = 2; 13.33%), it is used to refer to Macau, providing readers with the background information that Macau has been a Portuguese colony or enclave and the occurrence of *Portuguese* cannot be avoided as Macau has a long historical connection with Portugal as this small-size territory has been under the Portuguese administration for more than 400 years. Secondly, the occurrence of *Las Vegas* (N = 18; 6%), an American city famous for its gaming industry as well, is also not surprising as Macau is often called the "Las Vegas of the East".

In comparison to corresponding components in the Z2 tag of the *XH&CDC*, the *SCMPC* contains wider various items, appearing more than ten times in semantic field. The majority of words is similar to Z2 item in the *XH&CDC*, specific to Great China Region, such as *Macau* (N = 530; 1.10%), *Hong Kong* (N = 277; 0.58%), *HK* (N = 14; 0.03%), *Kong's* (N = 12; 0.02%) *Macau's* (N = 81; 0.17%), *China* (N = 65; 0.14%), *Beijing* (N = 56; 0.12%), *Beijing's* (N = 10; 0.02%), *Patacas* (N = 52; 0.11%), *Chinese* (N = 51; 0.11%), *China's* (N = 11; 0.02%), and *Hengqing island* (N = 10; 0.02%). Some of the above items, such as *Macau, Hong Kong*, and *China*, are not examined in detail as they have been analysed in top 20 lexical words. The item *Beijing* can only be found in the *SCMP*, which is used to denote the Chinese central government rather than the geographical location. A close look at concordance lines of *Beijing* shows that it frequently co-occurs with words and phrases with a negative meaning, such as *crackdown, control, launch, corruption, flow, illicit funds, dirty money, capital flight, money laundry activities, anti-corruption campaign,* and *fraudulent tractions.* This indicates that the *SCMP* has selected some reporting topics in relation to the negative impacts on Macau's gaming industry brought by measures or plans taken by Beijing (i.e., the Chinese Central Government) to combat corruption in Mainland China and the subsequently relevant illegal acts in Macau such as money laundering in the casinos of Macau. Here are some examples extracted from the *SCMP*:

24. **Beijing** launches major crackdown on flow of illicit funds to Macau
25. Watchdog to explain live monitoring of mainland transactions amid **Beijing** promoted crackdown that has seen gaming stocks plunge
26. High-rolling mainland gamblers held back on big-ticket punting since **Beijing** intensifies its crackdown on corruption
27. It is also the latest and clearest sign yet that **Beijing** is serious about stemming the capital flight problem it has with casinos
28. Regulators have called top bankers in Macau to a key meeting next month as part of a **Beijing**-inspired dirty-money crackdown that has rocked the city's under-pressure casino sector and sent gaming stocks tumbling
29. One long-time observer of the Macau gambling industry said that junket operators and casinos had made an effort to cut ties with people targeted in criminal investigations and increasing scrutiny from **Beijing**.

In addition, this key semantic field also covers some geographical places closely related to Macau historically, culturally or economically, such as *Portuguese* (N = 45) and *Las Vegas* (N = 38). The other regions or countries, such as *Asia* (N = 30), *Asian* (N = 17), *British* (N = 21), *Singapore* (N = 17), *Europe* (N = 16), *Australia* (14), *Philippines* (N = 12), *Malaysian* (N = 12), and *Japan* (N = 10), are also included in the news coverage.

G2.1. Law and Order

Table 5.9 presents the LL value, the raw and relative frequencies of the words, and the ranking in the key semantic field "LAW AND ORDER" in each corpus.

G2.1 only appears in the *SCMPC* (6th; N = 418; LL = 394.85) and the *MPDC* (10th; N = 699; LL = 460.21). As shown in Table 5.9, this key semantic field in the *SCMPC* contains a wide variety of lexical items, including *law* (N = 55; 0.11%), *anti-corruption* (N = 42; 0.09%), *security* (N = 35; 0.07%), *police* (N = 34; 0.07%), *court* (N = 14;0.03%), *prosecutors* (N = 13; 0.03%), *arrested* (N = 13; 0.02%), *lawyer* (N = 12; 0.02%), *arrest* (N = 11; 0.02%) and *legal* (N = 10; 0.02%). Specifically, investigating the concordance lines of *law* reveals that the most frequent co-occurrences is the phrase *Basic Law*[3] (N = 27; 49.09%). This suggests that this legal term is overused in the *SCMPC*. According to the finding in the previous analysis, the *SCMP* tends to emphasise the large differences between the Hong Kong SAR and the Macau SAR. The version of *Basic Law* of Hong Kong differs from that of Macau. Here are more examples that indicate that the *SCMP* repeatedly underlines the diversity of Basic Law between these two territories.

Specifically, examples 30 and 31 demonstrate that the *SCMP* cites the comments made by the high-ranking official Li from the central government. An iconic comparison in terms of practicing the Basic Law between Hong Kong and Macau is found. Residents in Macau, who do not like the Basic Law, are considered "rats" in the street, that will be despised, indicating that the speaker aims to emphasise that Macau is a good role model for adhering to, supporting and promoting the Basic Law, as shown in examples 32, 33, and 34. The SCMP interpreted these comments as a warning message from the Chinese authorities to Hong Kong. Contrary to "Macau's good performance", Hong Kong is situated amid the political storm, as shown in examples 33 and 35. Besides, example 30 shows the *SCMP's* concern on Macau's unfavourable political situation by using adverbs *regrettably* and *unfortunately* to show the regret that universal suffrage is not mentioned in the Basic Law of Macau.

30. Regrettably, our neighbours still have to put up with uncontested polls. Their desire for democracy can be found in a mock referendum in which about 95% of 8,688 citizens voted in favour of universal suffrage in 2019. Unfortunately, the Macau **Basic Law** does not make universal suffrage the final goal. Unfortunately, the Macau Basic Law does not make universal suffrage the final goal
31. One example was Macau's executive-led government, working hand in hand with the legislature. "The whole community adheres to, supports, learns and

[3] The Basic Law is a national law for the administration of the Macau SAR.

Table 5.9 The semantic field G2.1, "Law and order"

Semantic field	LL value XH&CDC	Word (raw and relative frequency)	Rank	LL value SCMPC	Word (raw and relative frequency)	Rank	LL value MPDC	Word (raw and relative frequency)	Rank
G2.1 Law and order	X	X	X	394.85	Law (N = 62; 0.12%) Anti-corruption (N = 42; 0.08%) Security (N = 35; 0.07%) Police (N = 35; 0.07%) Court (N = 14;0.03%) Prosecutors (N = 13; 0.03%) Arrested (N = 13; 0.03%) Lawyer (N = 12; 0.02%) Arrest (N = 11; 0.02%) Legal (N = 10; 0.02%)	6	460.21	Police (N = 161; 0.16%) Law (N = 97; 0.10%) Legislative (N = 39; 0.04%) Judiciary (N = 36; 0.04%) Security (N = 36; 0.04%) Arrested (N = 27; 0.03%) By-law (N = 25; 0.02%) Prosecution (N = 24; 0.02%) Legal (N = 20; 0.02%) Regulations (N = 18; 0.02%) Statutory (N = 17; 0.02%) Court (N = 16; 0.02%) Loophole (N = 14; 0.01%) Inspectors (N = 12; 0.01%) Arraignment (N = 11; 0.01%) Legislation (N = 11; 0.01%)	10

promotes the **Basic Law**," he said. Li's words on Macau contrasted with Chief Executive Leung Chun-ying's view of Occupy student protesters in Hong Kong, whom he said betrayed their lack of familiarity with the city's **Basic Law** in pressing for Beijing's withdrawal of conditions on the 2017 vote for Leung's successor

32. Macau help up as role model for **Basic Law**
33. Li said Macau was a place where "anyone who says the **Basic Law** is not good will be [as despised as] a rat on the street". "People in Macau thank the central government and thank the **Basic Law**"
34. Macau-based observer Larry So Man-yum saw Li's remarks as related to Occupy. "He has delivered a very clear message for Macau's youngsters, telling them not to do anything that departs from the Basic Law, like what is happening in Hong Kong
35. Earlier this month, Beijing official Li Gang described Macau as a place where if you don't like the **Basic Law** you will be "despised like a rat on the street". That seemed to sum up in succinct—if rather salty—terms the stark contrast between the body politic of the former Portuguese enclave and that of Hong Kong
36. All three spoke ahead of the former Portuguese enclave's 15th handover anniversary next week? and amid Hong Kong's political storm that is into its 10th week. "Throughout the past 15 years, 'one country, two systems' and the **Basic Law** has been implemented comprehensively in Macau," Li Gang, formerly deputy director of Beijing's liaison office in Hong Kong.

The lexical word *anti-corruption* collocates with *drive* (N = 21; 50%), *campaign* (N = 12; 28.57%), and *Xi* (N = 6; 14.29%), co-occurring with words and phrases with a negative meaning, like *pressure, worse, slowing, collapse, throttle, squeezed, warning, at risk, dampening, bite,* and *blow*. A closer concordance analysis reveals that the *SCMP* frequently mentions the side effects on Macau's casino-led economy brought by the Chinese President Xi Jinping's nationwide "tigers and flies" anti-corruption campaign,[4] which has also reaffirmed the findings of the above, namely, the *SCMP* tends to report on Macau's gaming industry from a negative perspective.

In comparison to the *SCMPC*, the semantic tag G2.1 in the *MPDC* includes a wider range of lexical words above 10 times than corresponding items in the *SCMPC*, including *Police* (N = 161; 0.16%), *law* (N = 97; 0.10%), *legislative* (N = 39; 0.04%), *judiciary* (N = 36; 0.04%), *security* (N = 36; 0.04%), *arrested* (N = 27; 0.04%), *by-law* (N = 27; 0.02%), *prosecution* (N = 24; 0.02%), *legal* (N = 20; 0.02%), and *statutory* (N = 17; 0.02%). Concordance analysis of *police* reveals that the word is mainly used as part of the name of local Macau's government organizations: *Public Security Police* (PSP) and *The Judiciary Police* (PJ). The word *police* also refers to Macau's local police. In comparison to *police* (4th rank) in the *SCMPC*, its reference is different, primarily denoting the Hong Kong Police. Besides, *law*, ranked 2nd in the

[4] "Tigers and Flies" Anti-corruption Campaign refers to a high-profile and large-scale national campaign targeting party, government, military and state-owned company officials suspected of corruption launched in 2012.

MPDC, primarily refers to Macau's regional law, rather than the national Basic Law in the *SCMP*. *Law* co-occurs with *smoking* (N = 23; 23.71%) and *tobacco-control* (N = 12; 12.37), revolving around a series of discussions on the amendment of smoking laws and tobacco-control regulations in the casinos of Macau. *Law* also co-occurs with phrases to do with occupation, such as *occupational safety*, *occupational disease*, and *employees' salaries*, referring to the Labour Relations Law of Macau. This indicates that Macau's local press is more concerned about the social impact of the gaming industry. In comparison to the predominant occurrence of *Basic Law* in the *SCMPC*, only two instances of *Law* refer to the *Basic Law,* only constituting 2.06%, implying that the use of *Law* differs between these two news article corpora: the *MPC* seems to deemphasise it and, by contrast, relevant topics related to the Basic Law are the key concerns in the *SCMPC*.

M7. Places

Table 5.10 shows the LL value, words' raw and relative frequencies, and the rank in the key semantic field "PLACES" in each corpus.

The key semantic field "M7, PLACES" is shared between the *XH&CDC* (4th; N = 471; LL = 338.27) and the *MPDC* (20th; N = 1121; LL = 296.41) (Table 5.10). In terms of M7 tag in the *XH&CDC*, *region* (N = 75; 0.26%), ranked 1st, mainly co-occurs with *special* (N = 28; 34.21%) at the N-2 position to denote Macau as a Special Administrative Region with an emphasis on its administrative status, namely Macau SAR being a part of the PRC. The next item *city* (N = 48; 0.17%) is mainly used to refer to Macau, with concordance analysis showing that the Chinses press is likely to represent a positive image about Macau as *special* co-occurs with words and phrases with a positive meaning, such as *charm, beautiful, progressing, prosperous,* and *good.* Besides, *city* is also used to refer to Hong Kong. The next item, *motherland* (N = 39; 0.14%) is used to refer to China. The exclusive use of *motherland* in the *XH&CDC* denotes that the Chinese mainland press emphasises the bond between China and Macau. *Motherland* co-occurs with *return* (N = 14; 35.89%) and *returned* (N = 7; 17.95%), implying that the Chinese mainland news articles focus on reporting Macau's return to China with the implication of patriotism and the close link between Macau and China, just like the mother and son's reunion. Besides, the recurrence of the phrase *loving motherland and loving Macao* (N = 4; 10.26%) indicates that the Chinese mainland press is conveying a value to the audience that loving the motherland is essential.

Besides, the word *motherland* is found to co-occur with phrases and clauses with a positive meaning related to achievements. Examples are *Macau has written a successful economic story*, *Macau SAR has constantly improved its governance system*, *remarkable achievements*, *fastest-growing period*, *great progress and achievements*, *rapid progress*, *more prosperous*, *changed dramatically*, *successful*, *dynamic*, *remarkable*, *more advantages*, *more development opportunities*, *quickly*, and *changed very much*, and *promising path.* The different forms of co-selection imply that the *XH&CDC* tends to emphasise the positive influence of China by presenting the achievements that Macau has made after its handover to the Chinese sovereignty since 1999 and holds a very optimistic attitude towards the present and

Table 5.10 The key semantic field M7, "Places"

Semantic field	LL value XH&CDC	Word (raw and relative frequency)	Rank	LL value SCMPC	Word (raw and relative frequency)	Rank	LL value MPDC	Word (raw and relative frequency)	Rank
M7 PLACES	333.82	Region (N = 75; 0.26%) City (N = 48; 0.17%) Motherland (N = 39; 0.14%) Local (N = 33; 0.12%) International (N = 31; 0.11%) Countries (N = 21; 0.07%) Regional (N = 17; 0.06%) Citys (N = 15; 0.05%) National (N = 14; 0.05%) Areas (N = 13; 0.05%) Area (N = 12; 0.04%) Place (N = 11; 0.04%) Province (N = 10; 0.04%)	4	X	X	X	296.41	Local (N = 340; 0.34%) Citys (N = 172; 0.17%) Venues (N = 94; 0.09%) Areas (N = 91; 0.09%) City (N = 79; 0.08%) Area (N = 49; 0.05%) International (N = 38; 0.04%) Place (N = 19; 0.02%) Campus (N = 18; 0.02%) Countries (N = 16; 0.02%) Cities (N = 13; 0.01%) Abroad (N = 12; 0.01%) Checkpoint (N = 11; 0.01%) Places (N = 11; 0.01%)	20

future development of Macau. The use of *motherland* specifically serves the purpose of appealing to Macau's sense of identity and belonging with the motherland (i.e., Mainland China), as evidenced by co-selected phrases to do with patriotic feelings, such as *sense of identity and belonging, close national bond*, the use of metaphor *blood being thicker than water, love for motherland and love for Macao, the fine tradition of loving the motherland, national pride, make contribution*, and *make special emphasis on Love.* Besides, *motherland* co-selects with words and phrases, such as *growing sense, ever strong, prevalent value, stronger, profound, stronger sense of national pride, better future*, and *deeper love*, emphasizing that Macau's citizens have increasingly strong patriotic feelings, such as the sense of belonging and identity and the national pride towards their motherland.

In the *MPDC*, by contrast, the most frequent word in the "PLACE" semantic field is *local* (N = 340; 0.34%), mainly co-occurring with *government* (N = 49; 12.56%), *gaming* (N = 45; 13.24%), *industry* (N = 27; 7.94%), *casinos* (N = 22; 6.47%), and *residents* (N = 20; 5.88%). The next item *city's* (N = 172; 0.17%) co-occurs with *gaming* (N = 78; 45.35%), *government* (N = 43; 25%), *smoking* (N = 35; 20.35%), *housing* (N = 29; 16.86%), and *operators* (N = 26; 15.12%). When considering these two words, it indicates that the news coverage in the *MPDC* pays attention to a wide range of local issues, from the government policy, gaming operators, the lives of its citizens, to housing problems.

Q 1.3. Telecommunication

Table 5.11 shows the LL value, words' raw and relative frequencies, and the rank in the key semantic field "TELECOMMUNICATION" in each corpus.

The key semantic tag Q1.3 is shared by the *SCMPC* (11th; N = 120; LL = 199.22) and the *MPDC* (9th; N = 282; LL = 477.33). In this key semantic filed 'TELECOMMUNICATION' of two corpora, the most significant item is the same, i.e., *operator*, as shown in Table 5.11.

In addition, the tag Q1.3 in the *MPDC* includes more word types compared to those in the *SCMPC* and this tag cannot be found in the top 20 key semantic fields in the *XH&CDC*, showing the item *operator* is not significantly overused in comparison to the other two corpora, suggesting the *XH&CD* tends to play down Macau's gaming industry, which also confirms to the above analysis. It is noted that *Operator* here is mistakenly tagged by the USUA tagged in the Wmatrix.

Concordance analysis shows that the word *operators* (N = 71; 0.15%) contains two meanings in the context of the *SCMP* concerning Macau's gaming industry in 2014. When it co-occurs with *casino* (N = 21; 29.58%), *gaming* (N = 4; 5.63%) or *gambling* (N = 5; 7.04%), it refers to the company that does a particular type of business. It also co-occurs with *junket* at the N-1 position, denoting the particular group of people *VIP junket operators* (i.e., VIP room promoters), who traditionally acted as a middle man to facilitate the gaming industry in Macau by bringing rich Chinese people to Macau and providing the credit lines necessary to circumvent currency controls. *Junket operator* is exclusively used in the context of Macau, rather than referring to someone who helps to connect people on a phone system. Thus, this word does not belong to the semantic field of "TELECOMMUNICATION". Concordances

Table 5.11 The semantic field Q1.3, "Telecommunication"

Semantic field	LL value XH&CDC	Word (raw and relative frequency)	Rank	LL value SCMPC	Word (raw and relative frequency)	Rank	LL value MPDC	Word (raw and relative frequency)	Rank
Q1.3 TELECOMNUICATION	X	X	X	199.22	Operators (N = 71; 0.15%) Operators (N = 35; 0.07%)	11	477.33	Operators (N = 162; 0.16%) Operators (N = 53; 0.05%) Phone (N = 23; 0.02%) Email (N = 15; 0.01%)	9

examination reveals that the lexical item *junket operator* has the semantic prosody of illegitimacy in the *SCMP*. The business of casino junket operator in Macau has been greatly impacted by the Chinese anti-corruption campaign and their target customers are always the VIP clients such as high-ranking officials from Chinese Mainland.

In the *MPDC*, *operators* (N = 162; 0.16%) mainly co-occurs with *gaming* (N = 125; 77.16%), signifying the gaming companies in Macau. By contrast, it only rarely co-occurs with *junket* (N = 4, 2.47%), signifying that this particular occupation *junket operator* is rarely mentioned in the *MPDC*. Likewise, its singular form *operator* co-occurs with *gaming* (N = 24; 45.28%) at the N-1 position, referring to the gaming companies based in Macau.

Z99. Unmatched

It is noted that the *SCMPC* is the only corpus, containing Z99 tag in the top-twenty key semantic tags, ranked by LL value, indicating that the corpus comprises a large number of items which cannot be recognized by the USAS tagger and in this case, many items specific to the context of Macau, such as people's surnames including *Chui* (N = 67; 0.14%) and *Cheung* (N = 23; 0.05%), company's names including *SJM*[5] (N = 51; 0.11%), *Wynn* (N = 29; 0.06%), and *UnionPay*[6] (N = 13; 0.03%), and also Macau's local place names including *Cotai* (N = 27; 0.06%), referring to the reclaimed area with many casino complexes. In addition, the footnote of News articles (i.e., *scmp. comscmcom*) cannot be identified by Wmatrix (Rayson, 2008). Another item, *anti-graft* (N = 13), which indicates the anti-corruption campaign mentioned before in the G1.2 semantic field cannot be identified either. In the *MPDC*, Z99 is also in the top 20 semantic fields.

Q2.1. Speech: Communicative

The key semantic field 'SPEECH: COMMUNICATIVE' is shared among three corpora, ranked the 2nd in the top 20 key semantic field list of the *MPDC* (Table 3.1), whereas the ranking of its corresponding semantic field in the remaining two corpora is relative low, 19th in the *XH&CDC* and 18th in the *SCMPC*, indicating the tag is significantly overused in the *MPDC*. This semantic field contains various word types. *Said* (N = 987), ranked 1st, shows the reporting style of the *MPDC* is unique when compared with the other two corpora, as it adopts a large number of quotation-related expressions in their news articles. Specifically, it co-occurs with *government* (N = 90; 9.11%) as its most frequent lexical collocate. Concordance analysis shows that Macau's local press tends to quote different people's utterances

[5] SJM refers to the Sociedade de Jogos de Macau S.A. ("SJM") which is one of the six companies authorized to operate casino games of fortune and other games of chance in casinos, under the terms of a concession granted by the government of the Macau Special Administrative Region in March 2002. SJM is the only casino gaming concessionaire with its roots in Macau.

[6] UnionPay is a bankcard association established under the approval of the State Council and the People's Bank of China.

concerning Macau's government. Moreover, *said* also co-occurs with *Chui* (N = 52; 5.16%), who is the current Macau's Chief Executive Fernando Chui Sai On, indicating that local newspaper the *MPD* prefers to adopt quotation of his views and regards him as the spokesman of Macau's government to present the government's latest policies and news. This reporting style is quite prevalent as citing the speech of powerful figures or celebrities is an important factor in gaining news value (Harcup & O'Neil, 2001). Furthermore, *said* co-occurs with *spokesman* (N = 44; 4.45%), which mainly refers to the spokesman of the Macao SAR's Judiciary Police (PJ), who primarily reports the crime process of investigations. *Said* also co-occurs with *Gaming* (N = 147; 14.89%) and *Government* (N = 145; 14.69%), indicating that quotation is the preferred way by the local media to report the news related to government and gaming.

T1.3. Time: Period

This T1.3 key semantic field is ranked 4th of the top 20 key semantic field list. The high presence of this field may be attributed by the relative high frequency of dates in its news articles, where the most predominant item is *morning* (N = 219) and the detailed examination of concordances reveals that it is mainly used as the part of corpus news source: *South China Morning Post* instead of referring to a certain time of a day.

5.4 Uniqueness in Topical Concerns Among Three Territories of the PRC: Analysis of Unique Key Semantic Fields

In the *XH&CDC*, 8 out of 20 semantic fields are unique. The following part shows the detailed analysis of these unique key semantic fields.

N3.2+ SIZE: BIG

As shown in Table 5.1, the key semantic tag: N3.2+ SIZE: BIG is unique in the *XH&CDC* (7th; N = 165; LL = 171.330), indicating that this key semantic tag is excessively used compared with the *SCMPC* and the *MPDC*. Specifically, the keyness of N3.2+ can predominantly be related to an extremely frequent lexical item: *Growth* (N = 91; 0.32%), which is also identified as the top 20 lexical word as well and followed by its other form *growing* (N = 15; 0.05%). *Growth* co-occurs with *economic* (N = 19; 20.87%) and *economy* (N = 10; 10.99%), indicating that Macau's economic growth is repeatedly and overly presented in the news articles of the *XH&CDC*, with its concordance lines revealing that the *XH&CDC* seems to display that Macau had been in a very good economic state since its sovereignty return to China in 1999. *Growing* primarily refers to the fast-growing period in example 36, growing sense of identity and belonging in example 37.

37. Uniting under the flag of Love Nation and Love Macao, the city has experienced fastest **growing** period in its history, including a rapidly developing economy,
38. Macao compatriots have gained a **growing** sense of identity and belonging with the motherland.

I 1.3-. Cheap

The tag I1.3- is a unique semantic field in the *XH&CDC* (8th; N = 111; LL = 166.28), where the most significant word is *economic* (N = 106; 0.38%). Concordance analysis shows several uses of *economic*. Primarily, 40.56% is used to portray Macau's economic development, 16.98% economic cooperation, 16.03% Macau's economic growth, and 10.37% about t Macau's economic diversification acceleration.

A 2.1+. Change

Another semantic tag is A2.1+ CHANGE (9th; N = 277; LL = 157.45) in the top 20 key semantic list of the *XH&CDC*. It is a unique semantic field in the *XH&CDC*, suggesting that the related words tagged as A2.1+ are overused compared to the reference corpus. Specifically, the A2.1+ contains six lexical items above the minimum frequency of 10; they are *development* (N = 130; 0.46%), *become* (N = 22; 0.08%), *develop* (N = 16; 0.06%), *developing* (N = 14; 0.05%), *reform* (N = 10; 0.04%) and *adjustment* (N = 10; 0.04%).

Concordance analysis shows that the use of *development* expresses different meanings and functions. It mainly co-occurs with *economic* (N = 46; 35.38%), reporting on Macau's economic development. Particularly, the bigram *economic development* co-occurs with adjectives containing a positive meaning, such as *leapfrog, sustainable, stable, smooth, rapid* and *sound* at the N-1 position, describing Macau's promising economic prospects. It also co-occurs with *cooperation* (N = 24; 18.46%), *mainland* (N = 16; 12.30%) and *government* (N = 12; 9.23%), denoting that the *XH&CD* highlights Macau's development benefits from the support from the Chinese Central Government and stresses the common mutual development through strengthening the cooperation between Chinese Mainland and Macau. Finally, *development* co-occurs with *sustainable* (N = 13; 10%), *diversified* (N = 13; 10%) and *new* (N = 11; 8.46%), showing that the use of *development* is related to Macau's future development directions and tendencies.

The second most frequent item is *become*, suggesting that the *XH&CD* highlights Macau's successful transformation over the past 15 years since its reunification to China, from the former Portuguese colony to become *big economy, world's top gaming destination, tourism destination, more prosperous,* and *important tourism resources.* In addition, the *XH&CD* specifically cites the Chinese President Xi Jinping's comment, as shown in example 38, to emphasise the patriotism of people in Macau concerning *the love for the motherland and love for Macao.*

39. President Xi Jinping made special emphasis on Love for the motherland and love for Macao have **become** a prevalent value in Macao society.

The next lexical item *develop* co-occurs with *tourism* (N = 4; 25%), *non-gambling element* (N = 3; 18.75%), and *travel products* (N = 1; 6.25%), together with its adjective form *developing* which primarily co-occurs with *tourism* (N = 7; 50%) and *cultural creativity* (N = 6; 42.86%), displaying Macau's future development plans. The plans involve developing other industries, such as tourism industry and culture creativity industry, that guide Macau's future development orientation and priority, rather than its gaming industry. In addition, *adjustment* co-occurs with *economic* (N = 7; 70%), relating Macau's adjustment of the economic structure with change; specifically, Macau's current casino-dominated economic structure needs to be adjusted. It is noted that the related topics concerning the development of Macau's gaming industry are seldom mentioned in the *XH&CDC.*

W3. Geographical Terms 13th

W3 is the unique semantic field (13th; N = 220; LL = 100.78) in the *XH&CDC* (See 5.2), and in which, the most significant component is *Mainland* (N = 111; 0.39%), refers to the Chinese Mainland, which predominantly co-occurs with *Macao* (N = 46; 41.44%) and the frequent co-occurrence of these two geographical locations indicates that the *XH&CD* underlines the close contact between Chinese mainland and Macau.

I4. Industry

I4 (12th; N = 85; LL = 112.46) is over represented in the *XH&CDC*, compared to the reference corpus BNC Sampler written. The most frequent item is the *gaming industry* (N = 25; 0.09%), which co-occurs with *new, nurture, supervision, regulation, strengthen, adjustment, and improve,* suggesting that the *XH&CDC* repeatedly underlines that the gaming industry of Macau is under stricter regulations and that Macau needs to develop new growth areas for the economy of Macau. Concordance analysis shows that the *XH&CD* specifically cites different opinions, ranging from the high-ranking officials from the Chinese authority, the government of Macau, casino operators to the local citizens in order to emphasise that Macau's gaming-led economy is not good for Macau and it needs adjustment as shown in the following examples:

40. Macao needs to solve difficult problems in its development, strengthen and improve regulation and supervision over the **gaming industry** and nurture new growth areas for its economy, according to Xi. (Chinese President Xi Jinping)
41. Li Gang, director of the Liaison Office of the central government in Macao, said the heavy reliance on one **industry** is not good for Macao. (Chinese high ranking official)
42. Macau Casinos shouldered hefty pressure as a senior Chinese official said the dominance of **gaming industry is** not good for the overall interests of Macau. (Chinese high ranking official)
43. Aware of the complaints that the booming **gaming industry** is killing the history of the region and overcrowding the city, the restaurateur, who arrived in 1978,

said the unusual marriage of an ancient Eastern culture with that of the West has always been Macao's most valuable trait. (Local citizen of Macau)

44. Although the gaming revenue in Macao has decreased in recent months, we still believe this is a healthy adjustment because any single industry cannot maintain rapid growth. The **gaming industry** has already experienced explosive growth in the past 10 years, so the slight adjustment is healthy. (Vice president of public relations from Macao's Galaxy Entertainment Group)
45. To make adjustments to attract visitors to stay in the city, which would have positive influences for the gambling-dependent **industry**, he said.

The next items are *Industry* (N = 18; 0.06%), *industries* (N = 10; 0.04%), and *tourism industry* (N = 8; 0.03%). The singular form *industry* is specifically used to refer to the Macau's gaming industry. *Industries* co-occurs with *cultural creativity* (N = 4; 40%), *developing* (N = 3; 30%), *cultivate* (N = 1; 10%) and *foster* (N = 1; 10%), implying that the *XH&CD* expresses their concerns on the development of industries other than the gaming industry.

S8+. Helping 14th

As shown from Table 5.5, the *XH&CDC* is the only corpus containing S8+, HELPING (14th; N = 240; LL = 80.39). In this key semantic field, there are six items whose frequencies are above 10 times. They are *cooperation* (N = 36; 0.13%), *support* (N = 24; 0.08%), *help* (N = 18; 0.06%), *promote* (N = 17; 0.06%), *service* (N = 17; 0.06%), and *services* (N = 10; 0.04%).

Cooperation is the most frequent word and it co-occurs with words related to business activities, such as *trade* (N = 10; 27.78%) and *economic* (N = 11; 30; 56%), representing 58.33%. This shows that the Chinese government wants to help Macau deepen the economic and trade cooperation between Chinese Mainland. The next most frequent lexical item is *support* and its most frequent lexical collocate is *central* (N = 12; 52.17%). Its recurrence in the news article indicates a positive outcome that Macau has obtained in the past 15 years since its handover to China, supported by the Central Government in recent years. *Promote* is ranked 4th. Concordance analysis suggests it refers to the promotion of Macau's social and economic development, the promotion of future economic diversification of Macau, and the promotion of Macau's tourism industry. However, the news article does not seem to show any clues concerning the promotion of the gaming industry of Macau and this proves that gaming industry of Macau has been weakened.

A6.1. Comparing: Similar/Different

A6.1 ranked 18th, is identified as the unique semantic field compared to the other two individual news article corpora and in which, *compared* (N = 20) is the only word, used to compare figures, displaying that the particular writing style of the *XH&CDC*.

Unique Key Semantic fields: Hong Kong (*SCMP*)

In the *SCMPC*, 7 out of 20 key semantic fields are identified as the unique semantic fields, which do not occur in the other two individual corpora. The following part is a detailed analysis of them.

G2.1-. Crime

The key semantic tag G2.1- is exclusively found in the *SCMPC* (9th, N = 165; LL = 270.79) as shown in Table 5.1, showing that corresponding words related to the illegal activities are overrepresented in the news coverage of the *SCMP* and specifically, in the semantic field, the most frequent item is *illegal* (N = 33; 0.07%) and the following items are *organized crime* (N = 23, 0.05%), *illicit* (N = 19; 0.04%), *criminal* (N = 16; 0.03%), and *crimes* (N = 10; 0.02%), whose frequency is above 10 times. *Illegal* co-occurs with business activities or participants specific to gaming, such as *bookmaking* (N = 9; 27.27%), *bookmaker* (N = 2; 6%), *online gaming sites* (N = 3; 9.1%), and *betting* (N = 2; 6%), referring to the local illegal betting syndicate, especially during the World Cup matches. *Illicit* primarily co-occurs with words such as *funds* (N = 14; 73.68%) and *money* (N = 5; 26.32%) at N + 1 position, with the concordance lines revealing that some controlling measures have been adopted by the Chinese authorities to curb the flow of illicit funds transfer to casinos in Macau.

I1.1. Money and Pay

The *SCMPC* is the only dataset containing another key semantic tag I1.1 (10th, N = 372; LL = 256.64) specific to the "MONEY" area, showing that the *SCMP* gives more attention to the financial aspect compared to the other two corpora. This semantic filed includes numerous lexical words *capital* (N = 28; 0.06%), *investment* (N = 27; 0.05%), *earnings* (N = 19;0.0 4%), *funds* (N = 18; 0.04%), *wages* (N = 17; 0.03%), *tax* (N = 15; 0.03%), *credit* (N = 13; 0.03%), *profit* (N = 13; 0.03%), *payment* (N = 12; 0.02%), *investors* (N = 11; 0.02%), *premium* (N = 11; 0.02%), *wage* (N = 10; 0.02%) and *profits* (N = 10; 0.02%). The most significant word *capital* co-occurs with *stemming* (N = 2; 7.14%), *stringent* (N = 2; 7.14), *conduit* (N = 4; 14.29%), *flight* (N = 6; 21.43%) and it is mostly used to refer the Chinese mainland economic situation and specifically, primarily denoting that the Chinese central government has adopted the stringent measure to control capital flight problem as Macau casinos are always regarded as a major conduit for a large amount of money sent out from Chinese mainland.

Y2. Information Technology and Computing

Y2 (13th; N = 183; LL = 158.72) is the unique semantic tag in the *SCMPC* and in which, *online* (N = 45; 0.09%) is the word tagged Y2 with the largest number, primarily co-occurring with words in connection with the risk money, such as *gaming* (N = 9; 20%), *gambling* (N = 12; 22.22%) and *betting* (N = 18; 40%). Following words are *analysts* (N = 33; 0.077%), *analyst* (N = 27; 0.05%), *websites* (N = 27; 0.06%) and *basic* (N = 21; 0.04%). The lexical word, *websites* is ranked 4th, similar to *online*. It co-occurs with *betting* (N = 12; 44.44%), and *gambling* (N = 8; 29.63%), demonstrating that themes and topics related to online gaming or betting are overrepresented in the news articles of the *SCMP*. It is noted that the word *basic* is mistakenly tagged by Wmatrix (Rayson, 2008). Instead, it exclusively co-occurs with *law* (N = 26; 100%), referring to the *Basic Law* of the Macao SAR.

N5-1. Quantities: Little

As shown in Table 5.5.1, N5- (15th, N = 266; LL = 135.43) is the unique key semantic tag in the top 20 list of the *SCMPC* in comparison to the other two corpora, in which the frequency of three items, such as *limited* (N = 153; 0.31%), *decline* (N = 42; 0.09%) and *declined* (N = 10; 0.02%), is above 10. *Limited* refers to *South China Morning Post limited* and this proper name is not examined. The next item *decline* co-occurs with *revenue* (N = 21; 50%) *and record* (N = 14; 33.33%), reflecting that the financial situation of Macau's gaming is the focus for the *SCMP*. Detailed concordance analysis shows that the topics and themes regarding the decline of Macau's casino revenue are found to be salient in the *SCMPC*. By contrast, the antonym of decline *growth* is tagged as overly presented in the *XH&CDC*, indicating Macau's economic growth, whilst the item *decline* appears saliently in the *SCMPC*, demonstrating that the reporting angles of the news coverage regarding Macau's gaming industry between the *XH&CDC* and the *SCMPC* are quite divergent.

Q1.2. Paper Document and Writing

The most significant word in this unique semantic field is *post* (N = 195; 0.39%), referring to the notice of copyright of the target source *South China Morning Post*. The second most frequent item is *document* (N = 22; 0.04%). Thus, this semantic field is not examined due to its significance reason.

I3.2. Work and Employment Professionalism

The semantic tag I3.2 (20th; N = 39; LL = 120.68) is unique in the *SCMPC* and in which, only two items namely *secretary* (N = 20; 0.04%) and *secretaries* (N = 12; 0.02%) are above 10. Specially, *secretary* in this context primarily refers to the Macau local government department *Secretary for Economy and Finance* (N = 14; 70%) instead of the actual occupation displaying the reporting focus related to the economic and financial affair of Macau.

Unique Key Semantic Tags: Macau (*MPD*)

In the *MPDC*, 6 out of 20 semantic fields are unique, which do not occur in the other two individual corpora. The following part shows a detailed analysis towards these unique categories.

I3.1. Work and Employment: Generally

I3.1 is a unique semantic field (5th; N = 1110; L = 885.94), which is not shared in the other two news article corpus (i.e., *SCMPC* and *XH&CDC*) indicating the *MPD* is likely to place the reporting focus on people's livelihood in terms of work and employment. Specifically, the salient components in I3.1 semantic field are varied, containing *employees* (N = 249; 0.25%), *workers* (N = 175; 0.17%), *staff* (N = 124; 0.12%), *working* (N = 116; 0.11%), *and work* (N = 104; 0.10%). Concordance examination reveals that *employees* co-occurs with *gaming* (N = 76; 30.52%), mainly referring to employees working in the gaming sectors of Macau and as the part of the local organization's name, as in *Gaming Employees Club*, *Gaming Employees Home*, and *Gaming Employees Association*. The next item *workers* is found to collocate with *gaming* (N = 53; 30.29%) and *casinos* (N = 47; 26.86%), referring to people who work in the gaming sector. In addition, the word *workers* also co-occurs with *construction* (N = 20; 11.43%), reflecting that the *MPD* draws attention to labour and employment in Macau. Besides, *worker* (N = 26; 14.86%) is used as the part of the organization's name called *Macau Gaming Industry Frontline Workers*. As for the followed item *staff*, it co-occurs with *Sands*[7] (N = 24; 19.35%), referring to the staff working in the Sands company.

F3. Smoking and Non-Medical Drugs

This key semantic field F3 is also unique (6th; N = 249; LL = 703.70) in the top 20 key semantic fields of the *MPDC*. Specifically, the most predominant item is *smoking* (N = 207; 0.20%). Specifically, it co-occurs with *gaming* (N = 86; 41.54%), *rooms* (N = 58; 28.02%), *areas* (N = 57; 27.54%), *ban* (N = 57; 27.54%), and *casinos* (N = 46; 22.22%), with the concordance of *smoking* revealing that the smoke ban has been frequently discussed by Macau's local media, mainly revolving around discussion on the implementation of new smoking ban regulation in Macau's casinos, including the need for setting up smoking rooms or areas in casinos.

S5+. Belonging a Group

The key semantic tag S5+ (8th; N = 1306; LL = 530.99) can only be found in the *MPDC*. In this key semantic field, the most predominant item is *public* (N = 181; 24%), primarily co-occurring with *housing* (N = 26; 14.36%), referring to the government's public housing programme, demonstrating that housing supply is a matter of concern for the *MPD*. The word *public* is also used as part of Macau's local official organization or institution, such as *Public Prosecution Office* and *Public Security Police*.

T1.1.1. Time: Past

T1.1.1(12th; N = 696; LL = 402.57) cannot be found in the other two news article corpora and in this key semantic field, it contains various time spots in the past, namely *yesterday* (N = 317; 0.31%), *last year* (N = 125; 0.12%), *yesterday's* (N = 49; 0.05%), *last month* (N = 39; 0.04%), *last week* (N = 30; 0.03%), *already* (N = 19; 0.02%), *last night* (N = 15; 0.01%), *past* (N = 11; 0.01%), and *history* (N = 10; 0.01%). *Yesterday* co-occurs with *gaming* (N = 62; 19.56%), *government* (N = 48; 15.14%), *Staff* (N = 36; 11.36%), *announcement* (N = 26; 8.20%), *Bureau* (N = 25; 7.89%), *Police* (N = 24; 7.58%) and *casino* (N = 23; 7.26%), indicating the coverage contents, including gaming and casinos, government announcement and related message conveyed by the police, are quite extensive. The next item *last year* primarily co-occurs with words used to describe the financial revenues concerning

[7] Sands China Ltd. is the leading developer, owner and operator of multi-use integrated resorts and casinos in Macao.

the gaming, such as *percent* (N = 47; 37.6%), *Patacas* (N = 22; 17.6%), *billion* (N = 17; 13.6%), and *gaming* (N = 19; 15.2%).

Q 4.2. The Media: Newspapers etc.

The tag Q 4.2 (15th; N = 350; LL = 382.43) is only found in the *MPDC* and in this semantic field. The word with the largest number is *reporters* (N = 157; 0.16%), co-occurring with *press conference* (N = 109; 11%), *newspaper* (N = 18; 2%), *journalists* (N = 12; 1%), *reporter* (N = 12; 1%), and *press* (10%; 1%).

N3.1. Measurement: General

N3.1 (16th; N = 245; LL = 369.18) is the unique semantic filed in the *MPDC*. It contains several items with the frequency above 10 times, namely *measures* (N = 75; 7%), *Ho* (N = 66; 7%), *Statistics* (N = 58; 6%), *HOS* (N = 17; 2%), and *measure* (N = 16; 2%). *Measures* co-occurs with *government* (N = 35; 46.67%), with the concordance lines representing a series of restrictive measures taken by the Chinese central government and the Macau government, namely the shorter days for transit visitors to stay in Macau and the tighter use of Union Pay card in Macau. *Measures* co-occurs with *gaming* (N = 10; 13.33%) and *house* (N = 10; 13.33%), showing some measures taken to regulate Macau's gaming and the housing problem in Macau. The *MPD* does not only focus on Macau's gaming, but also on Macau people's livelihood. The second most frequent word *Ho* was mistagged and it actually refers to the common surname in Chinese.

References

Culpeper, J. (2009). Keyness: Words, parts-of-speech and semantic categories in the character-talk of Shakespeare's Romeo and Juliet. *International Journal of Corpus Linguistics, 14*(1), 29–59.

Harcup, T., & O'Neill, D. (2001). What is news? *Galtung and Ruge Revisited, Journalism Studies, 2*(2), 261–280.

Rayson, P. (2008). From key words to key semantic domains. *International Journal of Corpus Linguistics, 13*(4), 519–549.

Chapter 6
Discussion and Conclusions

In this final chapter, the major research findings in the previous chapter are discussed (6.1) with other relevant studies and summarized (6.2). The contribution of this study is mentioned in (6.3) where the implications of this study are addressed theoretically, methodologically, and practically. The limitations of the present study and the further study are discussed in (6.4).

6.1 Discussion of Findings

The present study's findings make a meaningful comparison regarding the media representations of Macau's gaming industry in 2014 in three territories: Mainland China, Hong Kong, and Macau. Macau's gaming industry in 2014, the pillar industry of Macau, has attracted extensive media attention. This is evident from the wide range of topics and themes related to Macau's gaming industry being represented in the news media. In addition, 2014 proved to be a particular year for Macau, as many marked events, such as the 15th anniversary of Macau's return to China, the Chinese president Xi Jinping's visit to Macau, and the economic decline all happened in Macau in 2014. In neighbouring regions, both the Occupy Central Campaign in Hong Kong and China's anti-corruption drive in Mainland are reflected in the news discourse of the year.

The selection of newspapers published in the three territories of the PRC has been proven to be meaningful, based on the findings of this study. Through investigating the news discourse of these three regions, both topical and ideological differences in the newspapers of Mainland China, Hong Kong and Macau are found, as a result of the analysis of the patterns of co-selection of frequently occurring lexical items and trigrams and key semantic fields.

The findings of this study are consistent with those in previous studies mainly, the same news events or themes are found to be represented rather differently in the English-language newspapers published by Mainland China and those published

Y. Wu, *Media Representations of Macau's Gaming Industry in Greater China*,
https://doi.org/10.1007/978-981-19-7724-4_6

in other regions or countries (e.g., Joye, 2010; Li, 2009, 2011; Liu, 2017; Liu & Li, 2017; Yang, 2015). Liu and Li (2017), for example, found differences in media representations of China's smog between *China Daily* (*CD*) and three other western newspapers by examining the top 100 lexical keywords in the two corpora. Specifically, Liu and Li (2017) noted that the *CD* constructs China's smog as a severe natural phenomenon without reference to its affecting public health, whereas the western media frame the smog as a pollution disaster. By the same token, Wang (2009) found the media representations related to Lien Chan's visit to China between *China Daily* and *China Post* are not the same. *China Daily* (from Mainland China) depicts Lien's visit as a successful historical event with a positive attitude. By contrast, *China Post* from Taiwan reports some protest activities against Lien's visit to China with a mixed attitude towards this event. Liu (2017) examined the media representations of neoliberalism in the Sino-US currency dispute between *China Daily* (*CD*) and the *New York Times (NYT)*, with the findings showing that the *NYT* conveys a combative stance concerning China's exchange rate policies. In contrast, the *CD* underlines the stability value in their news reports with an ambivalent attitude towards neoliberalism. The ideological differences reflected in the divergent media representations concerning the same news events or themes are attributed to the different socio-political and economic contexts hidden behind these items of news discourse.

The ideological differences in terms of the media representations of the same news events or themes are not only found between two or more countries or territories, but can also be found in different newspapers published in the same region or country. Corpus-based CDA studies (Baker, 2010b; Baker et al, 2013; Baker & McEnery, 2005; Brindle, 2016b; Feng, 2017; Kim, 2012; Perera & Biachi, 2016; Teo, 2000; Zhang & Mihelj, 2012) have been applied to uncover the different types of ideologies in different contexts. In their studies, clear ideological differences are found between different newspapers in the representations of particular groups of people and particular events. The research findings of the present study concur with those in these studies. Specially, the themes related to Macau's gaming industry are represented differently in the context of Mainland China, Hong Kong, and Macau, respectively.

In the present study, corpus-based CDA has been applied effectively to achieve the same purpose of uncovering ideological differences in news discourse produced by Mainland China, Hong Kong and Macau. Despite the fact that all three territories have now joined and are part of the PRC, each is characterized by its own economic, social, historical and political backgrounds. The findings demonstrate ideological differences in the news discourse on Macau's gaming industry in 2014 produced by the three territories of Mainland China, Hong Kong, and Macau.

With regard to the methodological approach used in the present study, corpus-based CDA has been effectively applied to reveal the ideological differences and respective stances in the news discourse in different contexts.

Specifically, a number of corpus tools of CL are effectively applied in the present study to pinpoint the location for further analyses (i.e., the frequent or salient linguistic patterns with the examination of expanded concordance lines).

CL has been proven effective for the present study as CL tools, and programs offer researchers an overview of the corpus data, acting as a "map" to direct researchers to take a closer look at the corresponding concordance analysis (Baker et al., 2008), enabling researchers to "approach the text more objectively, free from preconceived notions, towards the content of the texts" (Gabrielatos & Baker, 2008, p. 3) when conducting corpus investigations. The news reporting has a cumulative effect and CL reveals its incremental effects through quantifying repetitive patterns (Baker, 2006a; Mautner, 2008, 2016; Stubbs, 2001).

Three corpus analysis methods, namely frequency, trigrams, and key semantic fields are applied in the present study to quantify the news discourse items of the three territories.

In relation to frequency, the word frequency lists of three news article corpora (i.e., *XH&CDC*, *SCMPC*, and *MPDC*) generated from WordSmith 7.0 (Scott, 2016) have indicated a good starting point (Baker et al., 2008; Brindle, 2016a; Cheng, 2012). Specifically, the top 20 frequently occurring single lexical words shown in each wordlist portray an overall picture of the news article corpus, in which constantly mentioned themes or topics are underlined in the three news article corpora.

The general differences among the three news article corpora have been outlined through the examination and comparison of each top 20 lexical single word frequency list of three news article corpus. Based on the frequency findings, the three news article corpora demonstrate respective preferences for the representations of particular issues. Specifically, the *XH&CDC* concentrates on the achievements that Macau has obtained over the past 15 years, especially on its economic growth since Macau's reunification with China, as evidenced by the unique prominence of top lexical words such as *development*, *economic*, and *growth*. The *XH&CDC* also dedicates their news articles to enhancing the national consciousness of Macau's citizens and their patriotism toward China as reflected by the unique lexical word *Chinese*. Besides, the *XH&CD* is noted for their preference for the top lexical word *tourism*, suggesting that this industry has been given special emphasis by the Chinese Mainland media, as this term is constantly mentioned in the *XH&CDC*.

In the *SCMPC*, the reporting preferences mainly cover financial aspect of Macau. The financial performance of gaming in Macau is the major focus in its news articles, as most of the top 20 lexical single words are semantically connected with business and financial fields. For instance, the most frequent lexical words *per cent*, *HK*, and *US* are used to report the financial performance in Macau's gaming industry.

In contrast, the *MPD*, as the regional news press, shows its reporting preferences for Macau's local affairs, particularly related to the gaming industry, as it has the largest number of unique lexical words such as *local*, *public*, *employees*, *smoking*, and *staff*, words about people's livelihood. This suggests that social problems, such as public housing policy, employment, benefits, and social welfare, are constantly discussed in Macau's local newspaper.

The wordlists of the top 20 trigrams of each news article corpus generated by the Wordsmith 7.0 (Scott, 2016) have been demonstrated to be a complementary phraseological analysis to the previous single lexical words analysis. The findings of trigram analysis are proved to be necessary in order to comprehend the surrounding environment as well as the contextual information of language, revealing subtle differences among three news article corpora. The finding of trigram analysis is consistent with Brindle's (2016a) findings that n-grams reveal "the representative ways of saying thing" (p. 43). Some interesting or marked trigrams are found in the respective news article corpus, which have not been highlighted in previous frequency analyses.

In the *XH&CDC* (Chinese Mainland), the trigram *in Hong Kong* is marked, as the collection of all news articles in each corpus is related to the gaming industry of Macau, indicating that the mainland Chinese press shows a special interest in reporting some particular issues and affairs happening in Hong Kong society purposely, with the aim of forming a strong contrast between Hong Kong and Macau by emphasising the construction of "good" and "bad" children when making a comparison between these two SARs. In the *SCMPC*, this trigram *in Hong Kong* can also be found. The co-texting information reflects that Hong Kong is in an unpromising situation and has received relevant warnings from the central government compared with Macau, combined with the trigram *to Hong Kong*. In addition, the high frequency of the 3-word n-gram *President Xi Jinping* in the *SCMP* indicates Xi, the Chinese political figure, has constantly been mentioned by the Hong Kong press in order to highlight his role as the initiator of the Chinese anti-corruption campaign, which is believed to have an impact on Macau's casino economy. Contrary to the *SCMP*, the trigram *the central government* was repeatedly mentioned in the *MPD*, which (rather than Xi JinPing) is emphasised by the Macau press as being the initiator of the anti-corruption campaign. Furthermore, the references to *the Central Government* are slightly different in the *XH&CDC* and the *MPDC*. The Mainland Chinese press underlines the Chinese Central Government's positive influence on the development of Macau, whereas the news coverage of the *MPD* is relatively comprehensive concerning the Chinese Central Government. For example, it mentions some relevant social discussions about adverse effects, such as the overload of tourists caused by the Individual Visit Scheme initiated by the Central Government, instead of simply speaking highly of it. Additionally, the high frequency of n-gram *slot-machine parlous* in the *MPDC*, reflecting the *MPD* demonstrates its reporting preferences for social issues related to the gaming industry.

Key semantic field analysis has also been effectively applied in the present study to "highlight differences between two or more corpora" (Potts, 2016, p. 69), achieved by the online interface Wmatrix (Rayson, 2008). Specifically, semantic similarities and differences among the three news article corpora are achieved by comparing the top 20 key semantic tags of the three corpora, as key semantic tags indicate the "usually prominent topics or themes" in a particular discourse (Prentice, 2010, p. 413). The findings related to key semantic field analysis are in accordance with those of other studies (e.g., Culpeper, 2009; L'Hôte, 2010; O'Halloran, 2017; Potts, 2016; Potts & Kjær, 2016; Prentice, 2010; Rayson, 2008; Sun & Jiang, 2014). Specifically, these studies employed semantic field analyses to reveal the predominant themes or topics in the particular corpus and underline the semantic differences between two or more corpora. For example, Potts (2016) compared four online question-and-answer forum corpora from four countries by comparing the top 2 key semantic fields in each corpus.

Rayson (2008) utilized semantic field analysis to highlight the semantic differences between Labour and LibDem Manifesto discourse. Sun and Jiang (2014) adopted semantic field analysis to compare the use of metaphor in the mission statements between the Chinese and the American companies.

The semantic differences between the three news discourse sources in the present study have also been highlighted based on key semantic field analyses used in the above studies.

The *XH&CDC* covers a number of themes pertaining to the achievements that Macau has made in the post-colonial period after its handover to China, implying that the *XH&CD* tends to portray Macau from a positive perspective. Specifically, the exclusive use of key semantic fields "SIZE: BIG" and "CHEAP" suggests that topics related to Macau's economic growth and social progress are emphasised by the media of Mainland China. The predominance of the key semantic field "CHANGE" together with the word *development* suggests the *XH&CD* not only outlines Macau's positive situation but also mentions its future development. The unique semantic field "INDUSTRY" not only illustrates Macau's pillar industry of gaming, but also demonstrates Macau's potential for industry diversification. This indicates that the Chinese Central Government's further policies are likely to support the development of other industries in Macau, rather than relying solely on its gaming industry. Besides, the key semantic field "HELPING" implies that the *XH&CD*, acting as the mouthpiece of the Chinese authorities, tends to construct a positive image of the Chinese Central government by stressing the support of the Chinese authorities for the development of Macau with the word *support*. In the *XH&CDC*, various key semantic fields refer to locations, namely "GEOGRAPHICAL NAMES", "PLACES", and "GEOGRAPHICAL TERMS". Specifically, the exclusive use of the word *motherland* from the key semantic field "PLACE" in the *XH&CDC* suggests that the Chinese mainland media have selected *motherland* instead of *China* to underline the bonding between Mainland China and Macau and to strengthen the patriotic sentiment of Macau's citizens.

The *SCMP* is found to have devoted more of its news content to Macau's financial performance in gaming, as shown in the key semantic fields "MONEY: GENERALLY", "BUSINESS: GENERALLY", and "MONEY AND PAY". Another key semantic field, "QUANTITIES: LITTLE", which exclusively appears in the *SCMPC* with the most salient item *decline*, represents Macau in relatively unfavourable financial circumstances, namely that the economy in Macau is on the decline. Additionally, the key semantic fields "MONEY GENERALLY" and "TELECOMMUNICATION" include more words, such as *money* and *operators*, with negative meanings connected with illegal activities, which are usages specific to the *SCMP*.

Analysis of key semantic fields in the *MPDC* demonstrates the important social problems related to Macau's gaming industry. Macau's local news (i.e., *MPDC*) naturally devotes much of its coverage to the local society, as evidenced by its use of unique key semantic fields "WORK AND EMPLOYMENT: GENERALLY", "SMOKING AND NON-MEDICAL DRUGS". In addition, the key semantic field, "BELONGING TO A GROUP" pertains to the Public Housing Program in Macau, reflecting that the *MPDC* also pays attention to the livelihoods of Macau's citizens.

The key semantic field "GOVERNMENT" is unique, containing various items related to Macau's local organisations and institutions. The key semantic field "SPEECH: COMMUNICATIVE" highlights the overuse of this quotation style in the news article in the *MPDC.*

In addition to the unique key semantic fields in each news corpus, the same key semantic fields shared by two or three corpora, such as "LAW AND ORDER" and "NUMBERS", are observed to carry items with different meanings through the examination of expanded concordance lines. Specifically, the number *two* in the *XH&CDC* and the *SCMPC* predominantly refers to the policy of "*One Country, Two Systems*" with a more political inclination. In contrast, *two* is mainly adopted in the *MPDC* to denote the exact figure in financial revenues. Similarly, the key semantic fields "BUSINESS GENERALLY" and "MONEY GENERALLY" are found to have different preferences in their news coverage. Notably, the *XH&CD* is observed to be more likely to accentuate Macau's overall economic development whereas the news media of Hong Kong and Macau, namely the *SCMP* and the *MPD*, seem to demonstrate their interest in reporting concrete statistics concerning fiscal revenue.

The majority of the findings reaffirm the results of the above frequency analysis, suggesting that key semantic field analysis can not only be utilised as an extension study of lexical analysis, but can also be a useful means of down-sampling the corpus data in order to achieve a more complete and more profound analysis (Potts, 2016; Rayson, 2008).

In addition, the value of analysing the extended units of meaning of a lexical item (Sinclair, 2004) has been highlighted in the present study. The findings in regard to the patterns of co-selection of single lexical words demonstrate that the analytical framework of Sinclair's (2004) descriptive model of lexical items is significant for the present study. The findings tie in well with Sinclair's (2004) descriptive model of the lexical item that language tends to be phraseological, that meanings cannot be created by the individual words instead of co-selection of words as "meaning resides in the extended units" (Cheng, 2012, p.154). Comparing the frequency/percentage of the single lexical words is not enough to comprehend the meanings in the news discourse. The findings related to the patterns of co-selection of the frequent single lexical words demonstrate that the same words in different news article corpora are found to have different co-selections and accordingly, the meanings that are expressed by the same words are different. The function of semantic prosody has proved to be significant in the present study to reveal the attitudes and ideologies embedded in each news discourse from the three territories, which confirms Sinclair (2004)'s descriptive model of lexical item that the semantic prosody is the most important category of co-selection, which is "the determiner of the meaning of the whole lexical item" (p.141), and that semantic prosodies can "express attitudinal and pragmatic meanings" (p.174).

The findings in terms of collocation, semantic preference and semantic prosody can be compared to those of previous studies (Cheng & Ho, 2014; Cheng & Lam, 2010, 2013). Their analyses, based on the model of five categories of co-selection of a lexical item (Sinclair, 2004), have revealed the topical concerns and attitudes between two or more different discourse items. Cheng and Lam (2010) found the ideological shift in the media representations associated with the lexical item *human rights* in the *SCMP* between 1993–1994 and 2003–2004 through comparing the semantic preferences and prosodies in two particular periods based on Sinclair's (2004) extended unit of meaning. Cheng and Lam (2013) observed the diachronic changes in the western perception of Hong Kong before and after Hong Kong's handover to China, based on examining the extended unit meaning of *Hong Kong/political*. Their findings demonstrate that western media organisations paid more attention to the general business environment of Hong Kong before its handover and in contrast, that politically-related issues are given greater emphasis by western media after Hong Kong's sovereignty was returned to China. Cheng and Ho (2014) observed divergent representations towards the introduction of the school subjects Moral and National Education (MNE) between two English-language newspapers published in Hong Kong and Hong Kong Government press releases by comparing collocation, semantic preference, and prosody in two different items of discourse associated with the lexical item *National Education*. Hong Kong media are found to portray a negative attitude towards this issue, as evidenced by using the collocates with negative meanings such as *brainwashing*, whereas Hong Kong government press releases tend to underline the potential positive influence on Hong Kong's younger generation.

In the present study, the contrastive analysis of the shared words between two or three news article corpora has revealed different co-selections. Accordingly, the diverse topical concerns and attitudes hidden behind these shared words in the three news discourses are uncovered through their respective media representations by examining collocation, semantic preference and semantic prosody.

The *XH&CD* constructs Macau positively, particularly accenting its economic growth and development over the past 15 years since its reunification with China. Besides, the image of the Chinese central government is framed positively by the media of Mainland China, emphasizing its key role in supporting Macau's development. These are reflected by the semantic preferences and prosodies of *Macau* in the *XH&CDC*. The representation of Macau's gaming industry is downplayed by the press of the Mainland media as the most frequent collocate of *Macau* is *SAR* in the *XH&CDC*, underlining the administrative status of Macau in China and by comparison, *gaming* is the top 1 collocate of Macau in both the *SCMPC* and the *MPDC*. The *XH&CD* places the emphasis on the diversification of Macau's gaming dominated economy.

The *SCMP* tends to construct Macau's economic outlook and Macau's financial performance in the gaming industry from a negative perspective, as reflected by the semantic preferences and prosodies associated with the lexical items *Macau* and *gaming* in the *SCMP*. Additionally, gaming-related illegal activities or crime is another matter of concern for Hong Kong's media, as evidenced by the semantic preference for *gaming* in the *SCMP*, and their activities are constructed as problematic for Macau's gaming industry to form a negative aspect.

In contrast, the *MPD* shows different reporting preferences. Macau's local press tends to be more concerned with local gaming-related issues, for instance, the working benefits and environments of employees from the gaming sector, with a critical attitude towards casino operators, reporting that they need to improve the unsatisfactory work environments for their staff as reflected by the semantic preference and prosody of the lexical item *gaming* in the *MPDC*.

The representations of *Hong Kong* are found to be different according to the source of the news discourse through their respective co-selections of *Hong Kong*. The *XH&CD* is inclined to represent Hong Kong as having an "unfavourable" situation to their readers. For instance, the *XH&CD* attributes this "negative" circumstance to interference from the former British colony's government. In contrast, the *XH&CD* constructs a more positive image of Macau by mentioning that "*Macao has surpassed Hong Kong in many ways*" and "*Macau has set an excellent example for Hong Kong in this regard*", with both setting Macau as a role model in upholding the policy of "One Country, Two Systems".

In contrast, the *SCMP* demonstrates its concerns about Hong Kong's political situation with an uncertain attitude towards Hong Kong's future political environment because of the Occupy Central protests. Besides, the *SCMP* tends to highlight the economic, political and social diversities between Hong Kong and Macau in order to imply that these two regions cannot be comparable.

The patterns of co-selection related to *China* between the *XH&CD* and the *SCMP* are also found to be different. In their respective representations of *China*, the *XH&CD* is found to highlight the role of China in Macau's success after its return to China's rule. China's image is also positively constructed in the *XH&CDC*, which proves the findings of the other studies that China Daily focuses on promoting a positive Chinese image to the outside world. By contrast, in the *SCMPC*, China is found to be consistently associated with gaming-related economic crime. The concordance lines suggest China is taking stricter actions to curb illegal funds going through China to Macau.

Based on the CL findings, the CDA approach's application is proven to be meaningful as CDA helps to make up for some shortfalls of CL. The corpus analyses cannot take the social, economic, historical and political context into consideration (Gabrielatos & Baker, 2008; Baker et al., 2013). Thus, CDA is applied to interpret the findings generated by CL as the major concern of CDA is "a relation between discourse and other social elements" (Fairclough, 2015, p. 35). According to Fairclough (1989, 1995, 2015), language is seen as discourse and a form of social practice and accordingly, CDA takes political and social factors into consideration (Baker et al., 2008; Fairclough, 1989, 2010, 2015).

Newspapers in the three territories: Mainland China, Hong Kong and Macau were found to have different reporting preferences and focuses regarding Macau's gaming industry. The divergent media representations towards Macau's gaming industry in the three different territories were expected, which conforms to the theory proposed by Fairclough (1995) that "language is a part of society and linguistic phenomena are social phenomena" (p. 23). The findings are consistent with previous studies (Bednarek & Caple, 2012; Conboy, 2006; Fairclough, 1995, 2001, 2015; Van Dijk, 1998) stating that news discourse as a form of social practice is ideological in nature, shaped and mediated by the particular political and economic structures. The findings also support Fowler's study (1991), which observes that "the news media select events for reporting" (p. 13), and that news imposes a structure of values, social and economic in origin, on whatever is represented. In addition, the findings support the studies (Brindle, 2016b; Fairclough, 1989, 2001, 2015) that media exert their hidden power through a cumulative effect: "repetition of particular ways of handling causality and agency" (Fairclough, 2015, p. 82) as the single text on its own is not quite significant. For example, based on the trigram analysis findings, the *SCMP* is found to have highlighted the agent *President Xi Jinping* frequently and his initiation of the anti-corruption campaign. By comparison, the *MPD* chooses the political institution *the Central Government* instead of highlighting the political figure of Xi Jinping to report its negative influence on Macau's gaming economy.

These diversities represented in the news discourse of the three territories are attributed to the different social, political, economic, and historical backgrounds of Mainland China, Hong Kong and Macau.

Mainland China has experienced an enormous transition from the previous fully planned economy to the market-oriented economy owing to its opening-up policy in 1978. However, the Mainland Chinese media industry is still under the control of the Chinese authorities and a strict censorship system is applied in Mainland China (Frisch, Belair-Gagnon, & Agur, 2018). Based on the literature, *China Daily* (*CD*) and *Xinhua News* (*XH*) in Mainland China perform the role of the Communist Party of China's (CPC) mouthpiece, aligning their news content with the interests of the Chinese central government to disseminate the government's policies and information. In the meantime, *CD* and *XH* are both national media organizations, which are considered to be propaganda tools for the Chinese authorities to serve their purpose of promoting patriotism as well as publicizing a positive image of China to the outside world (Liu, 2017; Liu & Li, 2017; Xin, 2006, 2012). This is also reflected in the findings towards the news discourse in the *XH&CD* that a positive image of the Chinese central government, patriotism and a positive image of China are highlighted in the *XH&CDC*.

Although the sovereignty of Hong Kong has been returned from Britain to the PRC, Hong Kong has preserved its economic system, British-style independence and judiciary free press (Frisch, Belair-Gagnon, & Agur, 2018). Hong Kong has been described as having the world's freest market economy (The Government of the Hong Kong Special Administrative Region, 2017). In contrast to the state-owned media in Mainland China, news media in Hong Kong are generally owned by conglomerates. The *SCMP* is considered to be the leading English-language newspaper in Hong Kong with a democratic and liberal stance (Cheng & Lam, 2010, 2013; Flowerdew et al., 2002). The findings of the *SCMP* are in line with the previous findings (Flowerdew et al., 2002) that the *SCMP* prefers to adopt metaphorical language to present its negative opinions in their news coverage.

Despite the fact that both Hong Kong and Macau have preserved their social and economic systems, these two Special Administrative Regions of the PRC differ greatly from each other economically, politically, socially and historically, as discussed in Chap. 1. These diversities are also observed in the media representations of Macau's gaming industry in 2014. The findings of the *MPD* are consistent with its introduction on its official website, stating "it is fully financed by its owners, who are determined to maintain a friendly equidistance vis-a-vis Macau's different political and economic interests" (Brüning, n.d.). Based on the findings in the *MPDC*, the regional newspaper shows greater interest in reporting local issues in regard to Macau's gaming industry with a relatively neutral attitude.

6.2 Conclusions

CL and CDA have been combined successfully to achieve my research objective and answer my research question. A comparative study of English-language newspapers published in Mainland China, Hong Kong and Macau has revealed ideological and attitudinal differences in their respective media representations of Macau's gaming industry in 2014.

The *XH&CD* places more emphasis on representing the economic achievements of Macau in the post-colonial period, and attempts to mitigate Macau's gaming elements in their news articles. Additionally, the Mainland Chinese press underlines the positive influence of China on Macau's development.

Although both *XH&CD* and *SCMP* tend to put Hong Kong and Macau together in news articles, it is interesting to observe that the Chinese press always praises Macau's good performance over the past 15 years since its handover to China. By way of contrast, the situation of Hong Kong in 2014 is depicted as "unfavourable" by the *XH&CD* due to its Occupy Central protest. Finally, the Chinese press constantly adopts *motherland* to refer to the PRC, aiming to underline the close bond between the Chinese Mainland and Macau in order to serve the specific purpose of promoting patriotism and a sense of belonging for Macau residents to the Chinese Mainland.

As for the Hong Kong Press, the *SCMP* tends to be more interested in reporting Macau's gaming industry with a special focus on the financial aspect of Macau's gaming, reporting on gaming revenues. In addition, the *SCMP* showed a marked interest in reporting gaming-related criminal and illegal activities such as organized crime and illegal online betting.

The *MPD*, as a regional newspaper, focuses on the social issues of Macau's gaming industry, such as employee benefits, working environments, and the social influence of gaming in the local community.

In addition to the different topical concerns or preferences reflected in three news article corpora, the noticeable attitudinal differences are observed. Specifically, the representation of Macau in the *XH&CDC* is portrayed very positively by underlining Macau's astonishing economic performance after its reunification to China. The *XH&CD* attributes Macau's success to the Chinese Central government's support. Besides, Macau is depicted by the Mainland media as a role model for successfully implementing the principle of "*One Country, Two Systems*" and the "*Basic Law*" in contrast with Hong Kong's "unfavourable" situation, namely the Occupy Central protests of 2014.

Conversely, the *SCMP* repeatedly underlines the differences between the Hong Kong SAR and the Macau SAR, indicating that these regions to some extent cannot be directly compared. The *SCMP* tends to hold a pessimistic attitude towards Macau's gaming-related economic situation by its use of metaphorical language with negative meanings such as *perfect storm* and a *death with a thousand cut*.

Macau's local press the *MPD* holds a relatively neutral attitude in reporting the events related to the Macau's gaming in terms of the selection of reporting topics, such as the local social affairs of Macau.

6.3 The Contribution of This Study

Theoretically, this is the first linguistic study that combines CL and CDA to compare the media representations related to Macau's gaming industry in the English-language newspapers published in Mainland China, Hong Kong and Macau. The analytical framework, based on the notion of the extended units of meaning of a lexical item (Sinclair, 2004), used in the present study can be used in other studies to reveal the ideological stances of a specific topic in the news discourse through comparing the patterns of co-selection of shared and unique words and phraseologies between two or more sources of news discourse.

This research suggests that the methods adopted in this study can be replicated to examine and compare the news discourse in different contexts. This study also has important practical implications for journalism and the media industry. The findings have confirmed that the news media of the three territories of the PRC are different from one another in their respective ideological stances.

6.4 Limitations and Further Study

The study has only focused on data related to news articles published in 2014. Future studies could extend the time span of the news articles in order to examine whether such a corresponding ideological shift occurs diachronically (Baker et al., 2013; Cheng & Lam, 2013).

Additionally, the literature review has shown that some corpus-based CDA studies are not limited to examining single-language news data. Instead, there have been some studies (Bayley et al., 2009; Fang, 2001; Freake & Sheyholislami, 2011; Morley & Taylor, 2009; Partingtong et al., 2013; Qian, 2010; Tabbert, 2015; Taylor, 2014; Vessey, 2013; Wang, 2013) that have used bilingual or multilingual data to compare how the same news events or themes are represented in the different language channels of the press. Their findings demonstrate ideological differences in newspapers utilising distinct languages. The present study only focuses on English-language newspapers published in the three territories of the PRC. For future studies, Chinese-language newspapers in the Greater China Region such as Chinese Mainland, Hong

Kong SAR and Macau SAR, where Chinese is still the mainstream language (Feng, 2017; Yao & Huang, 2014) should be compared, and the potential for finding differences in Chinese should not be underestimated.

In addition, for future research, I would like to select newspapers in Chinese and Portuguese languages published solely in the Macau SAR, as these two languages are prescribed by the Macau Basic Law as the official languages of the Macau SAR (The Basic Law of the Macao Special Administrative Region of the People's Republic of China, Art 9, 1993) and wield certain social impact. It would be especially meaningful to investigate how particular news events are represented by various news press agencies of multi-lingual societies (Moody, 2008; Yan & Moody, 2010) like Macau.

In addition to the lexical items used in the present study, future linguistic studies such as metaphor analysis can be conducted in the same set of corpora in the future.

References

Baker, P. (2006). *Using corpora in discourse analysis*. Continuum.

Baker, P. (2010). Representations of Islam in British broadsheet and tabloid newspapers 1999–2005. *Journal of Language and Politics, 9*(2), 310–338.

Baker, P., Gabrielatos, C., Khosravinik, M., Krzyżanowski, M., McEnery, T., & Wodak, R. (2008). A useful methodological synergy? combining critical discourse analysis and corpus linguistics to examine discourses of refugees and asylum seekers in the UK press. *Discourse & Society, 19*(3), 273–306.

Baker, P., Gabrielatos, C., & McEnery, T. (2013). *Discourse analysis and media attitudes: The representation of Islam in the British Press*. Cambridge University Press. https://doi.org/10.1017/CBO9780511920103

Bayley, P., Giuliani, D., & Serret, S. (2009). Semantic constructions of citizenship in the British, French, and Italian press. In P. Bayley & G. Williams (Eds.), *European identity* (pp. 153–189). Oxford University Press.

Baker, P., & McEnery, T. (2005). A corpus-based approach to discourses of refugees and asylum seekers in UN and newspaper texts. *Journal of Language and Politics, 4*(2), 197–226.

Basic Law Art 9. (1993). The basic law of the Macau special administrative region of the people's republic of China

Bednarek, M., & Caple, H. (2012). *News discourse*. Continuum.

Brindle, A. (2016a). A corpus analysis of discursive constructions of the sunflower student movement in the english-language taiwanese press. *Discourse & Society, 27*(1), 3–19.

Brindle, A. (2016b). *The language of hate: A corpus linguistic analysis of white supremacist Language*. Routledge.

Brüning, H. (n.d.). *Connecting Macau*. Retrieved from http://www.macaupostdaily.com/founding.html

Cheng, W. (2012). *Exploring corpus linguistics: Language in action*. Routledge.

Cheng, W., & Ho, J. (2014). Brainwashing or nurturing positive values: Competing voices in Hong Kong's national education debate. *Journal of Pragmatics, 74*, 1–14.

Cheng, W., & Lam, P. W. Y. (2010). Media discourses in Hong Kong: Change in representation of human rights. *Text & Talk, 30*(5), 507–527.

Cheng, W., & Lam, P. W. Y. (2013). Western perceptions of Hong Kong ten years on: A corpus-driven critical discourse study. *Applied Linguistics, 34*(2), 173–190.

Conboy, M. (2006). *Tabloid britain: Constructing a community through language*. Routledge.

Culpeper, J. (2009). Keyness: Words, parts-of-speech and semantic categories in the character-talk of Shakespeare's Romeo and Juliet. *International Journal of Corpus Linguistics, 14*(1), 29–59.
Fairclough, N. (1989). *Language and power* (1st ed.). Longman.
Fairclough, N. (1995). *Media discourse.* Oxford University Press.
Fairclough, N. (2001). *Language and power* (2nd ed.). Longman.
Fairclough, N. (2010). *Critical discourse analysis: The critical study of language* (2nd ed.). Routledge.
Fairclough, N. (2015). *Language and power* (3rd ed.). Routledge.
Fang, Y. J. (2001). Reporting the same events? A critical analysis of Chinese print news media texts. *Discourse & Society, 12*(5), 585–613.
Feng, W. D. (2017). Ideological dissonances among Chinese-language newspapers in Hong Kong: A corpus-based analysis of reports on the occupy central movement. *Discourse & Communication, 11*(6), 549–566.
Flowerdew, J., Li, D. C., & Tran, S. (2002). Discriminatory news discourse: Some Hong Kong data. *Discourse & Society, 13*(3), 319–345.
Fowler, R. (1991). *Language in the news: Discourse and ideology in the press.* Routledge.
Freake, R., Gentil, G., & Sheyholislami, J. (2011). A bilingual corpus-assisted discourse study of the construction of nationhood and belonging in Quebec. *Discourse & Society, 22*(1), 21–47.
Frisch, N., BelairGagnon, V., & Agur, C. (2018). Media capture with Chinese characteristics: Changing patterns in Hong Kong's news media system. *Journalism, 19*(8), 1165–1181.
Gabrielatos, C., & Baker, P. (2008). Fleeing, sneaking, flooding: A corpus analysis of discursive constructions of refugees and asylum seekers in the UK press, 1996-2005. *Journal of English Linguistics, 36*(1), 5–38
Joye, S. (2010). News discourses on distant suffering: A critical discourse analysis of the 2003 SARS outbreak. *Discourse & Society, 21*(5), 586–601.
Kim, S. (2012). Racism in the globalera: Analysis of Korean media discourse around migrants, 1990–2009. *Discourse & Society, 23*(6), 657–678.
L'Hôte, E. (2010). New labour and globalization: Globalist discourse with a twist? *Discourse & Society, 21*(4), 355–376.
Li, J. (2009). Intertextuality and national identity: Discourse of national conflicts in daily newspapers in the United States and China. *Discourse & Society, 20*(1), 85–121.
Li, J. (2011). Collision of language in news discourse: A functional–cognitive perspective on transitivity. *Critical Discourse Studies, 8*(3), 203–219.
Liu, M. (2017). Contesting the cynicism of neoliberalism. *Journal of Language and Politics, 16*(2), 242–263.
Liu, M., & Li, C. (2017). Competing discursive constructions of China's smog in Chinese and Anglo-American English-language newspapers: A corpus-assisted discourse study. *Discourse & Communication, 11*(4), 386–403.
Mautner, G. (2008). Analysing newspaper, magazines and other print media. In R. Wodak & M. Krzyżanowski (Eds.), *Qualitative discourse analysis in the social sciences* (pp. 30–53). Palgrave Macmillan.
Mautner, G. (2016). Checks and balances: How corpus linguistics can contribute to CDA. In R. Wodak & M. Meyer (Eds.), *Methods of critical discourse studies* (pp. 154–179). Sage Publications.
Moody, A. (2008). Macau english: Status, functions and forms. *English Today, 24*(3), 3–15.
Morley, J., & Taylor, C. (2009). Us and them: How immigrants are constructed in British and Italian newspapers. In P. Bayley & G. Williams (Eds.), *European identity* (pp. 190–223). Oxford University Press.
O'Halloran, K. (2017). *Posthumanism and deconstructing arguments: Corpora and digitally-driven critical analysis.* Taylor & Francis.
Partington, A., Duguid, A., & Taylor, C. (2013). *Patterns and meanings in discourse: Theory and practice in corpus-assisted discourse studies (CADS).* John Benjamins Publishing.

Pereira, F. H., & Biachi, M. M. (2016). Women in the 2010 Brazilian presidential elections: Two weekly magazines' discourses on women candidates. *Critical Discourse Studies, 13*(4), 411–428.
Potts, A. (2016). Semantic annotation. In P. Baker & J. Egbert (Eds.), *Triangulating methodological approaches in corpus linguistic research* (pp. 57–72). Routledge.
Potts, A., & Kjær, A. L. (2016). Constructing achievement in the international criminal tribunal for the former yugoslavia (ICTY): A corpus-based critical discourse analysis. *International Journal for the Semiotics of Law-Revue Internationale De Sémiotique Juridique, 29*(3), 525–555.
Prentice, S. (2010). Using automated semantic tagging in critical discourse analysis: A case study on scottish independence from a scottish nationalist perspective. *Discourse & Society, 21*(4), 405–437.
Qian, Y. (2010). *Discursive constructions around terrorism in the People's Daily (China) and The Sun (UK) before and after 9.11: A corpus-based contrastive critical discourse analysis*. Bern: Peter Lang
Rayson, P. (2008). From key words to key semantic domains. *International Journal of Corpus Linguistics, 13*(4), 519–549.
Scott, M. (2016). WordSmith Tools (Version 7) [Computer software].Stroud: Lexical Analysis Software
Sinclair, J. (2004). *Trust the text: Language, corpus and discourse*. Routledge.
Stubbs, M. (2001). *Words and phrases: Corpus studies of lexical semantics*. Blackwell publishers.
Sun, Y., & Jiang, J. (2014). Metaphor use in Chinese and US corporate mission statements: A cognitive sociolinguistic analysis. *English for Specific Purposes, 33*, 4–14.
Tabbert, U. (2015). *Crime and corpus: The linguistic representation of crime in the press*. John Benjamins Publishing.
Taylor, C. (2014). Investigating the representation of migrants in the UK and Italian press: A cross-linguistic corpus-assisted discourse analysis. *International Journal of Corpus Linguistics, 19*(3), 368–400.
Teo, P. (2000). Racism in the news: A critical discourse analysis of news reporting in two Australian newspapers. *Discourse & Society, 11*(1), 7–49. https://doi.org/10.1177/0957926500011001002
The Government of the Hong Kong Special Administrative Region. (2017). Hong Kong is ranked as the world's freest economy again [Press release]. Retrieved, from https://www.info.gov.hk/gia/general/201702/16/P2017021600208.htm
Van Dijk, T. A. (1998). Ideology: A multidisciplinary approach. London: Sage
Vessey, R. (2013). *Language ideologies and discourses of national identity in Canadian newspapers: A cross-linguistic corpus-assisted discourse study* (Doctoral dissertation, Queen Mary University of London)
Wang, F. (2013). *A social constructionist analysis of the discourse of mental depression in British and Chinese news: A corpus-based study* (Doctoral dissertation, University of Birmingham).
Wang, H. (2009). Divergent news representations of Lien chan's visit to China: A corpus-based lexical comparison between the China Post and the China daily. *Journal of Asian Pacific Communication, 19*(2), 179–198.
Xin, X. (2006). A developing market in news: Xinhua news agency and Chinese newspapers. *Media, Culture & Society, 28*(1), 45–66.
Xin, X. (2012). *How the market is changing China's news: The case of Xinhua news agency*. Lexington Books.
Yang, M. (2015). Olympism and the Beijing Olympic torch relay in the British and Chinese media discourses: A comparative study. *The International Journal of the History of Sport, 32*(3), 499–515.
Yao, S. Y., & Huang, Y. (2014). Aomen yu nei di xin weng yu pian chi hui cha yi de ji liang yan jiu [A quantitative study of the lexical differences in news discourses between Macau and Mainland]. *Yu Yan Wen Zi Yin Yong, 5*(2), 27–37.
Yan, X., & Moody, A. (2010). Language and society in Macao: A review of sociolinguistic studies on Macao in the past three decades. *Chinese Language and Discourse, 1*(2), 293–324.

Zhang, M., & Mihelj, S. (2012). Hong Kong identity and the press–politics dynamics: A corpus-assisted discourse study. *Asian Journal of Communication, 22*(5), 506–527.

Uncited References

Allen, W., & Blinder, S. (2013). Migration in the news: Portrayals of immigrants, migrants, asylum seekers and refugees in national British newspapers, 2010 to 2012. *Migration Observatory report*, COMPAS, University of Oxford

Baker, P. (2010a). *Sociolinguistics and corpus linguistics*. Edinburgh University Press.

Basic Law Art 12. (1993). The basic law of the Macau special administrative region of the people's republic of China

Basic Law Art 45. (1993). The basic law of the Macau special administrative region of the people's republic of China

Blinder, S., & Allen, W. L. (2016). Constructing immigrants: Portrayals of migrant groups in British national newspapers, 2010–2012. *International Migration Review, 50*(1), 3–40.

Gaming Inspection, and Coordination Bureau, The Government of the Macau Special Administrative Region. (n.d.). Macau gaming history. Retrieved from http://www.dicj.gov.mo/web/en/history/index.html

Gaming Inspection, and Coordination Bureau, The Government of the Macau Special Administrative Region. (n.d.). **Responsible gambling.** Retrieved, from http://www.dicj.gov.mo/web/en/responsible/responsible01/content.html#1

Godinho, J. A. (2015). Gaming in Macau: What reforms are needed? *Asian Gaming Lawyer*, 6–7

Rayson, P., & Garside, R. (2000). Comparing corpora using frequency profiling. In *Proceedings of the workshop on Comparing Corpora* (pp. 1–6). Association for Computational Linguistics

Scott, M. (2001). Mapping key words to problem and solution. In M. Scott & G. Thompson (Eds.), *Patterns of text: In honour of michael hoey* (pp. 109–127). John Benjamins Publishing.

Wan, Y. K. P. (2012). The social, economic and environmental impacts of casino gaming in Macao: The community leader perspective. *Journal of Sustainable Tourism, 20*(5), 737–755.

SPRINGER NATURE

GPSR Compliance

The European Union's (EU) General Product Safety Regulation (GPSR) is a set of rules that requires consumer products to be safe and our obligations to ensure this.

If you have any concerns about our products, you can contact us on ProductSafety@springernature.com

In case Publisher is established outside the EU, the EU authorized representative is:

Springer Nature Customer Service Center GmbH
Europaplatz 3
69115 Heidelberg, Germany